19 Minutes to Live - Helicopter Combat in Vietnam

A Memoir by Lew Jennings

Edited by Anneke Jennings

Lew Jennings
4O41 Soquel Drive # A243
Soquel, CA 95073
USA
www.19minutestolive.com

Publisher's Note: This is a work of non-fiction. Names, characters, places, and incidents are real. The author and contributors have done their best to accurately describe the events in the book, however, there may be discrepancies due to the march of time and failing memories.

Cover Photo by Michael Talton: Rearming an A/2/17th Air Cavalry AH-1G Cobra Attack Helicopter somewhere near the A Shau Valley, Vietnam, 1969. Michael Talton standing left with the submachine gun on his hip, Lew Jennings (author) standing right with the rocket across his shoulders and two armorer crew helping out.

Back Cover Photo by Michael Talton: Lew Jennings (author), Aircraft Commander, AH-1G Cobra Attack Helicopter, A/2/17th Air Cavalry, 1969.

19 Minutes to Live-Helicopter Combat in Vietnam/ Lew Jennings. -- 1st ed.
ISBN 978-1548484538

This book is dedicated to my heroes; the helicopter pilots and crews who served in Vietnam and especially my Brothers-in-Arms, the men of Charlie Troop, 7th/1st Air Cavalry and Alpha Troop, 2nd/17th Air Cavalry and those awaiting us on Fiddler's Green.

I would like to thank my fellow pilots and crewmembers for their incredible contributions to this book without which there would be no stories to tell:

Duane Acord, Dan Bresnahan, Len Constantine,
Tom Curtin, Dick Dato, Don Ericksen, Keith Finley,
Don Foster, Chris Genna, Al Goodspeed, Eddy Joiner,
Bob Larsen, Pat Lynch, Don McGurk, Dick Melick,
Tom Michel, Keith Reed, Mike Ryan. Mark Stevens and
Mike Talton.

"War is life multiplied by some number that no one has ever heard of."

— SEBASTIAN JUNGER, WAR

CONTENTS

PROLOGUE

KIRKUK, IRAQ 2008

It is cold and clear with temperatures hovering at freezing. The stars are glistening against a dark blue sky, silhouetting the before-dawn twilight. This is the quietest time of day.

The only interruptions to the silence are the melancholy sounds of calls to prayer being broadcast from the nearby mosque, and measured bursts of automatic weapons fire as the outgoing morning combat patrols "lock and load," making sure their equipment is in order before they head off into hostile territory.

A team of Kiowa Warrior helicopters swoops in low overhead. The Air Cavalry or "Cav" is returning from another night mission. One of our own planes comes in for landing too. They have probably been working together with the Cav, finding bad guys before they can do bad things or catching them in the act.

Many here at this sprawling military base are either just getting in from their patrols or just getting up to do their part to help out. The whole place will be a living, breathing beehive of activity by the time the sun comes up, all focused on one mission: bringing freedom and peace to the Iraqi people… and staying alive in the process.

It's my first time "down range", the term soldiers use to describe being here in the "sandbox". I've only been here two weeks and have already flown 33 missions with duty days up to 16 hours – like it was when I was a young combat helicopter pilot in Vietnam – except now I'm 62 years old, and this is Iraq.

I'm in a very select fraternity of pilots. Most are military retirees like myself hailing from all four Services and the Coast Guard. All volunteers. All combat experienced and well trained. Most in their 50s. Some, like me, in their 60s and even 70s. (Our Chief Pilot is 73.) All are expert at what they do.

Our mission is to find the bad guys. And, at that, we are very, very successful.

I can't tell you how we do it, or what kind of tactics and technology we employ. That's classified. I can tell you, however, we save **lots** of lives every day.

When you hear or read that insurgent attacks are at their lowest since the beginning of this war or that some key Al-Qaeda leader has been killed or captured, we probably had something to do with it.

My mission is flying support for our operations over here, ferrying people, supplies and equipment in and out of Iraq and to our bases around the country. I consider it an honor and a privilege and hope, in some small way, to help bring this conflict to a close and our troops home soon.

While I miss my lovely wife Anneke, my wonderful children and grandchildren, and holiday camaraderie with friends and family, this is where I need to be this Christmas morning.

Wishing you and yours a very Merry Christmas, Happy New Year, and a Joyous Holiday Season. –Lew

Matthew 5:9 "Blessed are the peacemakers: for they shall be called the children of God."

I wrote that note on my first of many combat support assignments in Iraq, where I flew 777 missions over the next two years. What I didn't reveal was that our base had been attacked over 20 times that December.

When I was invited to join an incredible group of gray-haired, mostly retired military professionals, to fly secret Intelligence, Surveillance, and Reconnaissance (ISR) missions in some pretty dangerous parts of the world, I immediately went to my own family to get their permission, or at least willingness, to allow Grandpa one final adventure after nearly a lifetime of service. To them, I owe immense gratitude.

And, to those friends and family who were concerned or upset that I was off to yet another war zone, I can only say that this experience was one of the most gratifying of my aviation career. I truly believe our ISR flights in Iraq helped save thousands of lives of our troops, coalition forces, and innocent Iraqi civilians.

When given the opportunity late in life to save lives on the battlefield once again, I jumped at the chance.

My name is Lew Jennings. I'm a retired US Army Officer, former airline pilot and business executive.

I was active military duty for 20 years with the US Army from 1967 to 1987 and served in Vietnam and Europe, at various bases in the United States and throughout the Pacific with the US Navy and Marine Corps. My combat experience included 726 helicopter combat missions flying Cobra Gunships in Vietnam, for which I was awarded over 50 combat decorations, including three Distinguished Flying Crosses and 36 Air Medals.

The war in Vietnam was known as The Helicopter War. There were very few roads in Vietnam and much of the terrain didn't allow the use of typical military modes of transportation like trucks, tanks, or other armored vehicles. The helicopter became the primary way to get troops into combat, to resupply them, to move cargo and equipment for them, and to evacuate the dead and wounded.

Over 12,000 helicopters would be used in Vietnam by all the US Armed Services, accumulating over ten million flight hours. In the process, 5,086 would be destroyed and 2,202 Pilots and 2,704 crewmembers killed. Helicopter crews would account for nearly ten percent of all the casualties of the war in Vietnam.

I was a Cobra helicopter gunship pilot in two Air Cavalry units in Vietnam from 1969 to 1970.

This is my story. I am honored to have served.

CHAPTER ONE

19 MINUTES TO LIVE

I had dreamed of flying since I was a toddler sitting on my mother's lap, watching my father crop dusting pineapple fields in Hawaii. My Dad was an Aviation Electrician's Mate with the Coast Guard at nearby Barbers Point Naval Air Station. He maintained the radios and electronics for the Coast Guard search and rescue aircraft there and flew crop dusters when he was off duty.

As he zoomed low over the rows of pineapples in a beautiful Stearman biplane, he would pull nearly straight up, do a slow half roll, turn, drop, and zoom low again, his wheels seeming to touch the very tops of the fruit. I was thrilled with it all and wanted to be just like him.

Dad encouraged me with his love of aviation. He had me flying gliders by the time I was twelve. I earned my Pilot's license at age 19 at the San Jose (California) Municipal Airport in 1966.

I was working fulltime and attending community college at night. My draft classification was IA, and I knew in the back of my mind that I could be called to serve in the military at any time.

The following year, in the spring of 1967, I thought the worst day of my life had arrived. I received my notice to appear for induction into the military. I was 20 years old.

The Vietnam conflict was escalating rapidly and the draft was in full force. Young men had to serve at least two years in the Army or Marine Corps. They could sign up or "enlist" for a longer term for specialty training or join the Air Force or the Navy. Most draftees trained as Army infantrymen and served in combat units carrying a rucksack and a rifle.

As I stared at my induction notice, I decided that if I had to serve, I would rather fly high with the Air Force than be an infantryman on the ground carrying a rucksack and a rifle into combat. I headed straight to the Air Force recruiter's office to sign up.

With my head held high and Pilot's license in hand, I strutted into the recruiter's office. "Hi, I'm Lew Jennings. I have a Pilot's license and I want to fly high with the Air Force."

The recruiter just stared at me for a moment, then, stifling a smile, said, "Okay, son. Are you a college graduate?"

"No," I replied. "I'm too young."

"Well then," the recruiter continued, "if you don't have four years of college, I'm afraid you can't fly high with the Air Force."

I was starting to feel a little nervous.

"We do have plenty of other great jobs for you in the Air Force though, if you qualify," he started explaining.

I told him I only wanted to be a Pilot.

"Tell you what then. Why don't you go next door and talk to the Navy!" he said, as he escorted me out of the office.

"Blue Angels! Hell, yes!" I thought and rushed next door.

As I entered the Navy recruiting office, there was a Chief Petty Officer at a desk to the right and a Marine Corps Gunnery Sergeant to the left. Both of them looked really sharp in their uniforms with lots of stripes on their sleeves and ribbons on their chests.

"Hi, I'm Lew Jennings," I announced. "I have a Pilot's license and I want to fly in the Navy."

They looked across at each other. The Chief smiled. The Gunny just rolled his eyes.

The Navy Chief looked me up and down and then asked if I had four years of college.

"No, I don't have four years of college. I'm too young. That's what I explained to the Air Force!"

"Well, son, if you don't have four years of college, you can't fly with the Navy or the Marine Corps either."

My lip started to quiver and my legs were getting weak. Visions of the Army with a rucksack and a rifle were filling my head.

Then, the Marine Corps Gunny, who had just stared at me without a smile, rose from his chair, came over and put his arm around my shoulder. As any Marine will tell you, he would only do that if you were **not** in the Marine Corps; otherwise, you would be in for a real ass chewing. The old Gunny must have been taking some pity on me.

"Son, if you're really set on being a Pilot, why don't you go next door and talk to the Army."

"The Army?" I stuttered as I tried to keep my composure. "Do they have airplanes?" I asked.

He hesitated. "Well, they have these things that fly called helicopters," he replied, "and they need a **lot** of Pilots." He smiled for the first time.

Little did I know that it was reported in the media at the time, that the average life expectancy of an Army Helicopter Pilot in combat was only 19 minutes!

I thanked the Gunny and the Chief as I left the Navy recruiting office and reluctantly headed next door to see the Army.

As I entered the door, there was a Staff Sergeant directly ahead, sitting at a desk with an American flag on a stand and recruiting posters behind him. One of the posters depicted helicopters filling the sky, flying soldiers into combat.

"Hi, I'm Lew Jennings. I'm a Pilot and I want to fly in the Army."

I had barely gotten the words out of my mouth when the Sergeant leaped out of his chair, extended his hand, and with a big smile simply asked; "Are you a high school graduate?"

I said, "yes," and he immediately exclaimed; "no problem! If you want to be a Pilot, we can make you a Pilot. Sit right down here son," as he pointed to a chair by his desk. Wow, what a change!

What followed was a whirlwind of paperwork and explanations about the Warrant Officer Rotary Wing Aviator Course. The Army needed Pilots, only a high school diploma was required, followed by a few tests and a physical examination, and I would be on my way to a career as an Army Helicopter Pilot. I was ecstatic and couldn't sign the papers fast enough.

With the paperwork completed and visions of flying helicopters firmly planted in my brain, I started to get up to leave.

"Hold on!" the Sergeant commanded. "There's something I need to emphasize before you leave."

Uh oh. I didn't like the tone of his voice.

"In the Army, you are a soldier first and a Pilot second." He was being very serious.

"What's that mean?" I asked.

"That means you are a soldier first and always. You will be sent to Fort Polk, Louisiana for Basic Combat Training as an Infantryman before you attend flight school. Then, if you fail flight school, you will be sent to Vietnam with a rucksack and a rifle."

I was in shock. My worst nightmare! What was I getting myself into?

"Not to worry," he said with the same sly grin that the Marine Corps Gunny had shown before. "You're already a Pilot and shouldn't have any trouble getting through flight school." With that, he sent me on my way and said he would be in touch.

As I got in my car, time came to a standstill. Wow! What the hell had I gotten myself into? I guess I had better tell my father.

I broke the news to my dad, Wilson Jennings, that I had signed up to become an Army Helicopter Pilot. I thought he was going to have a heart attack. He was furious!

My father was retired Coast Guard. He had served in the Merchant Marines as a young man, then in the Coast Guard and Navy during World War II, continuing his active duty in the Coast Guard after the war. His last assignment was Command Master Chief of the Coast Guard Air Station at San Francisco where he retired in 1957.

Dad had come from a long family lineage of service to the country. Three of his brothers had served with distinction in the Marine Corps. He was really upset that I had joined the

Army, although he calmed down when I told him I had been turned down by the Air Force, Navy and Marines and that the Army was my only option for flight training.

After a week or so, my father called me up and asked that I meet him at the airport in San Jose, California where I had learned to fly. He had arranged for my first helicopter flight so I could get a taste of what I was in for with the Army.

I sat in the helicopter marveling at the visibility provided by the plastic bubble surrounding us, trying to understand the mechanics of how it flew. A stick between your legs was called a *cyclic* to control movement forward, backward, left and right. That seemed pretty simple. Then, another stick down on your left side called a *collective,* you pulled up and down to make the helicopter go up and down.

Okay!

And, the collective stick had a throttle grip at the end of it like a motorcycle. Anytime you pulled up or down on the collective, you had to add or decrease throttle to keep the rotor blades overhead spinning at the right speed.

Hmmm, this is getting complicated!

Then, you had pedals for both feet like rudder pedals in an airplane, but not called rudder pedals in a helicopter; they are *anti-torque pedals*. In a helicopter, the pedals change the pitch or angle in the tail rotor blades to make the tail go left or right, or to keep it steady as you pull up and down on the collective, while rotating the throttle and moving the cyclic.

Wow, this is **really** complicated!

Needless to say, when the instructor asked me to try to keep the helicopter at a stationary three-foot hover, I lost control within seconds.

My father knew what he was doing that day. He wanted to make sure I was humbled with a taste of how hard it was to fly helicopters. I even entertained the thought that it might be an impossible task.

It wasn't long before I got the call from the recruiter to start my processing. Just as he had described, I took all the written tests, received a flight physical, appeared before an acceptance board, and received orders for my first assignment; Basic Infantry Combat Training at Fort Polk, Louisiana—the much-dreaded Boot Camp. And, if I successfully completed flight school, I would maybe have 19 minutes to live as an Army Helicopter Pilot in Vietnam!

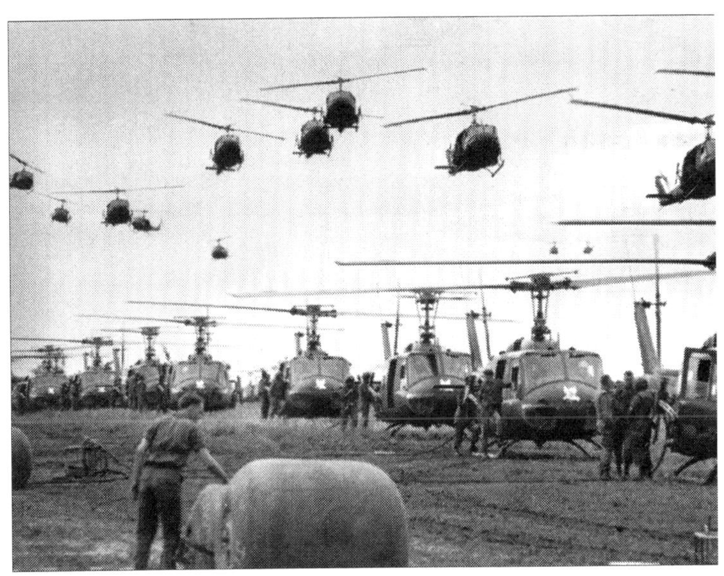

Basic Combat Training (Boot Camp) Fort Polk, Louisiana

CHAPTER TWO

RUCKSACK AND A RIFLE

On August 29, 1967 I reported to the Army Induction Center in Oakland, California. This was the real deal. No turning back now!

I was assigned to a ragtag group of young civilian men like myself and bussed to the airport to catch our flight to Dallas, Texas and on to Lake Charles, Louisiana where we would be further transported to Fort Polk for Basic Combat Training or BCT.

When the old DC-3 commuter plane landed at the airport in Lake Charles, we were immediately hit with the hot humid air common to the South that literally took my breath away. I thought I had stepped into an oven. It was definitely a far cry from the cool Pacific air of Monterey Bay back home.

I don't remember much about the hour and a half bus ride from Lake Charles to Fort Polk. I do remember our arrival. I had entered hell on earth!

We pulled up in front of a grassy parade field surrounded by two-story wooden barracks from the World War II era. There stood a line of Drill Sergeants waiting for us. They were impressive standing ramrod straight in their starched, tailored uniforms with spit-shined boots and highly polished brass glistening in the sun. Combat web belts snugged tightly around their waists. Smokey-the-bear hats tilted forward nearly covering their eyes. They looked like something right out of the movies or a recruiting poster.

But when the door of the bus opened, they morphed into screaming, diabolical maniacs! What ensued were the two longest months of my life!

"GET YOUR ASSES OFF THIS BUS! MOVE IT! MOVE IT! MOVE IT! FALL IN! LINE UP! YOU'RE TOO SLOW! MOVE IT! MOVE IT! MOVE IT!" they screamed and swarmed around us like angry wasps, yelling their orders directly into our ears and nearly nose-to nose in our faces. I was already sweating buckets.

Once they had us somewhat organized, we marched off towards the Company area. The "Company" in Army speak is your unit.

A Company usually consists of about 200 men with a Captain as the Commanding Officer, a First Sergeant (E-8) as the senior enlisted non-commissioned officer, and four platoons with 40-50 men each with a Lieutenant as Platoon Leader, Drill Sergeants as Platoon Sergeants (E-7) with Assistant E-6 and E-5 Drill Sergeants. In our unit, we even had an E-4 Drill Corporal.

Okay, okay, I know what you're thinking. What's with all this 'E' stuff?

Sorry, a little indoctrination here on military pay grades and ranks is in order. Also, a little orientation on Army combat organizations.

Here goes!

Everyone in the military is designated with a pay level grade and a corresponding rank or name for that pay grade.

Here are the grades and ranks for the Army and the positions they are normally assigned to in combat units, relative to their grade and rank.

O-1. Second Lieutenant (2LT). Also referred to as Butter Bar because of the yellow color of their single bar rank insignia. Platoon Leader, Gopher.

O-2. First Lieutenant (1LT) Rank Insignia = One silver bar. Platoon Leader, Company Executive Officer, Staff Officer.

O-3, Captain (CPT). Rank Insignia = Two silver bars. Company Commander, Battalion Staff Officer.

O-4, Major (MAJ). Rank Insignia = Gold Oak Leaf Cluster. Battalion Executive Officer, Brigade Staff Officer.

O-5, Lieutenant Colonel (LTC). Rank Insignia = Silver Oak Leaf Cluster. Also referred to as a 'Light Colonel'. Battalion Commander, Brigade Executive Officer, Division Staff Officer.

O-6, Colonel (COL). Rank Insignia = Silver Eagle. Also referred to as a 'Full Bird'. Brigade Commander, Division Chief of Staff or Staff Officer.

O-7, Brigadier General (BG). Rank Insignia = One Silver Star. Assistant Division Commander, Task Force Commander, Corps Staff Officer.

O-8, Major General (MG). Rank Insignia = Two Silver Stars. Division Commander.

0-9. Lieutenant General (LTG). Rank Insignia = Three Silver Stars. Corps Commanders, Senior Staff Officers at the Pentagon and other major headquarters.

0-10. General (GEN). Rank Insignia = Four Silver Stars. Not very many of these folks around. Commanders of Theater commands like US Army Europe and top-level staff positions such as Chief of Staff of the Army or Chairman of the Joint Chiefs of Staff.

0-11. General of the Army (GOA). Rank Insignia = Five Silver Stars. Only awarded in time of war; five generals have held this rank. Sadly, none of these Generals are with us anymore. Generals Marshall, Eisenhower, MacArthur, Bradley and Arnold were the last five-star Generals of the Army. General Hap Arnold was the only five-star general who was designated both a General of the Army during World War II and then General of the Air Force when that was established separate from the Army in 1947.

Enlisted Army soldiers have a structure similar to officers for pay grades and ranks.

E-1. Private (PVT).

E-2. Private (PVT).

E-3. Private First Class (PFC). Rank Insignia = One Chevron (inverted 'V').

E-4. Corporal (CPL). Rank Insignia = Two Chevrons. Team Leader.

E-5. Sergeant (SGT). Rank Insignia = Three Chevrons. Section/Team Leader.

E-6. Staff Sergeant (SSG). Rank Insignia = Three Chevrons plus One Rocker underneath (like a 'U'). Squad Leader.

E-7. Platoon Sergeant (PSG). Rank Insignia = Three Chevrons plus Two Rockers. Platoon Sergeant.

E-8. Master Sergeant (MSG). Rank Insignia = Three Chevrons, plus Three Rockers. Master Sergeant in a staff position. First Sergeant in leadership position. If filling First Sergeant position for the Company, will have a Diamond in the center of their rank.

E-9. Sergeant Major (SGM). Rank Insignia = Three Chevrons, plus Four Rockers. Sergeant Major in a staff position. Command Sergeant Major in a leadership position. If filling position of Command Sergeant Major, will have a Star in the center of their rank.

There are also Specialist designations (SP4, SP5) for ranks E-4 and E-5, for those assigned to technical positions.

Sandwiched in between Officer ranks and Enlisted ranks are Warrant Officers.

In the United States military, Warrant Officers (grades W-1 to W-4, in 1969; W-1 to W-5 as of 1992) are ranked as an officer above the senior-most enlisted ranks, as well as officer cadets and officer candidates, but below the officer grade of O-1.

Warrant Officers are highly skilled, single-track (as in Aviation) specialty officers. And while the ranks are authorized by Congress, each branch of the U.S. Armed Forces selects, manages, and uses Warrant Officers in slightly different ways.

For appointment to Warrant Officer (W-1), a warrant is approved by the Service Secretary of the respective branch of service (Secretary of the Army, or Secretary of the Navy for USMC warrant officers), while Chief Warrant Officers (W-2 to W-5) are commissioned by the President of the United States. Both Warrant Officers and Chief Warrant Officers take the same Oath of Office as Commissioned Officers (O-1 to O-10).

During the Vietnam War, the Army chose Warrant Officers as the primary pilots for the extensive helicopter fleet that was needed to fight the war because the use of Warrant Officers would reduce the manpower shortage then being experience among Commissioned Officers who were needed in the Combat Arms of Infantry, Armor, Artillery and other military occupational specialties.

Not lost on the Department of Defense was the fact that the military pay scale paid Warrant Officers less than it paid Commissioned Officers of comparable seniority of service and experience. Not only did the U.S. Army pay Warrant Officers less monthly "salary" (Base Pay) than Commissioned Officers, they paid them less for flying Army aircraft as well (Flight Pay), despite the fact that frequently both a Warrant Officer and a Commissioned Officer would share the same cockpit of an Army helicopter, and that the Warrant Officer, as a dedicated professional aviator, often performed the duties and carried the responsibilities of Pilot in Command or Aircraft Commander. It was not until 1974, after the war in Vietnam that U.S. Army Warrant Officer pilots finally received flight pay equal to Commissioned Officer pilots.

The mid-1960s saw a dramatic period of growth for Aviation Warrant Officers. Aviation Warrant Officer strength swelled from approximately 2,960 in 1966 to more than 12,000 by 1970. No one envisioned the huge impact that Warrant Officer aviators would have on the conduct of the war in Vietnam, nor the impact Vietnam would have on Army Aviation.

Warrant Officers proved themselves to be heroes of the Vietnam War and the backbone of Army Aviation. I couldn't wait to join their ranks.

While we are talking grades and ranks, here's a brief picture of sizes and names of organizations from small to large.

Team = 4-6 soldiers, Fire Team, led by a Corporal or Sergeant.

Squad = 9-10 soldiers, two Teams in a Squad, led by a Staff Sergeant.

Platoon = 40 soldiers, four Squads in a Platoon, led by a Platoon Leader (Second Lieutenant) and Platoon Sergeant.

*Company or Troop** = 200 soldiers. Four Platoons plus Headquarters led by a Captain as Company Commander and an E-8 First Sergeant. *In Cavalry units, the Company is called a Troop and is usually larger because of additional personnel and equipment assigned to accomplish their wide-ranging tasks of reconnaissance to find and fix the enemy.

*Battalion or Squadron** = 900-1,000 soldiers. Four Companies plus support elements and Headquarters, led by a Lieutenant Colonel as Commander and an E-9 Command Sergeant Major. *In Cavalry units, the Battalion is called a Squadron and usually a larger and more complex organization due to its missions.

*Brigade or Regiment** = 5,000 soldiers. Four Battalions plus support elements and Headquarters led by a Colonel as Brigade Commander and Sergeant Major as Brigade Command Sergeant Major. *In Cavalry units, the Brigade is called a Regiment and is usually larger and more complex due to its missions.

Division = 18-20,000 soldiers. Three Brigades in a Division plus a Cavalry Squadron, Artillery units, other support elements and a Headquarters led by a Major General and Division Command Sergeant Major.

Army = 100,000 soldiers. Several Divisions plus major support elements and a Headquarters led by a Lieutenant General as Army Commander and his Command Sergeant Major.

Theatre = One million or more soldiers comprising multiple Armies plus elements of other services led by a General or other four-star equivalent. Currently most Theatre commanders are referred to as Combat Commands such as Southern Command, Joint Special Operations Command, etc.

The 'highest ranking' officer in the Army is the *Army Chief of Staff* who leads the Army and serves on the Joint Chiefs of Staff. If an Army officer holds the position of Chairman of the Joint Chiefs, which is a rotating position held by four-star officers from all the Services, then he holds the highest position for an Army officer.

The highest position for enlisted soldiers is *Sergeant Major of the Army* where one individual is selected for that honor and serves alongside the Chief of Staff of the Army.

So that was your lesson in Army rank structure and organizations. From Second Lieutenant to General of the Army for Officers and Private to Sergeant Major for enlisted soldiers.

From units, as small as 4-6 man Teams to Theatre commands of a million troops or more.

There were nearly 200 of us newbies. When we arrived in the Company area, it was our first look at what we would call "home" for the next two months.

The Company area consisted of 10 or 12 World War II era wooden barracks. They looked in surprisingly good shape for being so old. The lawns and grounds were neat and tidy. Even rocks used for marking paths were lined up in order and painted white.

Of course, I had no idea that was due to the labor of those poor recruits who had gone before us. We would soon find ourselves spending lots of time cleaning the Company area. Even crawling on our stomachs under the barracks, picking up every little piece of trash and cigarette butt to make sure all was in order.

The barracks were two stories with a single stairwell inside and a fire escape staircase outside.

Each floor contained open squad bays running the length of the building, lined on both sides with steel bunk beds.

The bottom floor also housed the latrine (bath room) at one end and a separate single room for the platoon's senior Drill Sergeant.

The latrine was a huge shock compared to home. The shower at one end was one big steel stall for 8-10 guys. The urinal was one long steel trough. The sink was another long steel trough attached to the wall with a ledge above with reflective sheet metal for a mirror. The toilets were mounted on the floor beside the urinal trough arranged in a long row, side by side, no walls or doors. You would learn how to do the three "S's"; 'shit, shower and shave' on command in front of God and everyone!

We would learn how to make our bunks to the Army's exacting standard; sheets and blanket pulled tight to the 12th spring underneath, hospital corners, 6" collar, pillow fluffed, crease free and centered.

Our foot locker at the foot of the bunk contained nearly all our worldly possessions issued by the Army; socks, underwear, t-shirts, uniform brass, belt, belt buckle, razor,

razor blades, soap brush, tooth brush, tooth paste, bar soap, shoe polish, polishing cloth, towels, wash cloths, etc. It would be our *"Display"*; polished, clean, neatly organized, exactly the way the Drill Sergeant wanted it.

Our highly shined leather boots and shoes would be displayed alongside our shower sandals, centered under the bunk; left side for whoever was assigned the lower bunk, right side for the occupant of the upper bunk.

Our hanging lockers between the racks of bunk beds contained our fatigue duty uniforms (Army green), Khaki dress uniforms, Army dress green uniform, service hat and cap. All hangers equally spaced and everything neatly organized, exactly to standards.

The Drill Sergeants demanded that everything be clean and sparkling and ready for inspection. They spent untold hours teaching us how to do things the right way, the Army way, from cleaning toilets to cleaning rifles. They preached 'Attention to Detail' that could save your life and that of your buddies.

They would wake us up well before dawn by throwing the large metal trash cans the length of the squad bays while screaming at the top of their lungs; "GET YOUR ASSES UP! MOVE IT GIRLS! IT'S ANOTHER GREAT DAY IN THE ARMY! IT'S ANOTHER FINE DAY FOR THE CORPS! BEAT NAVY! FALL OUT FOR PT!"

We had two minutes to put on our fatigues and be down in the 'Company Street', in formation for physical training to start the day.

Physical training (PT) started with calisthenics, the Army "Daily Dozen"; Jumping Jacks, High Jumpers, Trunk Twisters, Push-ups, Sit-ups, Deep Knee Bends, Turn and

Bounces, Windmill, Lunges, Squat Thrusts, Bend and Reaches and Toe Touches.

That would be followed by Chin-Ups and Monkey Bars, then a run in formation, from one to five miles.

All physical training was done in full fatigue uniforms and combat boots back in those days.

Throughout the training day we would jog in formation from one training area to the next. Later in the training cycle it would also include jogging with our rifles (M-14s) held across our chests (port arms) and rucksacks on our backs as we went out to the ranges and other training areas.

Within a week or two we would be running a mile without throwing up and by the end of boot camp we would be running five miles or more and doing ten-mile "forced marches" in full gear.

After our morning PT, we would be allowed 30 minutes or so to do the three "S's", get our barracks all cleaned up and be ready for inspection. Of course, there was no way we could achieve their standards, so the Drill Sergeants continued their screaming and running us ragged, making us do the same things over and over again.

After inspection of the barracks and another inspection of each one of us "in ranks" out on the Company Street, we then marched to the Company Mess Hall for a quick high-calorie breakfast of eggs, bacon, potatoes, toast, oatmeal, or the infamous SOS, "Shit on a Shingle" (creamed beef on toast).

As we stood in line to enter the Mess Hall, we were constantly admonished to look sharp and keep quiet. Once inside, we each picked up our steel tray, napkin and utensils and proceeded down the serving line. Many of our fellow recruits were on the dreaded "KP" or Kitchen Police duty.

They had already been there for hours helping get all the food prepared and the mess hall cleaned, now serving us our portions as we headed down the line and proceeded to our tables.

The Officers and Drill Sergeants had their own table to enjoy their meal at their leisure with recruits serving them as waiters.

The rest of us sat at our tables while one or more of the Drill Sergeants would be roaming the mess hall screaming at us to instantly down our meals so we could get off to more inspections, classroom and field training.

The training curriculum was crammed full of indoor classroom and outdoor field training to teach us about the Army and the basic skill sets required of a soldier.

Learning the customs, courtesies and history of the US Army.

Learning how to take care of one's self through personal hygiene and maintenance of personal equipment and weapon.

Learning personal responsibility by achieving standards set by the Drill Sergeants.

Learning how to work together as a team through sharing of tasks, from cleaning the barracks to running combat obstacle courses.

Learning leadership by example and rotation through leadership positions as fire team leaders, assistant squad leaders, squad leaders, and continuous instruction and mentoring by the Drill Sergeants.

Learning how to shoot, move and communicate in a combat environment.

Learning basic battlefield first aid to help fellow soldiers survive when wounded.

And what seemed like a thousand other things. The most important of which, to me, was learning to work together, to support one another, to have each other's back regardless of race, creed, color or religion.

Each training day would begin before dawn and end well after dark.

And along the way I would gradually learn that the Drill Sergeants were not diabolical maniacs at all, but were actually the Army's "Best", physically and mentally tough professionals who guided and mentored us to achieve what we had thought was impossible.

Over those eight weeks, the job of the Drill Sergeant was to turn us rag-tag weaklings into combat-ready soldiers. And they did just that.

I will remember my Drill Sergeant for the rest of my life and have silently thanked him many times for helping me to become a good soldier and even better person.

I graduated boot camp as a Private E-1 in September 1967 and was awarded Military Occupational Specialty (MOS) 11B, (pronounced 'Eleven Bravo'), Combat Infantryman.

I was now a certified killer, able to carry a rucksack and rifle into combat and designated an expert in rifle marksmanship, machine gun and bayonet.

I couldn't wait to attend flight school.

The real heroes of the Vietnam War, those carrying a Rucksack and a Rifle, saw up to 240 days of combat in a one-year tour and casualty rates of four in ten or worse.

CHAPTER THREE

ARMY AVIATION

Leonardo da Vinci dreamed of it back in 1493. He even designed a model that he thought could accomplish it. He called it "The Air Screw" which looked like a screw that could, if spinning rapidly enough, accomplish the dream; Vertical flight.

Igor Sikorsky (1889-1972) is considered the father of the helicopter having flown the Vought-Sikorsky VS-300 he invented and constructed back in 1939.

Born in Russia, son of Russian psychologist Ivan and physician mother Maria, as a boy he studied the life and works of Leonardo da Vinci and Jules Verne. He built his first rubber band powered helicopter in 1901 at age 11. In May 1909, he began designing a real helicopter and conducted testing later that same year. Despite solving many technical problems, he realized the aircraft would never fly and disassembled it in October 1909.

"I had learned enough to recognize that with the existing state of the art engines, materials, and most of all, the shortage of money and lack of experience, I would not be able to produce a successful helicopter at that time."

Sikorsky turned his focus to airplanes. His first airplane design, the S-1, used a 15 horsepower Anzani engine that could not lift the aircraft. His second 25 hp Anzani model S-2 flew on June 16, 1910 at a height of a few feet. The following year he would fly his own two-place airplane, the 25hp S-5, earning Pilots license #64 from the Federation Aeronautique International in 1911.

His next airplane, the S-6 held three passengers and was selected as the winner of the Moscow aircraft exhibition in February 1912. Igor would go on to help build and test fly the world's first four-engine airplane, airliner and bomber in 1914.

After World War I, Igor Sikorsky immigrated to the United States in 1919, formed the Sikorsky Manufacturing Company in Roosevelt, New York in 1923 and produced America's first twin-engine airplane, the 14-passenger S-29.

The Sikorsky Manufacturing Company moved to Stratford, Connecticut in 1929 and became part of the United Aircraft and Transport Corporation. Igor Sikorsky would become famous for his design and manufacture of the S-42 "Clipper" flying boats used by Pan American World Airways to open Trans-Atlantic and Pacific air travel.

Sikorsky also continued his earlier work on vertical flight, eventually culminating in the first (tethered) flight of the Vought-Sikorsky VS-300 on September 14, 1939, with the first free flight occurring eight months later on May 24, 1940.

Sikorsky's success with the VS-300 led to the R-4 which became the world's first mass-produced helicopter in 1942 and would lead to the first recorded helicopter medical evacuation in Burma in 1944.

Sikorsky's final VS-300 rotor configuration, comprising a single main rotor and a single anti-torque tail rotor, would become the most popular helicopter configuration still being used in most helicopters produced today. Although, at this writing in 2017, Sikorsky corporation has introduced new technology with two main rotors stacked on top of each other and spinning in opposite directions, so no need for tail rotor and, instead, put a "pusher" propeller at the rear allowing speeds of over 200 knots – a new world record!

As previously noted, Sikorsky helicopters accomplished the first recorded combat search and rescue in 1944 in Burma. His helicopter designs would become the primary search and rescue aircraft for the Navy and the Air Force in the ensuing decades and the Marines would employ Sikorsky helicopters to carry Presidents from Truman and Eisenhower to the present.

Sikorsky's UH-60 Blackhawk helicopter would become the primary utility helicopter for the US Army in 1979, with many variants of that design providing specialized capabilities for all the Services and the Special Operations Command to this day.

I myself would be honored in 1975 as an Air Cavalry Captain assigned to the 2nd Armored Cavalry Regiment in Nuremberg, Germany, to host Igor Sikorsky's oldest son, Sergei Sikorsky, as a visitor and guest speaker at the inauguration of the "Red Catcher" chapter of the Army Aviation Association.

Igor Sikorsky enabled us to live the dream of vertical flight.

Other pioneers in vertical flight followed in his footsteps, developing incredible machines that allowed us to accomplish the unthinkable.

Frank Piasecki developed large tandem rotor helicopters that could move enormous amounts of people and cargo, move huge towers and equipment to the tops of buildings, and lift logged trees from mountain sides in minutes.

Larry Bell and Arthur Young developed the Bell 47 small bubble helicopter that would save thousands of lives on the battlefield as portrayed so well in the TV series MASH. The civilian version of that helicopter was used extensively for transporting people, equipment and cargo as well as crop dusting.

Bell would later develop the UH-1 "Huey" that would become the most combat proven aircraft in the history of warfare, accumulating nearly 10 million hours of combat flight time and performing over 500,000 medical evacuations during the Vietnam War.

Bell also developed the AH-1 Cobra, the first helicopter ever designed as a purely attack helicopter for combat operations.

Helicopters and their crews have save thousands of lives on land and sea. They are used throughout all the military services for hundreds of different missions.

And the helicopter continues to save untold lives in the civilian sector, from law enforcement and firefighting to search and rescue and medical transport.

It was little wonder that the Army, stripped of its aviation assets when the Air Force became a separate Service in 1947, started looking at the helicopter to move men, equipment and supplies on the battlefield.

Helicopters could magically transport anyone and anything anywhere on the battlefield within minutes. That was the concept. Now all that had to be done was to come up with the helicopters, tactics and techniques that could accomplish it.

The problem in 1947 was that there were no helicopters in the Army. And the few that existed in the military had very limited capabilities.

The Army was also severely restricted in its ability to add aviation assets, as that was now a responsibility of the Air Force.

The US Army had developed aviation since 1907 and kept the US Army Air Corps as an integral branch, like infantry or artillery. Aviation assets were usually divided up and assigned to ground commands.

General Billy Mitchell who was the Army's Deputy Director of Aviation Services back in the 1920's argued for independence of aviation. He believed that air power alone would win the next big war and needed to be autonomous; operated and developed solely by aviators experienced in the new technology.

General Mitchell became vehement in his views and after proving that bombers could sink battle ships, which was rejected by the Navy, wrote a paper he released to the media accusing Army and Navy leadership of "Incompetency, criminal negligence and almost treasonable administration of the national defense."

He was famously court martialed for his views in 1925 and resigned from the military. He would remain a hero to many and his concepts continued to surface in the military for many years.

In 1935 all Army flying aviation assets were centralized in one General Headquarters of the Air Force. This was the first step towards a separate Air Force.

President Roosevelt had become a staunch supporter of air power at the time and by 1940 called for production of 50,000 planes a year in the build-up to World War II.

By 1942 the US Army Air Forces had been created and had equal prominence as a separate combat command with the Army and Navy on the Joint Chiefs of Staff.

The use of numbered Air Forces was instituted for decentralized organization and command of aviation assets.

Strategic bombing became the strategy of the Air Forces in both the European and Pacific Theaters.

By the end of World War II, The US Army Air Force was itself autonomous as a separate organization and the United States Air Force was officially established on September 18, 1947. The National Security Act of 1947 also established the Department of Defense with three internal military Departments; Army, Navy and now Air Force.

Five-Star General of the Army Henry Harley 'Hap' Arnold, who had commanded the 20th Air Force in the Pacific and all US Army Air Forces during the war, would later be designated General of the Air Force in 1949. He was one of only five Generals to hold five-star rank alongside Marshall, Eisenhower, MacArthur and Bradley. Arnold would become the only person ever to hold both General of the Army and General of the Air Force ranks.

General Carl Spaatz, Arnold's protégé and commander of the 8th Air Force in Europe during World War II, would become the first Chief of Staff of the Air Force.

With the establishment of the Air Force as a separate service, Army aviation for the most part had been reduced to small two-seat reconnaissance airplanes made by Piper, Stinson, Aeronca and Cessna used for artillery spotting.

The Air Force had taken over responsibility for all aviation support to the Army including transport of troops, material and supplies and close air support to troops in contact with the enemy.

The Army was prohibited from developing aviation for roles that the Air Force now had responsibility, except helicopters. The Army naturally started focusing on the use of helicopters in combat and combat support roles.

The Army received their first helicopters in 1947; 13 OH-13 Sioux helicopters from Bell Aircraft Corporation. The OH-13's were the small bubble helicopters depicted in the TV series MASH that saw extensive service a few years later in Korea. The OH-13 would be used to conduct over 20,000 medical evacuations during the Korean conflict and be credited with helping reduce the combat casualty death rate by half, compared to World War II.

The rugged terrain of Korea forced the Army to increasingly look for helicopter support to be able to accomplish a variety of missions; medical evacuation, artillery observation, command and control, and movement of troops and supplies. The Army deployed the first cargo helicopters in Korea, the CH-19 Chickasaw made by Sikorsky.

The Army was constantly battling with the Air Force in the 1950s and '60s for aviation assets to support the ground commanders. The Army, on its own, continued to add more and larger helicopters and even started adding airplanes to the mix including a large tactical transport plane; the de Havilland CV-2 Caribou.

The Army was also prohibited from arming aircraft for close air support for the troops. However, there was no prohibition against using helicopters for that purpose.

The Army started testing helicopter "gunships" to escort the troop-carrying helicopters and provide close air support to soldiers in combat. The first armed helicopters were deployed in 1962.

The competition for aviation assets between the Army and Air Force came to a head in 1966.

The two Chiefs of Staff, Army General Harold K. Johnson and Air Force General John P. McConnell, signed the Johnson-McConnell Agreement on 6 April 1966, whereby the Army would agree to relinquish its tactical transport airplanes to the Air Force and the Air Force would agree to relinquish its claims to most forms of rotary wing aircraft.

The Army by then had amassed a huge fleet of helicopters as more troops were being deployed to the Vietnam conflict.

Secretary of Defense Robert McNamara had ordered a review of Army Aviation in 1962 to determine how helicopters could best be used in the insurgent warfare of Vietnam.

In response to the Secretary's orders, Army General Hamilton Howze formed the Howze Board and conducted a series of operational tests using large formations of troops and helicopters to conduct combat operations that became known as "Air Assault".

General Howze recommended entire Army Divisions be equipped with hundreds of helicopters and converted to "Air

Assault" Divisions to conduct this new type of airmobile warfare.

Various types of helicopters, big and small, would be used to find and fix the enemy, transport troops into battle, transport equipment and supplies, provide armed escort and close air support, and conduct medical evacuations.

Air Force Chief of Staff Curtis LeMay vigorously opposed the findings of the Howze Board, stating that the Air Force "should operate everything that flies, right down to the last puddle jumper."

Secretary of Defense McNamara rejected General LeMay's objections (thank God) and accepted the Howze Board recommendations.

Shortly thereafter, the 1st Cavalry Division was transformed into an Air Assault Division and renamed the 1st Cavalry Division (Airmobile) or more commonly known as the 1st Air Cavalry Division.

The Division was equipped with the latest in new helicopters.

UH-1 Iroquois "Hueys" to carry troops and supplies and perform medical evacuations.

CH-47 Chinooks to haul large amounts of equipment and supplies.

CH-54 Tarhe Skycranes to carry the largest loads.

The Division would later receive OH-6 Cayuse Light Observation Helicopters to conduct reconnaissance operations and AH-1 Cobra Attack Helicopters to provide gunship support.

Now organized with 16,000 men and over 400 helicopters the 1st Cavalry Division (Airmobile) started deploying to Vietnam in August of 1965.

The 101st Airborne Division followed suit, reorganizing as an Airmobile Division, and deployed to Vietnam in 1968.

The Army ramped up recruitment and training of helicopter Pilots, mechanics and crewmembers to meet the rapidly growing demand.

Industry also ramped up development and production of helicopters for the Army.

Bell Helicopter was producing thousands of UH-1 'Hueys' and developing the world's first attack helicopter, the AH-1 Cobra.

Boeing-Vertol was producing hundreds of huge tandem-rotor CH-47 Chinook cargo helicopters.

Hughes Tool Company was producing hundreds of OH-6 Cayuse light observation helicopters (LOH), or "Loaches".

Sikorsky was building dozens of the giant CH-54 Tarhe Skycrane heavy lift helicopters.

All these helicopters featured jet-like turbine engines instead of piston engines and other advanced engineering and materials to go higher, farther, faster and carry more cargo.

Army aviation was bursting at the seams and, with nearly 12,000 total aircraft in 1967, was rapidly on its way to becoming the largest air force in the free world.

Igor Sikorsky, "Father of the Helicopter" 1889-1972

Sikorsky VS-300

Sikorsky CH-19 Chickasaw 1949

Sikorsky CH-34 Chocktaw 1955

Sikorsky CH-53 Sea Stallion 1966

Sikorsky HH-53 Jolly Green Giant 1967

Sikorsky CH-54 Tarhe 1962

Kaman HH-43 Huskie/Pedro 1962

Piaseki CH-21 Shawnee 1952

Boeing Vertol CH-47 Chinook 1962

Arthur Young and Bell Helicopter Engineers 1944

Bell OH-13 Sioux 1945

Bell UH-1 Huey 1962

Bell UH-1 Gunship

Bell AH-1 Cobra Attack Helicopter 1967

Hughes OH-6 Light Observation Helicopter (LOH) 1966

CHAPTER FOUR

FORT WOLTERS

By the time I arrived at Fort Wolters, Texas in November of 1967, this sprawling military complex was running at full capacity, operating 24 hours a day, with tens of thousands of support personnel both military and civilian.

The sky was filled with hundreds of helicopters as they formed long lines, like weaving chains, to land at nearby heliports with the air reverberating to the sounds of thousands of rotor blades whirring overhead.

I gaped in awe and wondered how so many aircraft could operate in such close proximity without running into each other.

In advanced training and combat I would learn what real "close proximity" was; overlapping rotor blades with the helicopter next to you while descending into landing zones (LZs) in mountainous jungle terrain, with rockets exploding all around from the gunships prepping the LZ and the enemy trying to shoot you down.

For now, I was mesmerized by the spectacle of so many aircraft filling the west Texas sky.

This was the Army's Primary Helicopter School, where students learned the basics of flying helicopters in small two-seat trainers over a period of four months, before heading to Alabama or Georgia for an additional four months of advance training.

Fort Wolters is located 50 miles west of Fort Worth in the rolling hills and flat terrain of west Texas near the small town of Mineral Wells. The area provided lots of room for pesky helicopters to roam and was an ideal location for training helicopter Pilots.

Originally known as Camp Wolters, the base was one of the largest infantry replacement training centers in the country during World War II, credited with training some 200,000 infantrymen.

It was deactivated at the end of the war and later designated an Air Force Base in 1951, for training engineers.

The base reverted back to the Army in 1956 with the mission of training helicopter Pilots. It became a permanent military facility in 1963 and renamed Fort Wolters.

The school started with just 12 helicopters, one heliport (Main) and four outlying small airports called stage fields. The first class in 1957 graduated 35 students.

Now, in 1967, the school had more than 1,300 helicopters, three major heliports, twenty-five stage fields, and was graduating 600 students a month!

By the time Fort Wolters closed in 1973, the U.S. Army Primary Helicopter School had trained over 40,000 student Pilots.

All potential Army Helicopter Pilots received their primary training at Fort Wolters.

A 16-week Officer Rotary Wing Aviator Course (ORWAC) to train Commissioned Officers to be helicopter Pilots.

A 20-week Warrant Officer Candidate Rotary Wing Aviator Course (WORWAC) was offered to enlisted personnel aspiring to be helicopter Pilots. This course added an additional four weeks at the beginning of school for an intensive (read "brutal") Warrant Officer Candidate (WOC) Indoctrination Training Course - commonly known as "Preflight".

The first eight weeks, or Primary I, was dedicated to learning basic flight maneuvers; hovering, take offs, traffic patterns, landings, emergency landings (including autorotations), navigation and solo flights.

The flight training was conducted at the outlying stage fields, which were small airfields with multiple parallel runways, built to accommodate as many helicopters as safely possible.

The second eight weeks, or Primary II, taught students to apply those basic maneuvers while landing at small unimproved landing areas and introduced formation flying, air navigation and night flying.

The training here at Fort Wolters was intense and the attrition rate high. Some 25 percent or more wouldn't graduate.

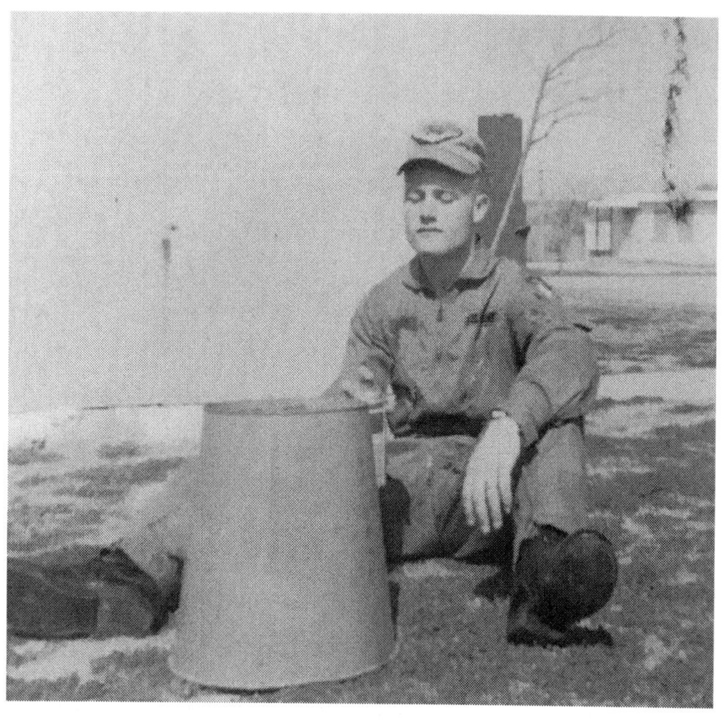

Warrant Officer Candidate Lew "Lower Than Whale Shit" Jennings. Gray Hats. Welcome to Flight School, Fort Wolters. Texas. 1967

CHAPTER FIVE

PREFLIGHT

"CANDIDATE!" screamed the TAC Officer. "Quit looking at the sky like you've never seen a helicopter before! If you want to fly one of those, you better get with the program! Come to attention and brace when you see an officer!" he continued yelling.

"You are a Warrant Officer Candidate. The lowest creature in the food chain. You are lower than whale shit! Do you understand Candidate?"

"Yes Sir," I responded.

"NOT YES SIR!" he screamed, turning almost purple from rage. "The first words out of your mouth will be 'Candidate Jennings, Sir!' Do you understand Candidate Whale Shit?"

"CANDIDATE JENNINGS SIR! YES SIR!" I screamed in response.

The four weeks of indoctrination known as "Preflight" had begun. Geez. I thought boot camp was over. This was going to be worse. Much worse!

The purpose of Preflight as I came to understand it, was several-fold.

First, to weed out those who didn't have the will, perseverance or strength to undergo the intense pressure of the program and future helicopter combat operations.

Second, to eliminate those who didn't have the capacity to work with others as a team.

Third, to impart the sense of personal commitment to those who carry a rucksack and a rifle, to do all we could to support them, even under fire. The motto of the school was "Flying Above the Best", to emphasize the focus on those fighting on the ground.

Fourth, to learn attention to detail to the extreme so as to predict, detect and eliminate failure.

Fifth, to learn and live by the Warrant Officer Creed. This Creed demands that, as a Warrant Officer, we:

Willingly render loyal services to superiors, subordinates and peers in every organization of which we are members.

Always set an example in conduct, appearance and performance that will make others proud to know and work with us.

Reliably discharge all duties with which we are confronted, whether such duties are expressed or implied.

Readily subordinate our personal interest and welfare to those of their organization and their subordinates.

Accept responsibility at every opportunity and acknowledge full accountability for our actions.

Never knowingly tolerate wrong-doing by ourselves or others, whether by commission or omission, design or neglect.

Teach other people in a way that effectively expands and perpetuates the scope of our technical competence.

Obtain breadth of perspective and depth of understanding beyond the limits of our specific responsibility.

Faithfull adhere to our oath of office in all respects, upholding and defending the nation's constitution by both word and deed.

Forcefully take the initiative to stimulate constructive action in all areas requiring or inviting our attention.

Improve ourselves both physically and mentally, professionally and personally, to increase our own abilities and value of our services.

Contribute our past experiences, service and knowledge to a dedicated effort of a betterment of the future.

Earn an ironclad reputation for the absolute integrity of our word.

Reflect credit and inspire confidence in ourselves, the Warrant Officer Corps, the military service of our nation and the United States of America.

Many in and out of military service ask, 'What is a Warrant Officer?'

Army Field Manual 22-100 puts this question in perspective with the following definition:

"Warrant officers are highly specialized, single-track specialty officers who receive their authority from the Secretary of the Army upon initial appointment. However, Title 10 U.S.C. authorizes the commissioning of Warrant Officers (WO1) upon promotion to Chief Warrant Officer (CW2). These commissioned Warrant Officers are direct representatives of the President of the United States. They derive their authority from the same source as commissioned officers but remain specialists, in contrast to commissioned officers, who are generalists. Warrant Officers can and do command detachments, units, activities, and vessels as well as lead, coach, train, and counsel subordinates. As leaders and

technical experts, they provide valuable skills, guidance, and expertise to commanders and organizations in their particular field."

The last sentence accurately describes the role of the Warrant Officer; a leader and technical expert that provides skills, guidance and expertise. Originally Warrant Officers couldn't be assigned to "Leadership" positions. That went out the window during Vietnam, but it didn't become official until years later, when Warrant Officers could be "Commissioned" and legally be in leadership positions, and even "Command" positions (usually reserved for W-5's).

"WHO JUST FARTED!" screamed the TAC Officer. He was a Chief Warrant Officer Helicopter Pilot recently returned from combat duty in Vietnam and had a passion for making sure only the best candidates survived "Preflight".

We were standing in line to enter the mess hall for our first meal at Fort Wolters. Even though once seated we only had ten minutes to eat, there were so many of us that the line was moving at a snail's pace.

Even standing in line had its own regimen. First, stand at "Parade Rest" with your feet shoulder width apart, stomach in, chest out, staring straight ahead, hands crossed behind your back, no talking. Then come to attention, take one step forward, then back to parade rest. That's when someone passed the gas.

"I SAY AGAIN, WHO FARTED?" screamed the TAC Officer as he stomped back and forth eyeballing each one of us for a clue as to who the culprit was.

"Okay, no one is going to fess up? Then we'll just have to have a funeral to bury that fart!" he hollered. We stifled any chuckles as we feared what was to come next.

"You, you, you and you!" he pointed at those at the head of the line "You will be grave diggers and dig the grave right over here," as he directed them to a patch of grass by the old World War II barracks.

"You, you, you and you will be the cannons! Kneel next to the grave!" as he directed the next four in line.

"You, you, you and you will be the cannon cockers! Stand at attention behind the cannons ready to fire on command!" he shouted.

"The rest of you will be mourners, so assume the dying cockroach position now and start moaning!" he commanded. (The "dying cockroach" position is on your back with your arms and legs waving in the air).

With that, the grave diggers started digging, the mourners started moaning, the cannon cockers cocked the cannons and the TAC Officer called the "Ready" and "Fire" commands until we were all hoarse from screaming BANG, BANG and moaning at the top of our lungs!

"Back in line!" he commanded and as quick as it had begun the ceremony was over. No one dared fart out loud again. We barely had enough time to get any food at all!

In the mess hall, each one of us grabbed a tray, received our portion of whatever was offered, marched to a table, set down our tray, napkin and utensils, and took a seat.

We were to eat a "square meal", meaning that you sit upright, stiff back, pick up a portion with your fork, lift it directly vertically in military fashion to a point just opposite and below your nose, then open your mouth, put the food in, take the fork out to the position in front of you, then lower it again for the next bite.

I was concentrating on doing this absolutely correctly when the TAC Officer halted right next to me and looked at the position of my butter knife. He then leaned down into my right ear and screamed "CANDIDATE JENNINGS, ARE YOU TRYING TO KILL ME?"

I nearly choked on my food as I screamed back in return "SIR, CANDIDATE JENNINGS NO SIR!"

"Then why is the blade of your knife pointed out at me rather than in towards your food?" he demanded.

"Sir, Candidate Jennings, I don't know Sir!"

"You don't know Candidate Jennings?" he roared. "On your feet!" he ordered.

I literally jumped to my feet, almost knocking over my chair. The whole mess hall went silent. Everyone had stopped eating and remained sitting at attention.

"Stand on top of your chair Candidate!" he shouted. I did so in an instant.

"Now, face your fellow candidates and repeat after me!" he directed.

"I Candidate Jennings do solemnly swear to uphold and maintain the integrity, dignity and manners of those of an officer and gentleman and never to allow my actions to cause distress, injury or death to those around me. I apologize for my reprehensible behavior at the mess today."

I repeated this word for word and, at the end, he simply commanded "Candidates, Fall In!" Everyone evacuated the mess hall at a dead run and assembled in formation outside, hence "Fall In", where we assembled four lines abreast, at attention, one arm length separation front and rear and to the side.

Geeezzz. I think I only got to eat two bites of food!

We marched off to the barracks for our room assignments, then to the Quartermaster for our gear; "Right Face! Forward March! Double Time March!" We started running. "You will run everywhere Candidates! The only time you will stop running is when you stop and come to attention to address an officer or senior candidate! Is that understood?" "Yes Sir!" we all replied in unison.

The next four weeks seemed like an eternity as we rose each morning before dawn, cleaned and polished our room and gear, made our beds so a quarter would bounce, sheets exactly twelve spring rows in under the mattress, shoes and boots exactly one inch apart, foot locker organized and gleaming like a museum piece, every hanger and uniform piece exactly equal distance and facing correctly in the locker, every button polished, every thread trimmed (no lanyards), everything exactly as directed only to be trashed sometime during the day, demerits assessed for not attaining standards and starting all over again.

We ran to breakfast, ran to lunch, ran to dinner, ran to classes, ran everywhere until we were near dropping and drenched in sweat. No rest. Constant harassment. Study until your brain fried. Clean until your arms fell off. Polish until your fingers were numb.

Four weeks later about 25 percent of the class had already dropped out or failed.

For the rest of us, it was time to learn to fly helicopters!

Hughes TH-55A Osage Training Helicopter

Hiller OH-23 Raven

CHAPTER SIX

PRIMARY FLIGHT TRAINING

"Helicopter Pilots Are Different" by Harry Reasoner

"The thing is, helicopters are different from planes.

An airplane by its nature wants to fly, and if not interfered with too strongly by unusual events or by a deliberately incompetent Pilot, it will fly.

A helicopter does not want to fly. It is maintained in the air by a variety of forces and controls working in opposition to each other, and if there is any disturbance in this delicate balance, the helicopter stops flying immediately and disastrously.

There is no such thing as a gliding helicopter.

This is why being a helicopter Pilot is so different from being an airplane Pilot and why, in general, airplane Pilots are open, clear eyed, buoyant extroverts, and helicopter Pilots are brooders, introspective anticipators of trouble.

They know that if something bad has not happened, it is about to."

I would soon find out that those great words by the late CBS correspondent and news anchor Harry Reasoner pretty accurately describe helicopter Pilots as introspective anticipators of trouble.

Over time, my own definition of a helicopter would be: "a thousand moving parts that happen to be flying in formation, any one of which can kill you."

The Warrant Officer Classes at flight school were numbered by the physical year you were to graduate, followed by an odd number. The Commissioned Officer Classes had the year, followed with an even number. My WOC class was number 68-19, Gray Hats.

The Commissioned Officers had already gone through their military training at West Point, College Reserve Officer Training Corps (ROTC) or Officer Candidate School (OCS). They were now Commissioned Officers; Second or First Lieutenants and even Captains for some who had been in the Army for a while and now wanted to be aviators.

The officers lived in their own quarters on post or off-post in rented housing. They collected flight pay even as students and many drove Corvettes.

Members of the Warrant Officer Candidate classes on the other hand were still Candidates. Lower than Whale Shit. We would not officially receive appointment as Warrant Officers until we completed all of our flight training, nearly a year to go. Even then, as soldiers, we would receive our appointment to Warrant Officer first, followed by award of our wings at graduation.

For the Warrant Officer Candidates or WOCs as we were referred to, flight training started out like every other day, living in the barracks. Military education. Physical training.

Cleaning the barracks until the floors glistened and the sinks sparkled. Arranging our gear to perfection. Being constantly harassed by everyone senior to us. Running here, there and everywhere until we were drenched in sweat. Only then would we be allowed to attend flight classes or actually fly a helicopter.

The daily routine was two hours of military readiness including inspections, physical training and breakfast, four hours of classroom instruction, lunch, four hours of flight instruction with two hours actually in the aircraft, then back to the barracks for more inspections, dinner, military training, preparation of your room and gear, study, and lights out at 2200 (10pm). This went on for 16 weeks.

The first eight weeks was introduction to basic helicopter flight.

In the classroom, we studied history of aviation, aerodynamics, weather, navigation, helicopter operations and maintenance, military and civilian aviation rules and regulations, safety and more.

We learned about precession, leading, lagging, translational lift, settling with power, retreating blade stall, ground resonance and a thousand other things peculiar to helicopter flight.

At the stage-fields we would practice basic flight techniques. Hovering, straight and level flight, traffic patterns, normal and steep takeoffs and landings, running takeoffs and landings, autorotation to touchdown in case of engine failure, and cross-country navigation.

Autorotations, landing the helicopter without power, were especially thrilling. Autorotations were a maneuver you performed to survive an engine failure.

You simulated an engine failure by closing the throttle, immediately lowering the collective to take the pitch out of the blades to keep the rotor spinning, keeping your airspeed up as you plummeted towards the ground, pulling back on the cyclic and flare at about 50 feet to get a big rush of air through the rotor to keep it at max rpm, pulling up rapidly (pop) a bit on the collective just before you hit the ground to reduce or halt your forward motion, then pulling up the remaining collective to get the rotor blades to take a last bite of air while pushing forward on the cyclic to level the helicopter as you gently settled to the ground.

If you were off by a foot or a second, you could crash or cut the tail boom off. Piece of cake!

We would perform straight-in autorotations, autorotations with a 90 degree turn to the runway, autorotations at night, autorotations while hovering and even pop-up autorotations from low level flight, all the way to the ground.

While many an Army aviator saved the day by performing a successful autorotation in an emergency, the Army wrecked so many helicopters in training, that years later practicing autorotations to the ground would be prohibited and we would recover the maneuver by adding power as we started the flare and not touching down.

My Primary instructor was a Chief Warrant Officer recently returned from a combat tour in Vietnam. He was great and had me flying the TH-55 'Mattel Messerschmitt' in no time at all.

I could tell he was proud of my accomplishments when, just after a few hours of flight instruction, he had me hover in front of the tower, then held his hands in the air to show the other instructors what his student could do.

Most of us would solo within 15 hours, however there were those who simply couldn't get the hang of it and we would lose another 10 percent of the class to attrition.

The second eight weeks we studied advanced helicopter flight techniques. Landing in confined areas or to a pinnacle or cliff. Landing on a slope. Take offs over 50 foot obstacles. Formation flight. Night flight. Cross country flight and more.

I especially enjoyed flying down the Brazos River with my instructor and landing on sand bars. The freedom of flight offered by a helicopter was amazing. I loved it!

Back at the barracks the intense military training continued.

We would lose another 10 percent of the class by the end of 20 weeks.

I was fortunate to graduate at the top of my primary flight training class at Fort Wolters and received orders for advanced helicopter training at Hunter Army Airfield, Savannah, Georgia.

UH-1 Huey Graduation Fly-By Formation

CHAPTER SEVEN

ADVANCED FLIGHT TRAINING

Most graduates from Primary at Fort Wolters went to Fort Rucker, Alabama, the official US Army Aviation Center and "Home of Army Aviation" for their advanced training.

I wanted Hunter Army Airfield at Savannah because at Hunter we were able to start advanced training right away in the infamous Bell UH-1 "Huey" helicopter that was being used so successfully in Vietnam. I couldn't wait to get started!

Upon arrival at Hunter, I reported to my new unit and advanced flight school class at an austere looking, but sparkling clean concrete barracks. I was a "Senior Candidate" by now when I left Fort Wolters, enjoying some semblance of achievement and respect. That was immediately dashed when I met my new tactical non-commissioned officer or TAC NCO.

"BRACE MAGGOT!" he ordered as I approached. "Who do you think you are just sauntering up here like you're on a Sunday stroll? Get all your shit out of your vehicle and up here, now! You have room A-6 Jennings. Consider yourself confined to quarters until further advised. MOVE IT SCUM BAG!"

I was in shock. But I wasn't alone as he treated everyone else who arrived the same way.

Some of the candidates had traveled across the country with their wives and children in tow thinking they would be allowed to live off post in residential housing like those candidates who had been assigned to Fort Rucker.

Not so. This was an entirely different regime that would insist on making it nearly unbearable for the Warrant Officer Candidates.

Even though we were confined to quarters and couldn't leave our rooms, we spent the rest of the day and that evening helping our married class mates haul their stuff up from their cars by tying their gear to sheets we had dangling from the upper story windows. This kind of tough treatment would continue for the next four months until graduation.

We had learned a lot in boot camp at Fort Polk and Primary Flight School at Fort Wolters. We knew how to maintain and present our gear. We knew how to make the floors shine like glass and the room presentable for the most exacting inspection. We were about to learn a lot more.

Our first day of classes at Hunter was an introduction to the UH-1 Huey helicopter and a dream come true. At the end of the day, we double-timed back to the barracks with smiles on our faces, until we arrived.

We "fell in" to our standard formation outside the barracks directly in front of our waiting TAC NCO (Tactical Non-Commissioned Officer or Sergeant). We looked up at the second floor to our rooms. Every window had some kind of nasty graffiti written on the inside in black shoe polish, OUR shoe polish. The TAC NCO's had conducted their first inspection. The place was a wreck.

As I entered my room, I remembered how it glistened when we left that morning. The floor had been polished and buffed to a mirror reflecting the clouds outside the window. A sparkle of sunshine gleamed off the sink faucet. Our gear and displays perfect.

Now it looked like a tornado had swept through. The TAC NCO's had disassembled the sink plumbing and dumped the contents of the sewer trap on the floor. They had ripped the beds apart, strewn our gear from one end of the room to another, did "360s" with their boots to ruin the floors, then took our boot polish and wrote inspirational messages on our windows. It would take hours to repair the damage. No problem, we had all night. Wake-up isn't until 0500. Look for this every day, they said, until you meet our standards. Welcome to Hunter candidates!

The classroom and flight instructors would secretly commiserate with us. We would arrive at flight training soaking wet with perspiration after hours of military drilling and running all over hell and back. It was our penance. Those of us who chose or were chosen to go to Hunter paid a dear price for a few more hours in the Huey.

Our classmates at Rucker rubbed it in when they wrote to tell us what a country club like atmosphere it was there.

Married candidates at Rucker did get to live off post with their families. Those candidates who lived in the barracks were treated as if they were already Warrant Officers.

We at Hunter were determined our training would better prepare us for combat. At least we wanted to think that was true.

In fact, the helicopter training at Rucker and Hunter was probably the best in the world. Combat seasoned Vietnam veterans were our instructors. And teach us they did!

We practiced combat formations keeping it tight. Performed low level and terrain flight following the contours of the earth. Practiced combat tactics and techniques learned through their experiences. Conducted troop pick-ups and drop-offs. Flew single ship, multiple ship and large formations in daylight, nighttime and marginal weather conditions.

Especially thrilling were low level and night auto-rotations to the ground where you chopped the throttle to simulate engine failure, pulled back hard on the cyclic to gain altitude and made the rotors go faster with the air streaming through, picking your landing target, maintaining rotor rpm and airspeed until 50 feet, then flaring to bring the helicopter to a stop in midair, and pulling the last remaining lift from the rotor blades as you settled to the ground. One mistake, one missed step, one errant calculation, spelled disaster. What fun!

At the end of nearly a year of training, we had accumulated around 200 hours flight time and thousands of experiences in all kinds of conditions and situations. We truly thought we were the best combat helicopter Pilots in the world! Time would tell.

Somehow, I managed to graduate number one in my class and was named Distinguished Graduate.

My father, Wilson Jennings, was now long retired from the Coast Guard and had been teaching electronics courses with the Navy at Treasure Island in San Francisco Bay. I called him with the good news. Dad told me he had recently fallen ill and didn't think he would be able to attend my graduation ceremony.

I informed my chain of command that there would be no family attending my graduation. They ran it up the flagpole and what happened next was unbelievable.

The Commanding General at Hunter personally placed a call to my father to let him know how well I had performed and how important it would be if he were able to attend.

My father rallied from his illness and the Air Force gave him a free ride out to Charleston, South Carolina from Travis Air Force Base in California.

I met him at Charleston and drove him down to the Army base at Savannah. Dad had brought his old Coast Guard uniform he had retired in as Command Master Chief at Coast Guard Station San Francisco. In the formal graduation ceremony at Hunter he was proudly wearing his uniform while he pinned the Warrant Officer bars on my shoulders along with the Commanding General and then pinned my wings on, designating me a bona fide Army Aviator.

After the graduation ceremony, I wanted to show my father the Company area. As we approached the barracks I would be treated to a totally different experience than when I arrived five months earlier.

The TAC NCO was drilling a new class of candidates out on the parade field. Like right out of the movie *An Officer and Gentleman*, when he saw us approaching he brought the entire class to attention, then turned and saluted me.

"Mr. Jennings (that's how Warrant Officers are formally addressed: "Mr."), congratulations on your selection as Distinguished Graduate and appointment to Warrant Officer. It would be an honor Sir to have you inspect the new class."

With that, he turned and ordered "Open Ranks March!", "Dress Right Dress!" and "Ready Front!", then escorted me down the line as I inspected each candidate of the new class with my father looking on. It was one of the proudest moments of my life.

I had a week off before my new assignment to Cobra School there at Hunter, so Dad and I took the opportunity to drive together to Kentucky and Tennessee to visit his family. We spent the next several days with aunts, uncles and cousins I hadn't seen in many years and bonding with my father as never before. It was a melancholy trip for us both when I returned him to Charleston to catch his flight back to California.

I felt I was following in his footsteps. I had always wanted to be just like him.

My Father and I at my Graduation from Flight School, Hunter Army Airfield, Savannah, Georgia, September 1968.

CHAPTER EIGHT

COBRA HALL

As Distinguished Graduate, I had a choice of further training in cargo or attack helicopters or heading straight to Vietnam, flying Hueys. I chose to attend Cobra School there at Hunter to qualify in the first-ever helicopter specifically designed and built as an Attack Helicopter, Bell's new AH-1G Cobra.

Cobra Hall, as it was known then, was the primary training school for this new machine.

The Cobra was designed by Bell Helicopter who also made the UH-1 Huey.

The engineers at Bell had taken the engine, transmission and drive train from the Huey, wrapped it up in a tight airframe only 36 inches at its widest point, put the Pilot and Copilot behind one another in a tandem seating arrangement, installed a rotating turret up front with an Emerson Electric Gatling Gun that fired up to 4,000 rounds per minute and a

Grenade Launcher that could fire 300 grenades a minute, plus little wings on each side that could carry up to 72 rockets.

The more streamlined fuselage saved weight and allowed the helicopter to fly faster than the Hueys it would be escorting into combat. And the lighter weight allowed the Cobra to carry more weapons and ammunition than other gunships that were overloaded and slower modified Hueys.

The Cobra looked like a jet aircraft with its sleek fuselage and tandem seating.

Unlike fighter jets of our sister Services where the Pilot sits up front, in the Cobra the Pilot sits in the back seat. He's a little higher up so he can see everything out front and has all the flight instruments and conventional controls to fly the helicopter. The Pilot can also control and fire all the weapons systems from his rear cockpit.

The Copilot/Gunner (CPG) sits in the front seat. There is a flexible gun sight the gunner can use to aim and fire a Gatling gun or grenade launcher mounted in a moveable turret under the nose of the aircraft.

The Copilot's station has miniature controls on either side of the cockpit to be able to fly the helicopter in the event something happens to the Pilot.

The Cobra was a fast, mean machine, loaded for bear. I thought it was the most beautiful helicopter I had ever seen (and still do).

Cobra school was four weeks long. The class was a mix of Commissioned Officers and Warrant Officers. The highest-ranking officer was our class leader. The training at this school was totally unlike all the previous training I had gone through. Here I was treated with respect as a Warrant Officer professional. It was a dream come true.

I lived off base in a house I rented with a fellow Warrant Officer and classmate, Pete Parnell.

No terrifying Drill Sergeants. No screaming Tactical Officers or NCO's. No one waking us at zero-dark-thirty hollering "TIME TO WAKE UP GIRLS, GET UP, GET UP, ITS ANOTHER GREAT DAY IN THE ARMY AND ANOTHER FINE DAY FOR THE CORPS!" No thunderous sounds of garbage cans being flung from one end of the barracks to the other to make sure we leaped out of bed. No falling out in the Company area for physical training and a five-mile run before breakfast.

Just the soft sound of a bedside alarm clock. I was in heaven!

Not to say Cobra school wasn't intense. It was! All the instructors were combat veterans and focused on teaching us how to best employ all the capabilities and firepower this incredible gunship could provide. They knew that when we graduated in just four weeks, our destination was Vietnam and our job would be to find, fix and destroy the enemy while supporting and protecting our troops, and to try and not get killed in the process.

We rose early each day to attend classes to learn all the intricacies of this new machine; electrical systems, hydraulic systems, engine, transmission, drive train, main rotor system, tail rotor system, aerodynamics, flight controls, stability augmentation system, and weapons, weapons, and more weapons systems.

The classroom instruction was augmented with daily flight training sessions to incorporate what we learned in a real-world environment.

We spent hours on the range learning how to properly load, aim and fire the rocket systems. We learned how to load, aim, fire and clear the Gatling gun. And we learned how to load, aim and fire the grenade launcher.

We flew day and night to learn the flight characteristics of the Cobra, conducting low level flight, high speed dives and low-level pop-up autorotations to simulate recovering and landing from engine failure. The training was intense and relentless. I loved every minute of it.

As I was getting ready to graduate from Cobra school and head to combat in Vietnam, I received word that my father was gravely ill. He had collapsed while teaching a class at Treasure Island Navy Base and lay in serious condition at Letterman Army Hospital, Presidio of San Francisco, California.

I rushed home to be by his side.

Bell AH-1G Cobra Attack Helicopter

The AH-1G Cobra was the first helicopter specifically designed as an Attack Helicopter. Tandem seating, two-place helicopter with the Pilot in back and Copilot/Gunner in front; 44.7 feet long, 13.5 feet high, fuselage is 36 inches wide, 5,810lbs Empty Weight, 9,500lbs Gross Weight, powered by a Lycoming T53-L-13 Gas Turbine Engine producing 1,100 Shaft Horsepower with a cruising speed of 149kts and maximum speed of 190kts.

Armament included 2-75" folding fin aerial rockets (FFARs) on the wing stores and a 40mm grenade launcher and six-barreled 7.62mm Gatling gun in the rotating turret up front. The grenade launcher could fire up to 300 grenades per minute. The Emerson Electric Gatling gun could fire 2,000 to 4,000 rounds per minute.

AH-1G Copilot/Gunner (CPG) position (Top). Small cyclic control visible on right and collective control on left. The flexible gun sight, upper right, allows the CPG to fire the Gatling gun or grenade launcher in the rotating turret. AH-1G Pilot position (Bottom). Full instrumentation and Pilot can control all weapons systems turret fixed in stow mode.

CHAPTER NINE

PRESIDIO OF SAN FRANCISCO

After graduating from Cobra school, I was given a 30-day leave to visit with friends and family before heading off to Vietnam. On arriving home to the San Francisco Bay Area, I immediately met my sister Gail and headed to Letterman Army Hospital at the Presidio of San Francisco to visit Dad.

His condition was far worse than he had let on. The doctors told us he was probably not going to make it. He had been diagnosed with Polyarteritis nodosa, a somewhat rare disease at the time that affected the arteries, heart and kidneys.

I was reeling in shock and dismayed at what to do. I had orders to Vietnam and needed to see if there was some way to delay my departure so I could be with my father and take care of things on his behalf.

There was a small airfield on the Presidio down by the water with some older looking airplanes and helicopters, called Crissy Field. I headed down there to see if there was someone I could talk to.

Crissy Field was built in 1920 and named after an Army Air Corps Pilot, Major Dana H. Crissy, who was then the commander at Mather Field and had died when his de Havilland DH-4B crashed at Salt Lake City on a "Transcontinental reliability and endurance test".

At the time Colonel Henry H. "Hap" Arnold, who would later become a 5-star General of the Army and Air Force at the end of World War II, was in charge of the construction of the airfield.

This beautiful location right on the water at the foot of the Presidio and below the Golden Gate Bridge had been used as a Coast Guard sea plane base and Army airfield from 1920 to 1936, when it was closed as a first line base and Hamilton Field opened across the bay in nearby Marin County.

Now in 1968, Crissy Field was being used to support the Sixth Army Headquarters at the Presidio. There was a small flight detachment on the field. It was a choice assignment for a privileged few.

I nervously entered a small Flight Operations building and approached what appeared to be a flight planning counter. I found myself facing a full bird Colonel sitting behind a desk.

As a 22-year old "Wobbly One" just out of flight school and having had my butt kicked for the last two years by Corporals to Sergeants, standing in front of a Colonel was like appearing before God. I was petrified!

As he looked up at me, I came to attention, saluted and stammered "Sir, Mr. Jennings, I have a serious problem I need to talk to somebody about."

"Relax Jennings. What's up?" he asked.

I started to explain my situation when he raised his hand "Hold on, let me check with the Commanding Officer," as he stepped into an office nearby.

Geeez, I thought, you mean there's somebody here that outranks him?

He motioned me to enter where I met another full bird Colonel. "Sir. Mr. Jennings reporting," I blurted out as I snapped to attention and saluted for a second time. He saluted, they both smiled and he asked me to take a seat. "What's this problem you want to talk to me about?"

"Sir, I'm here on leave from flight school with orders to Vietnam. My father is gravely ill in the hospital at Letterman and is not expected to live much longer. I would like to delay my orders but don't know what to do," I explained.

We spent the next 10 minutes or so discussing the situation, me describing my father's diagnosis and condition, what ward he was in, where I was staying with family in San Jose and when I was supposed to report to Travis Air Force Base near Sacramento, California for my flight to Vietnam.

He then looked over at the other Colonel. "Dan, would you ask Mr. Matthews to come over and show Mr. Jennings here our aircraft and facilities?"

Then to me, "Jennings, you did the right thing coming down to see us. Mr. Matthews will show you around while I make a few calls. Report back here in about an hour."

I couldn't believe it! Two Colonels and being treated like a fellow officer and no longer a boot or candidate in training. I must be dreaming!

Mr. Matthews met me at Operations a few minutes later. He was a tall, gray haired, good-looking guy with a ready smile and an aura of professional authority.

He was a CW4! That was the highest rank for a Warrant Officer in those days and I was immediately impressed. I was further impressed when I noticed he wore Master Army Aviator Wings. You don't get to wear those until you have attained several thousand hours of flight time and at least 15 years of service. He immediately stuck out his hand, "Bob Matthews".

We strolled down the flight line at Crissy Field towards the Golden Gate Bridge rising majestically just off the end of the runway. To our left the Presidio rose steeply up the hill, with its many structures dating back to before World War II, housing the Headquarters for the 6th Army and many supporting units. In the center and towards the top of the rise was a beautiful Spanish style building that was the oldest building in San Francisco and now served as the Officers Club.

"We have several missions and organizations we support here" Bob explained. "The primary mission is to support the Commanding General, Sixth Army. To fly the General, we have a nice UH-1 Huey with VIP package," he gestured as we approached the first aircraft on the flight line.

It was the most beautiful Huey I had ever seen, all polished and glistening in dark green and white. He pulled the sliding side door open to reveal a fully carpeted interior with plush leather seats and an array of radios in a pedestal mounted between the front seats. A nice ride for the Commanding General!

He then gestured to another helicopter nearby. Also gleaming in the sunlight. It looked like a totally restored vintage helicopter right out of a museum. It was a huge thing with a big, bulbous nose with clamshell doors hanging on the front, a tiny cockpit way up in the air above the nose, a huge sliding door on the side, and the whole thing perched on two massive wheels and a tiny tail wheel below the tail rotor.

"This is one of the few existing VH-34 Presidential Helicopters left," Bob revealed. "It was used to support President Eisenhower back in the late 50's. We now use it to support General of the Army Omar Bradley," he continued as he opened the sliding door to reveal an exquisite VIP interior with carpeting, stuffed chairs, a couch and lace curtains over the windows.

"This helicopter even has an autopilot and lots of back-up systems. It's so heavy we can only take aboard about five people max."

General Bradley was the only 5-star general still living and his residence was down in Beverly Hills outside of Los Angeles.

Even though retired, he was still supported by the Army and I heard an office and staff were maintained at his disposal in the Pentagon as well.

Bob continued to show me the rest of the aircraft on the line which consisted of a few small twin-engine airplanes, an OH-23 Hiller helicopter with floats and two more conventional CH-34 cargo helicopters.

"These CH-34's are our work horses." Bob continued. "They are equipped with floats as we fly across the Bay up to five times a day to pick up wounded at Travis Air Force Base coming in from Vietnam and transport them back here for treatment at Letterman."

Letterman Army Hospital I would learn was the largest military hospital on the West Coast and handled thousands of wounded returning from Vietnam for treatment.

When we returned to Operations, the Executive Officer motioned me into the Commander's office.

"Sir, Mr. Jennings reporting," I said as I came to attention and saluted.

"Have a seat Lew," he replied as he motioned me to a chair in front of his desk.

"Dan, would you ask Mr. Mathews to join us as well?" he asked.

When Bob entered the office a moment later, the Colonel directed his attention to me.

"I'm really sorry to hear about your father's condition. You're not to worry about your orders to Vietnam for the time being. You belong to me. You are now assigned to the 6th Army Flight Detachment on Compassionate Reassignment until further notice. Bob will help you with your new assignment and qualification in our aircraft so we can put you to work. I also want you to keep me posted on your father's condition. Welcome aboard."

With that he stood up and came around to shake my hand. Dan the Executive Officer and Bob also shook my hand and welcomed me aboard. I was shaking with relief as tears welled in my eyes. All I could muster was barely a whispered, "Thank you, Sir."

The next few weeks were a flurry of activity as I received qualification training in all the helicopters there at Crissy Field and settled into my new assignment flying support missions for Headquarters 6th Army and medical evacuations back and forth to Travis Air Force Base and spending quality time with Dad in the hospital every day.

My father, Wilson Jennings, was born in Paris, Tennessee on August 13, 1915. He had four brothers; Frank, Johnny,

Robert (Bobby) and James. He also had two sisters; Betty Lou and Grace.

Johnny, Robert, and James served with distinction in the Marine Corps, although James tragically died at age 19 in a drowning accident while on deployment in Panama.

Johnny stayed in the Marine Corps for over 20 years and retired as a Major and went on to a career in the defense industry in San Diego. His wife Flora founded the California Ballet Company there. Daughter Marlene became a ballet star and daughter Maxine still runs the Company today along with granddaughter Clarissa.

My uncle Johnny and I became very close when I was stationed in San Diego with the Navy late in my Army career. I was honored to give the eulogy at his passing in 1988.

Brother Bobby finished his initial tour of duty in the Marine Corps in the '50s and became hugely successful in the trucking industry in Los Angeles after several years of adventures in Alaska.

I went to live with Uncle Bobby for a while right out of High School and drove trucks in the LA area. I have many fond memories of times spent with Uncle Bobby. He retired back to Kentucky near his sister Betty Lou. He passed in 1994 and is survived by his wife Esther.

While at the Presidio, my sister Gail and I spent many hours with Dad as his condition worsened over the ensuing weeks and months. He passed peacefully at Letterman on November 20, 1968.

My father had insisted that he be cremated and that there be no elaborate ceremonies, funeral or burial, so I flew out over Monterey Bay where I scattered his ashes off the beautiful coast of Santa Cruz.

Then I headed to Travis Air Force Base for my flight to "Disneyland East for Adults", Vietnam.

Sikorsky VH-34 Presidential Helicopter with Float Kits

CHAPTER TEN

VIETNAM

Vietnam lies along the eastern edge of the Indochina Peninsula in Southeast Asia, surrounded by the Gulf of Tonkin and South China Sea on its eastern shore, with China to the north and Laos and Cambodia to the west.

The country is nearly a thousand miles long, from Ho Chi Minh City (Saigon) in the south to Hanoi in the north and is less than 50 miles across at its narrowest point, near the old demilitarized zone north of Hue. It's a subtropical region, starting in the south at just 8 degrees above the equator to nearly 25 degrees at the far north.

It is a beautiful country with vast rice paddies and picturesque villages in the Mekong River Delta of the south. Gorgeous beaches with crystal-clear water line the coast. The rolling hills, lakes and mountains of the central highlands and the steep jungles and mountains of the A Shau Valley are stunning, as are the great plains of Khe Sanh and the Red River Delta in the far north, home to Hanoi and Haiphong.

Vietnam Highlands

Fishing Nets in the Mekong Delta Region

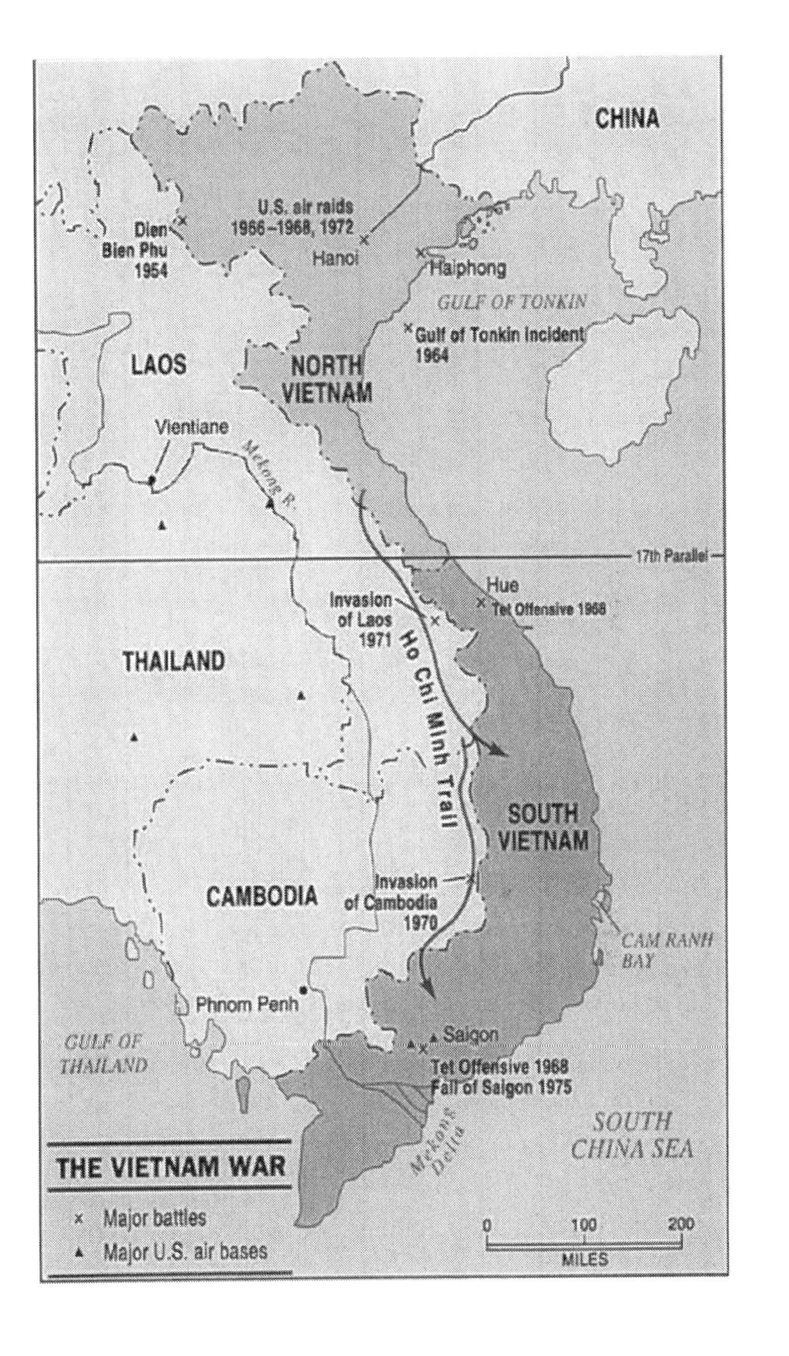

CHINA
U.S. air raids
1966–1968, 1972
Dien
Bien Phu
1954
Hanoi
Haiphong
GULF OF TONKIN
Gulf of Tonkin incident
1964
LAOS
NORTH
VIETNAM
Vientiane
Mekong R.
17th Parallel
Hue
Tet Offensive 1968
Invasion
of Laos
1971
Ho Chi Minh Trail
THAILAND
SOUTH
VIETNAM
Invasion
of Cambodia
1970
CAMBODIA
CAM RANH
BAY
Phnom Penh
Saigon
GULF OF
THAILAND
Tet Offensive 1968
Fall of Saigon 1975
Mekong
Delta
SOUTH
CHINA SEA
THE VIETNAM WAR
Major battles
Major U.S. air bases
0
100
200
MILES

Vietnam's history goes back thousands of years, however, our involvement can only be traced back to the late 1800s when France invaded and occupied that region of Southeast Asia for over 50 years. The French established their control of Vietnam and renamed it French Indochina in 1887. Laos and Cambodia were added in 1893.

Many resistance movements against the French occupation occurred over the ensuing years.

The initial uprisings were carried out by former officers of the feudal courts and Mandarin dynasties, while others were conducted by local peasants. However, all lacked modern weaponry and were effectively suppressed by the French.

During the 1920s and 1930s more radical movements emerged, backed by Vietnamese leaders based in China. Communist influence also increased with the establishment of the Vietnamese Communist Party (CPV). And Ho Chi Minh emerged as a prominent political figure and Communist leader in China in 1941. He would become a hero to his followers in Vietnam and a nemesis to the French and we Americans.

Born 19 May 1890 in the Vietnamese village of Hoang Tru, Ho studied Confucian teachings as a child and became proficient in Chinese writing. He attended High School in the ancient capital city of Hue (which includes the distinguished graduates; General Vo Nguyen Giap and North Vietnamese Premier Pham Van Dong). Ho then traveled the world while working on ships for several years; to France in 1911, the United States 1912-13 and again in 1917-18, to the United Kingdom in 1913 and 1919 and France again in 1919-1923.

It was during this last period in France that Ho joined a group of Vietnamese nationalists who had been publishing newspaper articles advocating for Vietnamese independence.

He attempted to petition the Western powers at the Versailles Peace talks after World War I to recognize the civil rights of the Vietnamese people and end French Colonial rule.

Although the group failed to gain consideration at Versailles, Ho became a symbol of the anti-Colonial movement at home in Vietnam.

Ho traveled to Moscow in 1923 where he met Lenin. He attended the University of the Toilers of the East, received formal training in Marxism and the techniques of agitation, participated in the 5th Comintern Conference and became a member of the Comintern's Southeast Asia Bureau.

From Moscow he went to Canton, China in November 1924. For several years he organized and taught youth education classes there and gave socialist lectures to young Vietnamese revolutionaries at the Whampoa Military Academy, whose members would later give rise to the pro-communist movement in Vietnam.

Ho was forced to flee China three years later in 1927 when Chiang Kai-shek, an influential member of the Kuomintang (KMT) Chinese National Party and close ally of Sun Yat-sen, led a successful coup in 1926, purging communist elements of the military. Chiang Kai-shek became Commandant of the Whampoa Military Academy, subsequently succeeding Sun Yat-sen as leader of the Chinese Nationalist Party.

Chiang Kai-shek continued further military actions against communist party activists in the Shanghai Massacre of 1927, solidifying his leadership of the country and suppressing communist uprisings.

Ho Chi Minh fled China that year and returned to Moscow. He returned to China in 1938 as an advisor to Mao Zedong's

Chinese Communist army that would later force Chiang Kai-shek's government into exile on Taiwan.

In 1940 Japan successfully invaded and occupied French Indochina, keeping the Vichy French Colonial government in place to maintain control under direction of the Japanese.

That same year Ho Chi Minh made his way south from China and re-entered Vietnam again for the first time in 30 years.

Once there, Ho took advantage of the Japanese invasion to piece together a coalition of Nationalist and Communist Vietnamese he called the Viet Minh. Under his leadership the Viet Minh created a 10,000-man guerilla force known as the "Men in Black" that battled the Japanese in the jungles of Vietnam with much success.

Ho became celebrated as the leading Vietnamese nationalist and ironically became an ally of the United States against the Japanese. "I was a Communist," he said then, "but I am no longer one. I am a member of the Vietnamese family, nothing else." Aided by the United States Office of Strategic Services (OSS), Ho would conduct many successful military operations against the Vichy French and Japanese occupation forces during World War II.

Support for the Viet Minh guerilla force also grew substantially due to the famine of 1944-45, caused by both natural and man-made disasters. Severe flooding reduced rice production and the occupying Japanese used much of it to feed the troops and supply fuel for the vehicles. Many thousands of Vietnamese peasants died as a result.

All this culminated in the "August General Uprising" on August 14, 1945, when the Viet Minh seized control of all of

Vietnam from the French occupation forces after the Japanese had surrendered.

Ho Chi Minh declared independence for the newly established Democratic Republic of Vietnam and was declared Premier of the new Republic headquartered in Hanoi, however, the new government was not recognized by any other countries, including the United States.

Unbeknownst to Ho, Vietnam's immediate future had already been decided by President Truman, Prime Minister Churchill and Premier Stalin as part of the Potsdam Agreement, ending the war with Japan.

The Potsdam Agreement stipulated that the northern half of Vietnam would be occupied temporarily by National Chinese forces to accept the surrender and removal of Japanese occupiers, while the southern half would initially be controlled by the British and then turned over to the French.

French forces arrived on British ships to retake control of Saigon while 200,000 troops from Chiang Kai-shek's Republic of China arrived in Hanoi to accept the surrender of the Japanese occupiers of Indochina.

The French also moved into the north in an agreement with the Chinese when they departed.

Ho Chi Minh's newly formed government was under intense pressure and sought an agreement with France to allow Vietnam to be an autonomous, independent state in the French Union. The French went along with the agreement to facilitate removal of the Chinese and signed it on 6 March 1946.

Both Ho Chi Minh and his college classmate and General of the Army Vo Nguyen Giap continued tenuous negotiations with the French, however the agreement quickly broke down.

The tense situation escalated dramatically on 23 October 1946 when the French bombarded Haiphong killing 6,000 Vietnamese and wounding another 14,000.

Ho Chi Minh concluded that France had no intention of allowing Vietnam independence and declared war against the French Union on 19 December 1946, signaling the beginning of the First Indochina War that would rage on for seven years.

In February of 1950, with the French blockade of the northern border successfully removed by the Viet Minh, the Soviet Union formally recognized the Democratic Republic of Vietnam. Ho traveled to Moscow where he met with Stalin and Mao Zedong and China agreed to recognize and provide support to the Viet Minh as well.

With weapons, supplies and training provided by the communist Chinese and Soviet Union, the Viet Minh, under the command of Vo Nguyen Giap, wreaked havoc on the French occupation forces.

French forces were spread out all over Indochina fighting the Viet Minh in what was becoming a protracted, unpopular war.

In December 1953, French General Henri Navarre established a large sprawling garrison way out at the western border of Vietnam at Dien Bien Phu to disrupt Viet Minh supplies lines south through Laos.

Viet Minh General Giap decided to attack the garrison and started covertly preparing the battlefield. While conducting a series of diversionary attacks, Giap placed covered and concealed artillery in the surrounding hills, employed Soviet antiaircraft weapons to disrupt resupply of the French garrison and built a series of camouflaged trenches and tunnels encircling the French forces.

When Navarre finally realized he was surrounded and called for help, US advisors recommended the use of tactical nuclear weapons while others called for strategic bombing to scatter Viet Minh forces. US President Eisenhower refused to intervene however, without agreement by the British and other Western allies. British Prime Minister Churchill declined, citing the on-going peace negotiations in Geneva. No support for the French at Dien Ben Phu was forthcoming.

Giap launched an intense 54-day offensive on 13 March 1954, defeating French positions one after another until the entire garrison was over run. The French garrison Commander, General De Castries, was captured in his bunker. French artillery Commander, Colonel Piroth, committed suicide by hand grenade. French casualties totaled over 2,200 men dead, 5,600 wounded and 11,721 taken prisoner.

The French forces surrendered on 7 May 1954 and the following day the French government announced that it intended to withdraw from Vietnam completely. Two months later, on July 21, 1954 the Geneva Accords were signed by the Democratic Republic of Vietnam, France, People's Republic of China, Soviet Union and the United Kingdom. The State of Vietnam in the south and its ally the United States were not signatories.

The Geneva Accords stipulated that a demarcation line and a 6-mile wide demilitarized zone would be drawn at the 17th parallel. French forces would regroup to the south and Viet Minh forces to the north of the demarcation line. There would be free movement of the population across the zone for 300 days. Neither zone was to join a military alliance or seek military reinforcement.

An International Control Commission comprising the countries of Canada, Poland and India would monitor the ceasefire. And general elections were to be held two years later to determine reunification of North and South Vietnam.

The aftermath of the Geneva Accords would lead to a series of events that seared the conscience of America and the world for generations to come and would result in the destruction of governments and the deaths of millions.

French forces departed from both the South and the North. The United States became the primary support for Ngo Din Diem and his government of the State of Vietnam in the South. Nearly two million people migrated to the South right after the initial ceasefire while 52,000, mostly Viet Minh soldiers and their families, migrated to the North.

In the ensuing years, both sides repeatedly violated the accords and elections were never held, neither in the North nor the South.

General Giap continued strengthening the North Vietnamese Army (NVA) with weapons, materials and supplies from China and the Soviet Union, nearly doubling the size of the North Vietnamese Army.

North Vietnam invaded Laos and Cambodia and built supply lines through those countries to support the Viet Cong forces in the South. The complex of these supply lines became known as the Ho Chi Minh Trail.

The US continued to support Diem's Army of the Republic of Vietnam (ARVN) in the South with money, equipment, supplies, training and advisors.

Fighting in the South continued to escalate between the Viet Cong and ARVN and thus began the Second Indochina

War or, as we know it in the West, the Vietnam War, in the late 1950's.

By 1964 North Vietnam had committed 30,000 troops to attacking South Vietnam and that number increased to 100,000 in 1965.

The US, in response to fears of spreading communism in Asia and confrontations with the Soviet Union in the growing Cold War between East and West, increased its military support to Vietnam from 900 advisors under Eisenhower to 16,000 under Kennedy by 1963.

Celebrated economist John Kenneth Galbraith was a close advisor of President Kennedy and warned him at the time of the "danger we shall replace the French as a Colonial force in the area and bleed as the French did".

US Special Forces advisors were imbedded at almost every level of the South Vietnamese Army however, ARVN forces had been defeated in several battles with the Viet Cong who were the local communist sympathizers recruited, advised and supplied by the North Vietnamese Army.

While the majority of the population was Buddhist, South Vietnam's President Ngô Đình Diệm was a devout Roman Catholic and appointed other Catholics throughout his administration including key military posts.

Diệm's older brother Ngô Đình Thuc was the Archbishop of Huế and his younger brother Ngô Đình Nhu was placed in charge of the secret police and military special forces.

Diệm's regime favored Catholics and lashed out at Buddhists for perceived opposition to government policies. The tensions exploded with the killing of Buddhist activists by ARVN Special Forces, orchestrated by Diệm's younger brother, causing widespread damage and a death toll in the hundreds.

The government was becoming dysfunctional with widespread corruption. The military was ineffective with low morale and high desertion rates. The population was becoming more and more opposed to Diệm's regime and favoritism afforded the Catholic minority. The Viet Cong were taking advantage of the situation and making sweeping gains in influence and territory in the South.

With tacit approval of President Kennedy and support from the CIA, Diệm's regime was overthrown in a military coup on 2 November 1963. Diệm and his brother Nhu were summarily executed.

The next two years witnessed chaos in the military and government as coup after coup took place.

The Gulf of Tonkin incident in 1964, where the North Vietnamese attacked US Navy ships with torpedo boats, propelled Congress to pass the Gulf of Tonkin Resolution giving then President Lyndon Johnson far ranging authorization to use conventional forces in Vietnam without officially declaring war.

Viet Cong strength had risen from 5,000 in 1959 to over 100,000 by 1965. North Vietnamese Army strength had increased to nearly a million soldiers. The Viet Cong had by then destroyed over 7,500 hamlets in South Vietnam.

Hesitant to commit American combat troops to the fight, President Johnson initiated bombing of North Vietnam (Rolling Thunder) and the Ho Chi Minh Trail in Laos and Cambodia in 1965.

US Army General William Westmoreland however, sounded the alarm calling for US ground troops to combat the

Viet Cong in the South and NVA forces infiltrating from the North saying, "I am convinced that U.S. troops with their energy, mobility, and firepower can successfully take the fight to the NLF [National Front for the Liberation of South Vietnam a.k.a. the Viet Cong]."

General Westmoreland's plan called for three phases.

Phase 1 was commitment of U.S. (and other free world) forces necessary to halt the losing trend of the ARVN forces by the end of 1965.

Phase 2 called for U.S. and allied forces to mount major offensive actions to seize the initiative to destroy guerrilla and organized enemy forces.

Phase 3 was a 12 to 18-month extension of phase 2, calling for the final destruction of enemy forces remaining in remote base areas if the enemy persisted.

General Westmoreland predicted victory would be won by 1967.

Secretary of Defense Robert McNamara visited Vietnam to see first-hand the situation there and confirmed Westmoreland's need for US troop support. President Johnson approved General Westmoreland's plan and preparations proceeded at a rapid pace to deploy US forces in strength to Vietnam.

At the same time, McNamara had ordered the Army to study how it could better use helicopter assets to rapidly move, support and resupply troops in combat.

Robert S. McNamara, Secretary of Defense 1961-1968

That study, conducted by General Hamilton Howze and known as the "Howze Board", recommended entire combat divisions be converted to "Air Mobile" divisions, supplied with up to 400 helicopters of all types; Observation Helicopters to conduct reconnaissance, Utility Helicopters to transport and resupply troops and perform medical evacuations, Attack Helicopters to escort the Utility helicopters and provide close air support and large Cargo Helicopters to move heavy equipment and supplies.

The tactics these new helicopter combat organizations would use to rapidly deploy large troop units into combat would become known as "Air Assault".

These new airmobile units, with their helicopter assets, were deemed perfectly suited to rapidly move personnel, equipment and supplies throughout Vietnam to meet and defeat the threat posed by North Vietnam and Viet Cong forces.

The 1st Cavalry Division was the first division to be converted to Air Mobile. It deployed to Vietnam in July 1965.

Other smaller helicopter combat units were quickly formed and deployed while the 101st Airborne Division was being converted to an Airmobile Division as well. It deployed to Vietnam in 1968.

US troop strength in Vietnam rapidly increased to over a half a million, supported by thousands of helicopters and the conflict would become known as "Vietnam - The Helicopter War".

I knew very little of this as I arrived at Travis Air Force Base in California for my flight to Vietnam.

Pan Am Charter. Travis AFB to Vietnam

7/1st Air Cavalry Squadron Unit Crest

CHAPTER ELEVEN

BULLET CATCHER

Dressed in my starched khaki uniform with a duffel bag slung over my shoulder, I reported to the duty clerk at the huge Military Airlift Command Terminal at Travis Air Force Base just outside Vacaville near Sacramento, California for my flight to Vietnam the first week of February 1969. The place was packed with what seemed like hundreds of other guys just like me.

"I'm Mr. Jennings. Here's my travel orders," I said as I checked in and handed the paperwork over to the Airman.

It was just after 5pm in the afternoon, a good two hours before my flight at 7pm.

"Uh, Mr. Jennings, your flight was at 1700 hours," he clarified, pointing out the large windows to a lumbering jet taxiing out to the runway.

"What?" I stuttered. "How did that happen?" I questioned.

It happened because in all the tension of the last few days, my brain took the "7" in 1700 hours (which is 5pm civilian time) and kept telling me it was 7pm. I was two hours late!

DAMN! I missed movement! That's what the military formally calls missing your time and place to move out on assignment. It's a serious offense under the Uniform Code of Military Justice and subject to Court Martial, especially in time of war. I could end up in prison for years.

I couldn't believe this happened. My budding military career was over. I would be court martialed in disgrace, reduced to Private and sent packing for a long tour in Fort Leavenworth!

"The next flight leaves at 10, that's 2200 hours, Mr. Jennings," the airman said next as he looked down at the flight schedule.

Then he looked up and said with a wry smile. "I'll make room for you on that flight. In the meantime, please have a seat in the waiting area. We'll start the boarding process at 2130," as he stamped my orders and handed me my boarding pass.

Smart-ass Air Force Airman. Now I was on my way to Vietnam as a Helicopter Pilot with 19 minutes to live. Maybe Leavenworth was a better option.

The chartered Pan Am flight was nearly full as we taxied out for the long flight to the other side of the world. We would cross the Pacific and stop for fuel in Guam before heading on to Tan Son Nhut Air Base near Saigon, Vietnam.

The Pan Am Captain came over the public-address system as we entered Vietnam's airspace. "We're now in a combat zone," he explained, "and our arrival into Tan Son Nhut will be a bit different than what you're used to. Please tighten your seatbelts. Flight attendants, please be seated," he ended abruptly.

With that he started a steep, spiraling, rapid descent over the airport to avoid flying low and slow over possible enemy locations before landing at the air base.

We held on to our seats while he maneuvered the big jet as we circled down. His touchdown was smooth though and we all cheered his expert landing.

The flight attendants had been especially attentive during the long flight and now said warm farewells as we departed the plane. Soon they would be greeting those who would be heading back home, their tours of duty in hell finally over.

Ours was just beginning though as we stepped down onto the tarmac. The heat of the tropics surrounded us and our nostrils immediately filled with a strange, pungent odor that we would endure for the rest of our time in country.

The peculiar odor was the smell of burning feces excreted by tens of thousands of military personnel, soaked in fuel oil and set afire in thousands of barrels from hundreds of outhouses. Plumes of smoke dotted the horizon nearly everywhere you looked. A daily regimen performed at every military base throughout Vietnam.

We boarded buses that would drive us to the nearby Army base at Bien Hoa. The scariest part of the ride was looking at the heavy wire grates covering the windows. We had been told those were there to help protect us if we were attacked by rocket propelled grenades.

Geeez, a few minutes in-country and I'm already nervous as hell. Stupid really. This was paradise compared to where I would be going.

The Army had a huge reception facility at the base at Bien Hoa. We would spend several days here undergoing in-processing and in-country orientation.

First up was issuing our jungle fatigues, boots, hats, mosquito netting and personal combat gear.

Then began the daily medical regimen of taking huge pills to ward off malaria and salt pills to help keep us hydrated.

And warnings to never have sexual relations with the local girls of the night as you would become combat disabled. Your dick would fall off!

We attended lectures on the history, customs and courtesies of Vietnam.

We were briefed on the US military organization in Vietnam and the division of the country militarily into four Corps; I Corps (pronounced eye-core) in the far north from Da Nang to the DMZ, II Corps (2-core) in the Central Highlands, III Corps (3-core) in the middle and IV Corps (4-core) in the south.

This was followed by an orientation on the enemy and his weapons, tactics and capabilities including a live demonstration outside by a former North Vietnamese soldier, now on our side as a "Kit Carson" scout, who infiltrated his way into the base through all the defenses, in broad daylight, totally undetected until he stood up just a few feet in front of us!

That was followed by demonstrations of our weapons for both offensive and defensive operations including the Claymore mine.

And it all wrapped up with assignments to our combat units. I was assigned to Charlie Troop, 7th of the 1st Air Cavalry Squadron or C/7/1 at Vinh Long in the Mekong Delta.

That evening I was notified to pack up. A helicopter would be picking me up soon to take me to the unit.

The Huey never stopped running as I hunched over to keep clear of the rotor blades and fought against the wind it created to load my gear and myself into the helicopter, under the watchful eye and direction of the crew chief. Once I was aboard the crew chief gave a thumbs-up to the Pilot and we lifted off, nosed over and in seconds were out of there and flying over the Vietnam countryside.

I couldn't see much in the dark and had no idea which direction we were heading or where we were going. I just trusted the helicopter crew to get me there alive.

The flight was less than an hour and proved uneventful. When we landed at the air base at Vinh Long and parked the helicopter and shut down, I was greeted by some of the other Pilots in the unit and escorted to my quarters.

The quarters or "hooches" as they were referred to, were actually really nice one-story buildings made of plywood and wire screen mounted on concrete pads and topped off with tin roofs. The facilities at Vinh Long had been there for several years and had been constantly improved over time by the soldiers who resided there, past and present.

Our hooch for the Cobra Pilots or "Weapons Platoon" had four-man rooms inside, built from plywood and rocket boxes. Some were really decked out with nice bunks, lockers, stereos and refrigerators. I was impressed.

First Lieutenant Don Ericksen, who had arrived just a few weeks earlier, showed me to my room, pointed out my bunk and where to stow my gear, and then showed me where the showers, latrine and shitters were located. He then agreed to meet with me at 0630 for breakfast and help get me in-processed into the unit.

I stowed my gear, made my bunk, flopped down and fell fast asleep. It had been a long day.

The next morning at breakfast in the mess hall I was introduced all around to the fellow Pilots in my platoon and following breakfast, formally met with the Commanding Officer. The First Sergeant and Company Clerk then took over and in short order got me in-processed and issued my weapons and ammunition; an M-16 automatic rifle and .38 caliber pistol. And an armored chest protector called a "Chicken Plate" that I would wear every time I flew.

After a tour of the base, our facilities and the flight line and introduced to the aircraft crew chiefs and maintenance support personnel, the next order of business was an "In-Country Check Ride".

The check ride was conducted by the unit Standardization Instructor Pilot or SIP for Cobras. His job was to provide me with instruction on unit flight procedures, maintenance and safety and to conduct an in-flight examination of my ability to perform basic flight maneuvers to make sure I was competent to fly as a Copilot in the Weapons Platoon.

The Cobras in the 7/1st Cav had been in the unit for quite a while and had already seen lots of combat. They were all painted Army green, however had been adorned on the front with a gaping red shark's mouth and huge white teeth. Scary!

After giving the aircraft a thorough preflight inspection and review of aircraft systems and weapons loading procedures, we climbed aboard for our flight to the nearby air base at Can Tho for the check ride.

He directed me to the back seat where the Pilot-in-Command or PIC normally sits as he took the Copilot/Gunner front seat. We went through the prestart and start checklists and soon were hovering out for takeoff. He continually talked and explained things as we took off from Vinh Long on our short flight to Can Tho.

The Instructor was flying from the front seat and talking to the control tower as we entered the traffic pattern at Can Tho. He cleared with the tower for a practice engine failure and told me he would demonstrate a straight-in autorotation and then it would be my turn to do the same.

"I'll maintain pattern altitude and 90 knots as I line up with the intended area of landing," he started explaining as he set up for the maneuver.

"About here on final with a steep approach angle I'll reduce the throttle to flight idle to simulate engine failure, reduce collective to maintain rotor rpm, maintain 90 knots forward airspeed and continue scanning the instruments."

We were coming down fast. Helicopters glide like a brick.

"As we approach 50 feet I'll bring in aft cyclic and flare to maximize rotor rpm, being careful not to over speed and about here - BAM!"

He never finished his sentence as he had waited too long to pop the collective to arrest our descent.

We hit the runway hard, bounced back in the air, and started wobbling sideways as the rotor rpm rapidly decreased. My life passed before my eyes as I peered through the canopy thinking we were crashing sideways onto the perforated steel planking.

We hit again at about a 45-degree angle to the runway as he pulled the remaining collective for a last gasp of lift.

The aircraft lurched off the runway and climbed a few feet, just clearing a barrier of concertina wire.

With no lift left and low rotor rpm, we flopped down into a muddy rice paddy, immediately sinking several feet up to our wings and rocket pods.

We came to rest totally splattered in a mud bath, but safe with no injuries, and the helicopter still running with the rotor blades spinning.

Personnel in the air traffic control tower had watched the whole thing and fire trucks were already on their way. The tower called us and we reported safe with little apparent damage.

After the fire trucks arrived and stayed on the other side of the concertina wire barrier, the now totally embarrassed Instructor Pilot notified the tower he would lift the aircraft to a hover out of the mud and back to the runway to further inspect for any damage.

We did just that and with the help of the fire trucks and their high-pressure water nozzles gave the aircraft a complete bath and spent a long time examining the helicopter. With no apparent damage, he terminated the check ride and we flew back to Vinh Long.

Even though I hadn't flown a single maneuver, the Instructor signed me off as competent to fly with the promise I wouldn't reveal to anyone in the unit what had happened. I didn't and he shall forever remain unnamed.

My first real mission was with Chief Warrant Officer Ed Bobilya. He had been in country quite a while and was an experienced Aircraft Commander. He would become my primary mentor while flying for the Charlie Troop "Comanches". We took off from Vinh Long and headed to a US Special Forces camp named Moc Hoa to conduct reconnaissance operations near the Cambodian border.

This was the Mekong Delta of Vietnam where the insurgent Viet Cong forces transported weapons and supplies, infiltrating in small boats called sampans from Cambodia on the many rivers, canals and tributaries throughout the region.

We were to team up with another Cobra and two OH-6 LOHs or Loaches as Scouts, plus a Huey flown by the Commanding Officer or Operations Officer to provide command, control and communications to coordinate our mission.

The Scouts flew extremely low, sometimes less than 10 feet, continually bobbing and weaving to avoid being hit by enemy fire as they looked for enemy personnel, supplies and equipment.

The Cobras flew overhead at around a thousand feet keeping a close eye on the Scouts and ready to lay down horrific fire power if they ran into trouble.

Scout Pilots were well known for their extreme bravery flying low and slow to ferret out enemy positions. They even had a different anatomy than the rest of us as their testicles were as big as basketballs and their sexual prowess was, well, let's just say they were men of much bravado!

And they depended on us Cobra Pilots to watch out for and protect them whenever they needed some help, which was often.

I was thinking about our brave Scout Pilots and anxious to prove myself and gain Ed's confidence as a good Copilot.

I climbed into the front seat and got my gear sorted in this little confined space; Chicken Plate in place over my chest, pistol between my legs to protect the family jewels, large tactical maps carefully folded so I could help with navigation and at the ready to call in position reports, adjust artillery fire, request medical evacuation or just keep us informed of our location, grease pencils to write notes on the Plexiglas that I would wipe clean after the mission, and the gun sight at the ready in case I had to respond to enemy fire with the devastating Gatling gun.

As we cranked up to head out and did radio checks over the intercom, I told Ed how excited I was to be his Copilot on my very first mission.

He hesitated a moment, then told me, "Lew, your position up front is not Copilot, it's Bullet Catcher. Your job is to protect me, the Pilot. You will fly for three months up front as bullet catcher and if you live, you will get to be Pilot".

With that, he laughed as we lifted off to join the team. Me, I was totally silent thinking about what he just said and wishing I had a bigger Chicken Plate!

We flew all kinds of missions, day and night, throughout the Delta region, staging out of places like Moc Hoa and Chi Lang. We constantly provided cover for our Scout Pilots as they discovered enemy locations. We prepped landing zones (LZs) for large formations of troop-carrying Hueys and escorted them into and out of danger. We provided close air support to troops of the 9th Infantry Division. We conducted reconnaissance operations to find and fix enemy locations and when we did, fought pitch battles for hours, returning to the battles again and again after refueling and rearming at remote locations. And we performed a peculiar mission called "Heroes Hooch", where we would sleep out under the helicopters in full gear at night to instantly respond to incoming mortar fire or rocket attacks on our base at Vinh Long.

I learned a lot from Ed Bobilya, Damon Cecil and many of the other Aircraft Commanders I had the privilege of flying with and being their Bullet Catcher. After two months, I was nominated early to become an Aircraft Commander myself and having survived my time in the front seat, started flying Cobras from the back seat as Pilot. Don Ericksen was the first to volunteer to fly as my personal Bullet Catcher and we would become life-long friends.

The guys would laugh at my routine flying in the back seat. I was just 5 feet, 9 inches tall but would put my seat all the way down so all you could see were my eyeballs peeking out the bottom of the windows.

I was one of the few Pilots to wear the new "Ballistic Helmet". It was supposed to be strong enough to repel small arms fire, however most Pilots didn't like the damn thing as it was very heavy and wouldn't wear it. Not me! I always wore my ballistic helmet even though within a few minutes, my head would flop over to one side or the other from the weight and stay that way for the remainder of the flight. I didn't care as long as it would help me survive and complete the mission.

And even flying in the back seat with Bullet Catchers up front, like my dear friend Don Ericksen, I always wished I had a bigger Chicken Plate. We were always getting ourselves into trouble with the bad guys. That was our job.

I flew as Aircraft Commander with the "Comanches" of C/7/1 for just a few weeks when a new unit of the 101st Airborne Division (Airmobile) arrived in country and needed experienced Aircraft Commanders. I was selected to join the new unit way up north near the demilitarized zone at a base called Camp Evans. It was Alpha Troop, 2nd of the 17th Air

Cavalry, 101st Airborne Division (Airmobie). My new call sign would be Assault 23.

I would not see Don Ericksen again for 20 years.

7/1st Air Cavalry Cobras over the Mekong Delta

CHAPTER TWELVE

SCREAMING EAGLES

There were a bunch of us Loach, Huey and Cobra Pilots from throughout the 7/1st Air Cavalry Squadron at Vinh Long that would be "infused" with the new air cavalry squadron up north near the DMZ and the ancient city of Hue.

2/17th Air Cavalry Squadron

Most everyone in the new unit, which had come over from Fort Campbell, Kentucky, had arrived at the same time so all had the same DEROS date (Date Estimated Return from Overseas Service) which meant they would all be leaving at the same time 12 months later.

It was necessary then to transfer many of the new arrivals to other units in Vietnam and infuse experienced folks into the new unit. This would make the unit combat ready quickly while at the same time reduce personnel turn over due to similar DEROS dates.

The familiar term "short-timer" refers to counting down the days you have left in country to your DEROS date. When you get within weeks or days to your Date of Estimated Return from Overseas Service, you officially become a Short-Timer.

Ed Bobilya and I were the chosen ones from the Weapons Platoon to join the others from our Squadron and head north. We packed up all our gear into our Hueys at Vinh Long. We were flown to the nearby base at Can Tho where we loaded aboard Air Force C-130 cargo transports for the several hundred-mile flight north to Hue Phu Bai in I Corps (pronounced Eye-Core).

The rear loading ramp was down as we climbed aboard with the Air Force Load Master directing "40 to a pallet" over and over again as we sat down on the plane's hard steel floor and squeezed together as tight as we could.

Finally, he raised the loading ramp as the four huge turboprop engines cranked up and we were off. I don't remember much about the trip other than it was uncomfortable as hell, alternating between a sweatbox on the ground and a cold meat locker at altitude. I loved being a Pilot but hated being a passenger, especially being treated like cargo and squeezed together like sardines "40 to a pallet".

It didn't take the C-130s long to fly us north for our rendezvous with destiny with the 101st Airborne Division (Airmobile). The decorated Division of World War II fame, known as the Screaming Eagles with the bald eagle as its combat patch, also has the battle motto; "Rendezvous with Destiny".

The 101st Airborne Division (Airmobile) in 1969 was a huge organization with over 15,000 soldiers in three combat Brigades, an Air Cavalry Squadron, an Artillery Battalion, an Aerial Rocket Artillery Battery, a Ranger Company and a host of Transportation, Communication, Intelligence, Medical and other Support and Special Operations units.

The Division Headquarters and main base was located at Camp Eagle just outside of Hue in I Corps, the most northern military sector of South Vietnam. Other units of the Division were spread throughout the region at Camp Evans, LZ Sally, Phu Bai, Quang Tri and temporary forward locations called firebases, with names like Bastogne, Blaze, Zon, Berchtesgaden, Rendezvous, Currahee, Airborne, Ripcord and more.

My new unit, Alpha Troop, 2nd Squadron, 17th Air Cavalry was located at Camp Evans just north of the ancient city of Hue.

We arrived at the Hue Phu Bai airport where we were greeted by our new Squadron Commander, Lieutenant Colonel William "Bill" DeLoach. He went down the line as we stood in formation, shaking our hands and welcoming us to the new unit. When he got to me, he looked me in the eye and thanked me for coming aboard as a combat experienced

Aircraft Commander. Little did he know I only had a few weeks experience as an "AC" and hadn't fired a rocket in anger yet, however that would quickly change.

We loaded our gear aboard trucks and then climbed aboard Hueys to fly to nearby Camp Evans. When we arrived in the new Alpha Troop area, it was a sight to behold. Organized chaos!

Unlike our old unit down south at Vinh Long with manicured grounds, palm trees, clean comfortable quarters and lots of amenities, Camp Evans looked like the aftermath of some terrible storm that had left small buildings strewn on a sea of mud. The whole base was a series of scattered structures on small hills of dirt and valleys of sand and mud.

The hooches were 20 by 30-foot plywood structures with tin roofs, precariously arranged in rows on the sides of hills and gullies. Their walls were 4 by 8-foot single plywood sheets laid horizontally, with sandbags piled up 3 to 4 feet around the base. Then screen mesh for ventilation from the top of the plywood up another four feet to the tin roof. And more sand bags had been thrown up on the roof to keep the tin sheets from blowing off during the monsoon season's wind and rain.

Small shower and latrine buildings of similar construction known as "shitters" could be seen scattered throughout the area, with their distinctive 50-gallon drum and diesel immersion water heaters mounted up on the roofs, to provide hot water for showers, and an adjacent latrine that could accommodate up to five patrons.

The headquarters building and mess hall looked the same as the other hooches.

The location of the Tactical Operations Center (TOC) which is the communications center and heartbeat of the unit was easily identified by the cluster of antennas nearby, however, the center itself was a steel Conex container buried under the ground, with layers of sandbags on top and around the narrow entrance for protection from rocket or mortar attacks.

The aircraft were located a few hundred feet away on the top of a small ridge. Perforated Steel Planking (PSP) are large mats of steel with holes in them and easily hinged together, that had been laid on the ground in rows of 10 by 20-foot sections, each section bordered on the sides with 4-foot high sand bag walls. Each section was called a revetment and spaced far enough apart to park the helicopters side by side with room for the turning rotor blades.

Compared to Vinh Long, Camp Evans looked like a garbage dump. It was our new home though and in typical GI fashion we set to work to make it our own.

Each one of us had a cot, sleeping bag, duffel bag with our gear, and a mosquito net which we set up in our hooches along with stringing lines to hang laundry and we pounded nails near our cots as hooks for our gear. Then we started searching the base camp, scrounging materials to build out the interior of the hooches to include small night stands, wall lockers, foot lockers, card tables and even a bar with a refrigerator in ours!

In short order, we were pretty well settled in and it was time to get down to the serious business of getting the unit combat ready. We would move to Camp Eagle a few weeks later.

Alpha Troop was a large, complex organization of 26 aircraft and nearly 300 personnel.

The aircraft included 8 UH-1 Hueys, 9 AH-1 Cobras and 9 OH-6 LOHs (Light Observation Helicopters or "Loaches").

The aircraft, Pilots and support personnel were organized in Platoons; LIFT for the Hueys, WEAPONS (also called GUNS) for the Cobras and SCOUTS for the LOHs.

In addition to the aircraft platoons were a Headquarters section for our command and admin personnel, a Maintenance section for aircraft and vehicle support and, unique to Air Cavalry Troops, a Platoon of infantry known as the BLUE Platoon.

Colors were also associated with the platoons; RED for Guns, WHITE for Scouts and BLUE for the Infantry and Lift.

The Troop was commanded by a Major, with a Captain as Executive Officer, a Captain as Operations Officer and more Captains as Platoon Leaders. Most of the Pilots were Warrant Officers with enlisted men as helicopter crew chiefs, door gunners, maintenance and support personnel and infantry.

Major Tom Curtin was our commanding officer. He was a cigar chomping, combat-seasoned leader and much older than the rest of us. At the ripe age of 34, Curtin had commanded the Troop at Fort Campbell, Kentucky while it was being organized and prepared for deployment to Vietnam. He was well respected by his troops and definitely knew his stuff.

Curtin was now faced with the formidable task of getting Alpha Troop combat ready within 30 days. He started a daily regimen of briefings on combat tactics, unit procedures, and enemy intelligence and orientation of our area of operations (AO).

The daily briefings were supplemented with flight training in our particular aircraft, check rides from the unit Standardization Instructor Pilot (SIP) and one-on-one orientation flights with experienced Pilots like Roger Cauble of Delta Troop, 1st Squadron, 1st Cavalry Regiment, who had been there for about a year and knew the area well.

We spent hours and hours building our map books, memorizing procedures, orienting ourselves to the Division area of operations, prepping our gear and aircraft and getting to know and trust one another.

It was April 1969. We had already performed some reconnaissance and convoy cover missions up north, as the 9th Marines had wound up Operation Dewey Canyon in the northern A Shau Valley and Khe Sanh plain and were recovering back to their bases at Vandergrift and Quang Tri. It would be the last major combat operation for the Marines up there.

I had a really close call while supporting the Marines that almost ended my tour of duty before it could even get started. It was one of those things you don't expect to happen that gets you. And this one classifies as a true near disaster.

We were refueling at Firebase Vandegrift (the Marines owned it and called it Combat Base Vandegrift) up by the DMZ covering their pullout from the Khe Sahn plain. I was lounging in the back seat as Aircraft Commander Supreme with the helicopter running at "flight idle" while the lowly Copilot, today it was John Bacic, had the duty of refueling the aircraft.

The fuel port was right next to my cockpit on the right side of the aircraft, outside and just behind my right shoulder. Even though it was close to me, the standard operating procedure at the time was for the Copilot to exit his front cockpit on the left side and come around and perform the refueling behind me on the right side. A matter of seniority or something I suppose.

John's a little guy like me and had to stand on his tippy-toes to put the nozzle in the port to start the refueling process. The fuel bladders and pressure pump were probably a hundred feet or more away from us. He started pumping the gas (JP-4 jet fuel like kerosene) and everything was going smoothly as I sat there, fat, dumb and happy, just watching the engine gauges.

Then, unbeknownst to us, the pump started surging, sending a huge bubble of fuel down the line towards us. The nearby fire crew heard the pump, saw the bulge in the hose heading our way, leaped into the fire truck and started racing towards us.

When the high-pressure fuel bubble reached us, it hit with such force that John was thrown backwards and the nozzle he was holding came out of the fuel port and started whipping around, gushing fuel everywhere.

First, the hose and nozzle turned him left, blasting a torrent of raw fuel directly into the engine intake and the engine roared to life, trying to drink it all in.

Then the nozzle whipped him to the right, sending a waterfall of fuel into the cockpit, nearly drowning me!

I instantly closed the throttle, hit the console switches closed and in a nanosecond, dove out of my seat and hit hard, head first in the dirt, rolling over and over.

By some miracle I didn't catch on fire but the JP-4 was caustic, burning my skin, as I started ripping my clothes off faster than a professional stripper.

The fire crew arrived a second later and started hosing the helicopter with fire retardant as the engine and rotor were slowing down. Then they turned the hose on me and washed me down with water to cool the burning chemicals.

John was okay. The helicopter was a mess and had to be "hooked out" with a Chinook to home base and I was transported in my underwear back to base too.

Whew! That was a close one. My incident, along with several other tragic refueling accidents, caused a change in operating procedures for hot-refueling Cobras throughout the Division and maybe all of the Army. From then on, the Pilot did the refueling while the Copilot manned the controls. A **lot** safer.

Helicopter on fire at a Forward Area Refueling Point

We moved late in the month to our "permanent" home base over at Camp Eagle at the "Scabbard Pad". We set to making it our home as we needed to get ready for combat operations in a big way.

We would soon have the first of many "Rendezvous with Destiny" ourselves in the infamous A Shau Valley with battles at memorable places like Hamburger Hill, Firebase Airborne, and many more.

Alpha Troop, 2/17th Air Cavalry Scout and Weapons Platoon Hooches. Shower and Shitter, Camp Eagle, 1969

CHAPTER THIRTEEN

A SHAU VALLEY

I had just gotten a glimpse of the A Shau Valley the month before in early April on one of my orientation flights with Chief Warrant Officer Roger Cauble of Delta Troop, 1st Squadron, 1st Cavalry Regiment. Roger had been flying combat operations in support of the 101st Division for many months before our arrival and was now temporarily assigned to our unit to teach us the ropes.

"That's the infamous A Shau Valley," Roger explained, as he climbed the helicopter high above the surrounding mountaintops and pointed to a valley about five miles to the west. "I can only give you a glimpse of it for now" he continued, "as we don't have any troops or support out there and it has historically been a very dangerous place."

We had been flying along a new road being built by our Division's 326th Combat Engineer Battalion in the foothills west of Camp Eagle, that would continue into the higher terrain to the A Shau Valley.

Firebases were already constructed on hilltops along the road every few miles; Birmingham, Bastogne, Veghel,

Cannon, Zon and Blaze. Artillery batteries were located at several of the firebases with 105mm Howitzers, 155mm and long range 175mm cannons and self-propelled 8-inch guns, to provide support to ground combat operations anywhere within 20 miles.

Some of the firebases also provided fuel and ammunition supplies for our helicopters so we could do quick turnarounds, without having to go all the way back to home base. We would end up visiting them frequently and some would become our second homes.

As we approached each firebase, Roger took me through the procedures necessary to safely land at the proper locations, where to refuel or rearm, and best procedures for take-off, all while avoiding outgoing artillery fire.

Wow, things sure were different here from flying down south in IV Corps. There we had thousands of acres of flat land with rice paddies. There had been lots of places to land in case of emergency, although no cover or concealment, so we flew the Cobras high, usually above 1,000 feet to avoid small arms fire.

Up here in the north, we flew over steep valleys and jungle covered mountainous terrain. We also flew low, around 300 feet, so the enemy could only get a glimpse of us through the trees and jungle when we flew overhead and maybe not have enough time to get a bead on us. Not many places to land in case of an emergency or engine failure.

The Scouts with their light observation helicopters always flew extremely low to find and fix the enemy, usually at 50 feet or less. They did lots of yanking and banking and maneuvering to keep from getting shot down.

Our job in the Cobras was to always keep our little birds in sight and be in position to provide them instant covering fire in case they got into trouble, which was frequently.

The A Shau Valley ran north to south for some 30 miles, with the Laotian border just to the west. The valley was surrounded on both sides by mountains to the east and west and a river meandering down the middle.

The lush and beautiful valley floor was covered with elephant grass up to 10 feet tall and the surrounding hills and mountains were covered in dense jungle and forest.

The A Shau also straddled the Ho Chi Minh Trail and was a main route used by the North Vietnamese to infiltrate troops and supplies into South Vietnam and they used it as a staging area for their own combat operations.

Which was why we were gathered here, in the mess hall this morning, for a mission briefing from our Commanding Officer, Major Tom Curtin. We were going into the A Shau Valley.

Major Curtin had brought the unit over from Fort Campbell. He was stocky like a bull with a ruddy flushed complexion and a cigar perpetually clamped in his mouth. He reminded me of a young Winston Churchill. He was a combat veteran and seasoned Scout Pilot with a previous tour under his belt. Tom Curtin was very professional, mission oriented, and dedicated to his troops.

"Gentlemen, I will not sugar coat it, we will be going into enemy territory to find, fix and fight elements of the North Vietnamese Army. The NVA has been using the A Shau Valley as a primary route of the Ho Chi Minh Trail to move troops, supplies and equipment into South Vietnam and conduct combat operations in our area," he emphasized pointing to a large tactical map.

The A Shau had been the scene of many fierce battles over the years. US Special Forces suffered 100 percent casualties back in 1966 when their camp in the A Shau was over-run by NVA forces. The NVA had used the A Shau as a major staging area to attack Hue City the year before, during the Tet Offensive of 1968.

The 1st Cavalry Division had conducted Operation Delaware in the A Shau Valley the previous year and hundreds of bomb craters still pock marked the valley floor. Some of the old landing zones used by the 1st Cav still held carcasses of Hueys that had been shot down in combat.

The 9th Marines had just completed a sweep of the northern A Shau and Khe Sanh plain the month before as part of Operation Dewey Canyon.

As Roger Cauble had warned me earlier, it was a dangerous place.

"The 101st is launching Operation Apache Snow to conduct combat operations in the A Shau to stop the enemy from using it as a major supply route and staging area," Curtin continued.

"As you know, Captain Reed led the Blues in an assault near LZ Airborne on the east side of the valley two weeks ago where they met intense enemy opposition."

Boy, was that an understatement, in typical Tom Curtin fashion.

Some Air Force fighter jets returning from a mission two weeks earlier still had ordnance on board and were directed to the eastern ridge of the A Shau by a Forward Air Controller (FAC) to drop their bombs on the way home. When the bombs hit the top of the ridge, huge secondary explosions took place and were reported by the FAC to the Army. The 101st Division decided to send in ground troops to investigate and 2/17th Air Cav responded, flying in two platoons of infantry from C and D Troops below the ridge. They met fierce resistance as they tried to assault up the ridge and the call went out for reinforcements.

Captain Keith Reed, Platoon Leader of our Alpha Troop Blues, and 25 of his men were air lifted into a tiny landing zone below the eastern ridge just before dark on 25 April to reinforce elements of C and D Troops.

"The weather was iffy with low clouds and fog, and visibility was a problem with the impending darkness," Keith recalls. "It was a one-ship landing zone and I was on the first Huey being flown in by Lieutenant Lou Herrick. He told me the visibility was bad, so after we got out of the helicopter, I stood on a stump and used my emergency strobe light to guide in the other three birds, one at a time".

"The first two made it in okay," he continued. "Mike Ryan and Mark Stevens were flying the last bird in, however were not lining up on my strobe and were way too low. They thought they were being guided in by my light, but it must have been a deception by the bad guys luring them in with their own light. I called them on the radio and warned them to climb immediately, which they did. They saw the correct light, came in and off loaded the last of the troops."

"It was dark by then so we joined up with the rest of C and D Troops to reinforce our perimeter for the night and would try another assault up the hill in the morning."

"The next morning, we moved out and headed uphill through the dense jungle. My lead squad soon found a trail.

When they told me that they had spotted a bunker further up the hill, I told them to get off the trail to avoid being ambushed."

"I then told the lead squad to attack the bunker with a LAW (Light Anti-Tank Weapon) they carried that would provide the punch to get through the thick walls."

"I waited for the explosion. Nothing happened."

"Crouching low, I headed up to the front. The guys were still trying to set up to fire the LAW. I took the LAW myself and went up beside the point man to engage the bunker. Machine gunner Specialist Four, Jerry Knighten, was beside me laying down covering fire when they opened up on us with automatic weapons and grenades."

"Jerry was wounded immediately and Sergeant Rich Smith threw his pack on a grenade and saved all of us, as we dove for cover."

"More grenades landed around us. One exploded next to me and I lost consciousness."

"When I came to a few minutes later, all was quiet. I stayed still trying to assess the situation. I found myself just eight to ten meters from the bunker and my platoon had formed a defense line about 25 meters down the hill from me."

"I located my rifle beside me and watched as an enemy soldier emerged from the bunker, heading slowly towards me. I quickly got off three rounds killing him and headed towards my guys, but was immediately engaged by enemy automatic weapons. A bullet tore through my shirt, grazing my chest."

"I dove to the ground, returned fire, and emptied my magazine of bullets. As I was getting more magazines from my bandolier, one dropped to my side and was hit by an enemy bullet that ricocheted into my hip. Thankfully it had turned sideways and didn't penetrate, although it left a bruise the size of a softball."

"Rocked on my side from the impact of the bullet to the hip, I rolled back over, slapped in a magazine and returned fire, while scrambling back down to the platoon."

"We tried to advance and recover the weapons and equipment we had lost in the ambush, however, several more automatic weapons engaged us, resulting in more of us being wounded. I directed the platoon to withdraw and resume our previous defensive positions with D Troop. I carried SP4 Pedro De Armas with me, who was seriously wounded."

"Back in our makeshift perimeter and the wounded cared for, I asked our medic, SP4 Wayne Widman, for some aspirin as I had a terrible headache. It didn't seem to help and I kept taking more and more until he refused my requests, saying I had had enough. Then my Platoon Sergeant, Staff Sergeant Ernie Leach, had me take off my helmet and found a large grenade fragment, the size of a marble, imbedded in my skull. No wonder it had been hurting so bad."

"The doc back at home base would later joke that it's a good thing I'm hard-headed!"

At about the same time Keith was air assaulted in to reinforce C and D Troop, Companies of the 3rd Battalion, 187th Airborne Infantry had also been tasked to air assault into the area to reinforce the 2/17th Air Cavalry. They were carried in by Hueys from A Company, 158th Aviation Battalion "Ghost Riders" out of Camp Evans into a single-ship LZ at the top of the ridge. They met with disaster in the upper LZ, with five Hueys getting shot down over the next three days with many of the aircrews wounded, including their

Commanding Officer. Two pilots and one of the crew chiefs were killed.

Amazingly, crew chiefs of the 158th trapped in the LZ were able to repair one of the Hueys by scavenging parts from the other downed aircraft.

That Huey had been shot down when a round went through the hydraulic reservoir and the crew lost hydraulic power freezing the controls. It had settled to the ground intact and, while still running, soldiers and crew members had stood on the forward part of the landing gear to keep the aircraft from tumbling backward off the landing zone while others propped up the tail boom with logs.

Sergeant O.B. Carlson, one of the Huey crew chiefs, retrieved a hydraulic reservoir off one of the other wrecked Hueys, installed it within minutes and filled it with hydraulic fluid that he still had in containers on board his own wrecked aircraft, all while being protected by fellow crew members as they were repeatedly attacked. Warrant Officer Bill Parsons cranked the aircraft up again, loaded it with some of the surviving crewmembers and wounded and flew it out of the LZ, making room for others to be able to land.

Lieutenant Dan Bresnahan, an Infantry Platoon Leader with A Company, 3/187th Airborne Infantry recalls landing in LZ Airborne after Parsons had managed to take off.

"We were briefed we would be inserted onto a secondary LZ well down the East Wall of the A Shau, below LZ Airborne."

"We started the next CA (combat assault), with me in the first helicopter but Murphy reared his ugly head, and I was mistakenly inserted into LZ Airborne, the hot LZ. I made it onto the ground uneventfully. It was a one-ship LZ, with several upside-down Hueys, and bodies everywhere. I crouched down on the spot."

"The second ship landed okay but the third ship, while still at a 3-foot hover, was hit by an RPG which passed right over my head. The crew chief was killed, several of my men were wounded, and the CA was again halted."

"Now we had an LZ with many wounded and killed, and parts of three platoons of two Infantry Companies, and several aircraft crewmembers. We were there several days and each time we patrolled outward, in every direction, we were attacked."

The courageous Ghost Riders and Lancers of the 158th Aviation Battalion continued to land 3/187th Airborne Infantry soldiers into two landing zones on the ridge as they fought their way towards our Blues of the 2/17th Air Cav.

Elements of the two forces linked up and pushed the enemy from the ridge, capturing large caches of enemy weapons and ammunition. The upper landing zone was secured and over the next few days was built out with artillery pieces and personnel and became Firebase Airborne.

Keith Reed of Alpha Troop, 2/17th Air Cav received the Silver Star for his courageous efforts in that operation and his second award of the Purple Heart. His Blues had suffered nine wounded, five seriously.

The aircrews that had repaired and flown the Huey out of the hot LZ were also awarded Silver Stars for valor.

Whew! And we were just getting started.

Aircrews and Soldiers stand on the front of the skids of the stricken Huey in LZ Airborne to keep it from toppling back down the mountainside when the hydraulic system was damaged by ememy fire. Others prop up the tailboom with logs while Crewchief Pat Lynch provides covering fire. Sergeant O.B. Carlson would scrounge a replacement hydraulic reservoir from another downed Huey in the LZ to repair the damage and "Ghost Rider" pilot Warrant Officer Bill Parsons would fly this one back out. loaded with wounded, to clear the LZ for more inbound Hueys. Photo by Pat Lynch.

CWO Elton Searcy, one of the crewmembers of another downed Huey, guides a rescue bird into the LZ. Tragically, Searcy would lose his life to enemy fire shortly after this picture was taken. Photo by Pat Lynch.

Post Script: Lieutenant Dan Bresnahan of A/3/187th here on LZ Airborne would become one of the few surviving Platoon Leaders of Hamburger Hill. When he returned stateside after his tour, he attended flight school and Cobra school and returned to our own little Alpha Troop, 2/17th Air Cav just 18 months later where he distinguished himself again as a Cobra Aircraft Commander with the Air Cav.

Back at the Mess Hall, Major Curtin was wrapping up the operations briefing when he reminded us "Let's not forget Al Austin who we lost out there."

Sp4 Al Austin was flying as a door gunner in one of our Scout birds with Captain Ben Thornal. We were initially employing three people in our Scout birds; a Pilot in the right seat, an Observer in the left seat with an M-16 and a door gunner manning an M-60 machine gun in the rear compartment behind the Pilot. Al had been killed during one of our first missions in the A Shau when hit by enemy fire. We stopped using a third man door gunner after that experience and installed pilot-operated minigun systems instead.

"We suspect elements of the 29th NVA Regiment are out there in force," Major Curtin continued. "And it's our job to find them. "Let's get with it," he said as he picked up his gear and we all stood at attention and followed him out to our aircraft.

Today is 5 May 1969 and Day One of my first missions into the A Shau. I was flying a Cobra with Warrant Officer Mike Talton up front as my Copilot.

Mike and I were roommates, sharing a hooch back at home base. He had come over with the unit from Fort Campbell. We were both in our early 20's and about the same size and build. I was 5 feet 9 inches and maybe 150 pounds. I think Mike had an inch on me at 5 feet 10 inches and maybe another pound or two.

He was from Charleston, South Carolina and talked with a slow drawl and a quick smile. He was smart as a whip. We hit it off as soon as we met. I was glad he was flying with me today.

"Assault 23, this is 18, over." That was Captain Al Goodspeed checking in with me on the Company VHF radio. Al was flying the little Scout bird with Staff Sergeant John Hayden as his Observer. We were a single Cobra and LOH (pronounced Loach) known as a hunter-killer or Pink Team (the combination of "Red" Cobras and "White" Scouts). Our mission today was to conduct a reconnaissance of the northern part of the A Shau Valley.

"18, 23, you ready?" I responded.

Al Goodspeed was a combat experienced Scout Pilot having come up with us from the 7/1st. He was also a good old southern boy from Sanford, Florida and well-liked by all of us. And although he was "Captain" Goodspeed, rank among the Pilots was like virtue among whores and we called each other by our first names or nicknames. In his case, we mostly just called him "Speedbird" or simply "Speed" for short.

It never ceased to amaze me that the biggest guys in the unit usually flew the smallest aircraft. "Speed" was no exception. As a matter of fact, I think he was the poster boy for that observation.

At over six feet tall and nearly 200 pounds with all his gear, it seemed he could barely squeeze into the Pilot's seat of that tiny helicopter. His body would fold to the contours of the egg-shaped cockpit as he hunched over the controls with his helmet crammed against the overhead Plexiglas.

Speed loved being a Scout Pilot, flying the OH-6. He flew close by us with a huge smile and thumbs up signaling he was more than ready. We were off into the wild blue yonder on our first mission together into the dreaded A Shau.

Many of our helicopter units in Vietnam had varied tactics and procedures individually developed for their particular area of operations and their own experiences. Ours was no different.

Down south we flew as full Heavy Teams; two Cobras, two Scouts and a Command and Control (C&C) Huey overhead to coordinate the operation and provide immediate rescue capability if one of us got shot down.

The Blues (Six Hueys and a platoon of approximately 40 Infantrymen) were usually on standby ready to do a mini combat assault into a hot area, if we found ourselves battling the enemy.

Up north we had a vast area to operate in and lots of reconnoitering to do to try and find and fix the elusive NVA in the mountainous and jungle covered terrain. Major Curtin intentionally decided to split us up into four to six Pink Teams of one Cobra and one Scout each to operate independently and cover as much area as possible.

Two to three Pink Teams would be flying while the other two or three would be at a nearby firebase ready to relieve one another when low on fuel or ammo.

Major Curtin or his Operations Officer, Captain Roy "Bud" Dowdy, would stay in contact with all of us via our unit radio frequency and fly the Command and Control (C&C) Huey around the area checking in on us. The C&C Huey was also loaded with lots of rescue gear in case one of us got into more trouble than we could handle.

The Cobra in the Pink Team was the high bird providing cover for the little bird down below. The Cobra crew would do all the navigation chores and mission coordination with ground infantry units, artillery units, air traffic control,

Tactical Air Command (TAC air) fighter jets, search and rescue and unit operations, so the Scouts could concentrate on their job of finding the bad guys and identifying the good guys.

Today in the A Shau we had multiple operations going on.

Speed and I were a Pink Team assigned to reconnoiter the A Shau from the middle of the valley near the old A Luoi air strip, to the far north end past Tiger Mountain.

Other Pink Teams would recon the south end of the valley while the Hueys and Blues were on standby at a new staging area, a clearing the size of a football field bulldozed in the floor of the valley called LZ Rendezvous at the eastern entrance to the A Shau.

There wasn't much chatter on the radio going out. We were well trained and disciplined to stay off the radios as much as possible and concentrate on our flying and the mission.

As we neared the A Shau the other teams and Hueys broke off while Speed and I dropped down low to crest the east ridge and then down on the deck to start reconning the valley floor.

"Geez, this is incredible!" I said to Mike over the intercom, our private radio link in the aircraft to converse with one another. The huge jungle trees, the swift running river, the rich green tall elephant grass, the beautiful foliage and what looked like banana trees. It was something out of the *Lost World*, an amazingly beautiful place and eerily quiet as we continued north, back and forth, looking, searching, straining, and anticipating trouble.

The A Shau Valley from the east rim looking northwest with Aloui Airstrip middle left, Hamburger Hill behind it upper left and Tiger Mountain in the distance upper right

Speed flying low in his little Scout bird startled a deer from the elephant grass. It was huge! It was the size of an elk as it ran across the plain and into a small depression where it could hide. We held our fire.

Then I saw what appeared to be an alligator lumbering out of the river and onto a sand bank. I called Speed to check it out. He radioed back it wasn't an alligator. It was a lizard! We all chuckled. Incredible. Back to the business at hand trying to find the bad guys.

We continued our reconnaissance north past Firebase Airborne which was high up the ridge to our right.

We were following a well-camouflaged trail that meandered up the center of the valley, back and forth, looking for anything that might detect recent enemy activity. When we reached the end, still nothing except an old bomb crater with a fifty-gallon drum perched on the edge.

Now we were feeling a sense of quiet relief. We had traversed the valley from south to north and had not found any signs of enemy activity. I radioed Speed.

"18, 23, How about we conduct some recon by fire?" I asked.

Sometimes, if we are in an area that does not have friendly forces nearby, and designated a free fire area, if we don't find anything, we will intentionally start shooting up the area to see if the enemy is actually there and hiding from us.

"23, 18, Sure! What do you have in mind?" he radioed back.

"Let's see which one of us can knock over that barrel on the edge of the bomb crater with our mini-guns. You first." I responded.

"Okay! Here goes!" he replied, as he whipped the Loach around and started blasting away at the barrel, immediately filling it full of holes and kicking up a lot of dirt as he fired off a few hundred rounds in a short burst with his Gatling gun.

The barrel still stood right where it was.

"Hah!" I laughed. "My turn," as I arched high and lined up a gun run "remain well clear, I'm in hot," I warned.

"Mike," I whispered over the intercom, "I'm going to fire a pair of rockets instead of the mini-gun. We'll blow that thing sky high," as I let off a pair. Direct hit!

I pulled off and banked hard right, gloating over my expert shot as the Best Cobra Pilot alive. I looked over my shoulder for Speed and saw he was hauling ass away from us heading back down the valley with smoke pouring out of the side of his Scout bird.

"Aw Geez Mike, what's he doing?" I said.

I depressed the radio switch as I chased after him.

"18, 23, where are you going?" No answer as he continued flying low at full speed.

"18, 23, you okay?" No answer.

"Speed, what's going on?" I pleaded.

It was at this point that we saw his rotor blades stop in midair. He plunged into the ground doing nearly 100 miles an hour. His helicopter pitched end over end. The rotor blades flew off. The tail boom flew off. The machine continued disintegrating as it finally rolled to a stop in a cloud of dust and smoke.

My body reacted violently. I wanted to throw up. Oh God, Oh God, Oh God. This can't be happening!

"MAYDAY! MAYDAY! MAYDAY! THIS IS ASSAULT 23 IN THE NORTHERN A SHAU, MY SCOUT BIRD 18 IS DOWN. I REPEAT 18 IS DOWN!" I screamed over the unit frequency as I swooped low over the wreckage trying to see any sign of life.

"23 this is Assault 12, I'm on my way." It was Tom Michel, another one of our great Scout Pilots.

Before I could answer, Mike was hollering at me over the intercom: "Lew, land here, land here! There's a spot down here by the trail. Land here so I can go over and help!" he continued as he pointed to an area below us.

The Hughes OH-6 was beloved by all of us who had a chance to fly it. It was nimble, quick, fun to fly and best of all for Scout Pilots, had a built-in roll cage that made a crash survivable, even when hitting the ground at a hundred miles an hour. We could see someone was still alive down there and the cockpit was relatively intact.

I did a tight circle, checking out the landing area for obstacles and slowed down to set up for an approach.

"6 this is 23, we're landing on the trail near the crash. We think we can see survivors." I radioed to Major Curtin as I landed in the small clearing on the trail.

Mike was out of his front seat in a heartbeat and immediately disappeared into the tall elephant grass to our left heading to the wreck, while I kept the Cobra running at full speed in case we were attacked while on the ground. I could then pull pitch to a hover and start firing our weapons in all directions.

Al Goodspeed recalls the crash. "We went down fast, landing on our skids and flipping end over end for about 150 feet or so before coming to rest with the aircraft lying on Hayden's side. I was able to get out relatively quickly. We were in the middle of the elephant grass in about 18 inches of water and deep mud. I immediately crawled back into the aircraft and removed Hayden's seatbelt and pulled him from the aircraft. He was in shock, bleeding profusely, but conscious. That is when I realized that sometime during the crash the first aid kit had been lost."

"We were in the mud in the high elephant grass and had no visibility except straight up," he continued. "I knew we had to get Hayden out fast or he'd bleed out. I lifted him on my shoulder to try to carry him to the trail that I figured was about 50 meters to the west. The problem was that the mud was so deep, I could hardly take a step. I could hear Lew's Cobra nearby toward the trail but couldn't see him."

"About that time Mike Talton came running through the elephant grass to help. Mike was a sight for sore eyes at that point. We laid Hayden back down and decided to use a tourniquet to stop the bleeding. I ripped off my shirt and removed my t-shirt for Mike to apply a makeshift tourniquet. While he was doing that, I tore off one of the engine bay doors from my Loach to use as a sled to make it easier to transport Hayden over the mud and elephant grass. We had Hayden on the sled when Tom Michel arrived in another LOH. Mike and I then started stomping enough elephant grass down so that Tom could hover close enough to the ground to load Hayden."

Back in the Cobra I was catching my breath and trying to make sense of what had happened, when I noticed small poles beside the trail that had communications wire strung on them. Holy moly, this must be one of those major enemy supply routes where the NVA had set up communications lines hidden by the elephant grass! We were right in the middle of it! The trail we had landed on was actually known as Highway 548, a major NVA infiltration route in the A Shau.

In less than five minutes that seemed like hours, Tom Michel swooped in low overhead in his Scout bird and set up for an approach to land near the wreck.

"23, 12, I can see the guys next to the wreckage. For sure one wounded. I'll call on the way out," he radioed as his little bird disappeared in the tall elephant grass maybe 50 yards to my left.

"6 and 23, this is 12, coming out with one WIA. 18 Oscar (Sgt. Hayden) is seriously wounded. Heading direct to 18th Surg at Evans".

Al Goodspeed appeared out of the elephant grass a few minutes later like an apparition, covered in dirt and blood. He lurched toward me and planted a big kiss on the Plexiglas canopy by my left shoulder, gave me a big thumbs-up, and disappeared back into the grass as a Huey approached.

Al relates what happened next. "Mike returned to the Cobra and Lew and a short while later a Huey was able to land on the trail where Lew had landed and flew me to the 85th Evac Hospital at Phu Bai."

"John Hayden had survived, but lost his leg. I remember he had shown me pictures of his new baby before we took off on that mission. I recall that all I could say while pulling him from our aircraft was 'It's okay you're going home to see your baby!' I've often thought about that day and regretted that I was so young and inexperienced in life that I didn't appreciate the excitement he was enjoying about his newly born child. Much later, once I had become a parent, it haunted me that I was unable to convey to him that day how excited he must have felt," Speed reminisced.

By then Mike appeared and climbed back into the front cockpit. "LET'S GET THE HELL OUT OF HERE!" he yelled over the intercom.

The Huey landed to pick up Speed as Tom Michael took off in the Scout bird.

"12, 23, right behind you," as I pulled pitch for take-off.

Mike started explaining what had happened.

"You wouldn't believe it! There was an NVA 12.7 machine gun near that 50-gallon drum. When we started firing on it, the bad guys thought we had discovered them and fired at Speed when he flew nearly directly overhead. He took rounds through the cockpit, radio console and transmission. It knocked out his radios, so he couldn't talk to us and then the transmission froze and he crashed."

"One of the rounds nearly severed Hayden's leg," Mike continued. "I used my pistol and a t-shirt as a tourniquet to try and stop the bleeding, while Speed got one of the engine doors that had been ripped off the helicopter to use as a stretcher to load him aboard 12's Loach."

"Speed seems to be okay. I don't know if Hayden is going to make it," Mike sighed.

The Chicom 12.7mm machine gun is approximately the same size as our .50 caliber machine gun. It fires BIG bullets that easily tear through the aluminum and Plexiglas of a helicopter, not to mention the skin and bone of our bodies.

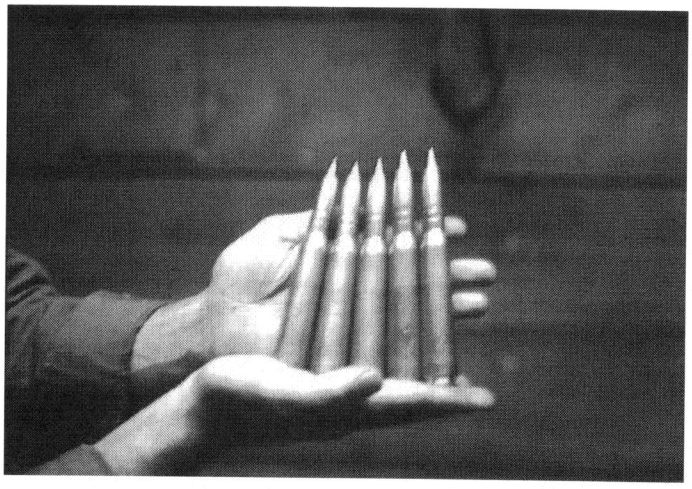

Mike Talton holds CHICOM 12.7mm/.51 Caliber Anti-Aircraft Rounds or what he describes as Great Balls of Fire (GBOFs) later in Chapter 22

I called our CO, Major Tom Curtin and gave him an update on the radio. He called me back with word that he was in contact with an Air Force FAC (Forward Air Controllers flew in small light observation airplanes) who was bringing fast movers inbound with CBUs (Cluster Bomb Units).

And then he asked if I would direct them to the location of the enemy machine gun position and mark it for the attack.

"Yes, Sir!" I could hardly get back there fast enough.

I broke off from escorting Tom Michel and dove to fly fast and low back up the valley along the trail to muffle the direction of the sound of my rotor blades pounding the air and to stay out of sight of the enemy's anti-aircraft guns.

"Mike, we'll come in low and fast, do a cyclic climb as we near the target, then a single run to mark the area with rockets for the FAC. We'll break early to stay well away from the gun emplacement. Be ready to cover us on the break with the mini-gun to keep their heads down."

"Roger that," Mike replied as I saw him squaring his shoulders and getting the flexible turret sight ready and fingers on the triggers.

The Air Force FAC was circling high to the west and had me in sight coming up the valley. I fired a series of several pairs of rockets on the single run, marking the target area, then dove for a low exit while Mike poured lead towards the gun emplacement with the mini-gun at 2,000 rounds per minute.

As we cleared the target area and rapidly climbed to altitude, the first of the Air Force fighter jets appeared and started their bomb runs.

The cluster bombs look similar to conventional bombs however, they break apart in the air as they descend, scattering hundreds of bomblets over a wide area. Each bomblet was like a huge hand grenade with a killing radius of maybe 20 meters. Perfect for taking out enemy troops and disabling vehicles and equipment caught in the open, like the NVA manning the machine gun and who knows what, all still hidden there.

After helping out with the Air Force raid on the machine gun emplacement and surrounding area, it was time for us to head to Firebase Blaze just east of the valley to rearm, refuel and prepare for our next mission. We had been airborne less than two hours.

The adrenaline was finally starting to seep out of our bodies as we landed at Blaze, hot refueled and rearmed, then shut down for a quick break as another Scout was flying out from home base to replace Goodspeed as our hunter-killer team mate.

As we were grabbing a bite to eat from the box of C-rations I carried behind my seat and a drink from a jug of water I always kept on hand, the CO landed nearby in his Huey and headed over to us.

"Oh Man, what a day," he sighed. "You scared the crap out of me Lew, landing like that, and you too Mike. But you guys did the right thing and I think saved Hayden's life. He's already on the operating table at 18th Surgical. I don't know if they will able to save his leg though."

"I've got to get back up and head to a LRRP (Long Range Reconnaissance Patrol) extraction in the south valley," he said as he turned to leave. "In the meantime, as soon as your Scout arrives, I want you to escort and cover Goodman who is coming out with a maintenance bird and a recovery team to sling out what's left of the Loach before it falls into enemy hands."

With that, he climbed into his waiting Huey and was gone.

A few minutes later Eddy Joiner and his Observer "Smitty" Smith arrived to join up with us and shortly after that "Goody" Goodman arrived with the Huey and recovery team.

We briefed on the spot, going over the details of what happened that morning, looking at the wreckage site on our maps, going over the enemy situation, weather, obstacles, radio communications and artillery, air and medevac support if we needed it.

I would be coordinating all from above while providing initial prep of the landing zone by doing a series of gun runs, laying down rocket fire around the crash site. Then Eddy would come in with the little bird, do a short reconnaissance, and mark the landing site with a smoke grenade.

Mike and I would then escort Goodman in the Huey on his approach and landing and continue circling the area to provide instant fire if they ran into trouble.

The whole operation took about half an hour as the team rigged the remains of the wreckage for sling load.

The Huey has a large, electrically operated cargo hook in the middle of its underbelly. The recovery team ties the wreckage together with ropes and straps and hooks the end of the strap into the cargo hook.

Once it's all ready to go, the Huey slowly and carefully comes to a hover directly over the cargo until the strap is tight, then carefully lifts the cargo to make sure it is stable and not too heavy for the Huey to lift.

Then the Huey slowly takes off with the cargo slung some 10 to 20 feet beneath it.

If the cargo is too heavy or starts swinging violently in flight, the Pilot can push a button on his cyclic control stick that instantly opens the cargo hook and drops the load. It's called "Pickling the Load", which is not a good thing.

And that's exactly what would happen to Speed's little bird, as we hit some afternoon turbulence crossing the eastern mountain ridge and Goodman pickled the load from 1,000 feet.

As Tom Curtin had sighed earlier, "What a day!"

OH-6 Scout Wreckage Recovered

And it wasn't over yet. Little did we know that the LRRP extraction in the south A Shau, that the Boss was going to check on, had turned into a disaster.

Specialist 5 Don Foster was the crew chief of the Huey from our Lift Section that was going in for extraction of the Long Range Reconnaissance Patrol (LRRPs). Roger Courtney and Bob Craig were the Pilots. Here's how Don describes what happened.

"We had a 0530 wake up call. It was going to be another hot Vietnam day. On the way to my Huey helicopter, 67-17663, I met up with Captain Roger Courtney who was going to be the Mission Commander and his Pilot, Chief Warrant Officer Robert Craig. Specialist 4 Larry Lyles joined us too, as he would be our other door gunner for the mission besides me."

"I told all three of them that I had a really bad feeling about the mission this morning and feared someone was not going to survive the day. Captain Courtney slapped me on the shoulder and said not to worry, it's just a routine extraction. Maybe so, I replied, but I still have a strange feeling."

"Little did I know," Don recalls, "that a few short hours later, my helicopter 67-17663 would crash into the mountainous jungle and one of the LRRP Rangers would die."

"We departed Eagle with two helicopters to do the extraction, mine and Rosie's (crew chief John Rosenback). We would extract three of the LRRP team members with my helicopter and Rosie's would extract the other three. However, before we reached the pick-up point, our commanding officer (CO) Tom Curtin, decided only one helicopter, mine, would be used to extract all six members of the team."

"When we arrived at the landing zone, it appeared to be a very tight mountainside LZ with no place to land. We would have to use a rope ladder to do the extraction as Captain Courtney maneuvered us in close and would come to a hover above the pick-up point."

"I left my position manning one of our two M-60 machine guns and dropped the rope ladder over the left side to the ground below, then assumed my position back at the machine gun. The LRRP team was instructed to allow only one man at a time on the rope ladder as it was hot, high and we might not be able to carry the full team at one time. The first Ranger climbed the ladder and scrambled aboard. A second Ranger was already on the ladder and he got aboard too. Then a third started climbing the ladder and a fourth man got on the ladder too, while the third one was still only half way up. Uh oh."

"I could hear the engine and transmission starting to whine as the Huey struggled to handle the load, with two Rangers aboard and two still on the ladder. Old 663 then started oscillating violently. It was losing power and the rotor blades started slowing. We were going down and the only thing I could do was hang on and pray."

"The helicopter started to corkscrew down as the Pilots lost tail rotor control. Dirt, grass and tree limbs were flying all around us as the rotor blades cut into everything in their path."

"There is a seat support post attached between the cargo deck and the roof and I was holding on to it with a death grip. I was being thrown from my seat out and into the machine gun on its pivot mount, then back into and against the transmission bulkhead, never letting go of that seat support while we spun toward the ground."

"We crashed to the ground and came to rest with the Huey on its right side and the nose high pointed uphill. The seat post I was holding on to had broken free from the floor and ceiling, still in my hands. Larry was looking at me and yelling my name. My first thought was, so this is what it feels like to die."

"As my brain cleared and Larry came into focus I could hear what he was trying to tell me. One of the LRRPs was trapped under a rotor blade and we needed to help him. As I clambered out, it only took one look to see he was beyond need of our help. He had been hit in the head by the rotor blade and was obviously dead. It was a sight I would remember a thousand nights or more over the next 48 years."

"We gathered at the front of the helicopter for a head count to see how many of us were left. That's when I realized I didn't have my M-16 rifle or M-79 grenade launcher. I scrambled up and over the helicopter to find my weapons and that's when I saw an NVA soldier down the mountainside. He jumped for cover and disappeared at the same time I found my M-16 and M-79. I also found a PRC-25 portable radio to call for help and my Instamatic camera that I used to take some pictures of the wreckage before we were extracted."

"Our CO, Major Curtin, arrived high overhead in his C&C bird. He was coordinating our rescue and called down asking me to check 663 over to see if it could be lifted out. I examined the chopper from top to bottom and discovered the transmission had broken loose from its mounts. Old 663 would never be leaving this mountain."

"She was a great helicopter and she was mine. A few Pilots had flown her, a few door gunners had protected her, but I was the only crew chief ever assigned to her. I felt like I had lost my best friend."

"We waited to be extracted with the remaining crew members and Rangers. The dead Ranger was extracted first by medevac helicopter. The rest of us would wait our turn and be extracted by rope ladder, only three at a time."

"I volunteered to go last. The first three were out and it seemed like hours before a Huey returned to take the rest of us. I was standing on top of Old 663 and grabbed the rope ladder. I climbed up and at the top was greeted by my dear friend and fellow crew chief John 'Rosie' Rosenback as his hand reached for mine."

"Once inside and looking down at the wreckage, the tears started flowing. I couldn't stop crying as the others climbed aboard. Rosie slapped me on the back and gave me a thumbs-up signaling, everything's going to be okay."

Don Foster continues; "After we were all clear of the crash site, Cobra gunships came in and put Old 663 to rest with rockets through and through. She was a part of history now. I was assigned a new aircraft, Triple Nickel, that would become my second-best friend. To this day, I still have an empty feeling about that fateful day when we lost courageous Ranger Sergeant Keith Hammond and the loss of a good friend, 67-17663. May they rest in peace."

CHAPTER FOURTEEN

HAMBURGER HILL

Needless to say, it was with much trepidation that Mike and I continued operations in the A Shau over the next few days following Speed's crash.

With our Scouts, we reconned the valley and adjacent ridgelines and supported A Company, 3/187th "Rakkasans", that had replaced our Blues from 2/17 Cav to build out Firebase Airborne.

Artillery was helicoptered into the firebase by huge CH-47 Chinooks to provide support anywhere within 20 miles. We would need it and much more over the coming days.

We had encountered sporadic enemy activity and called in Air Force F-4 fighter jets to destroy some hooches we found on a jungle covered ridgeline near Hill 937 and Tiger Mountain.

One of our teams engaged a 12.7mm anti-aircraft machine gun emplacement in the western hills and killed the crew. Major Curtin wanted to extract the enemy anti-aircraft machine gun and take it back to Squadron Headquarters. Probably not a good idea but what the hell, as the saying goes; "If you ain't Cav, you ain't shit!"

Eddy Joiner flew his Scout bird in low to make sure all the bad guys were dead and then hovered over the gun to hoist it out with a line and grappling hook. Their plan was to have his Observer, Sergeant Hyden, hook on to it, fly it a few kilometers away, then land and transfer it to the Boss's Huey.

Mike Ryan in his Scout bird and Don McGurk in a Cobra came in to provide cover for Joiner.

Just as Joiner and Hyden had the anti-aircraft gun hooked and started to lift it out, Ryan spied an arm come out of a nearby spider hole with an automatic rifle. The NVA soldier unleashed a burst of fire and Joiner's bird took several hits in the engine and transmission area. They just had time to drop the line, hover over to a grassy area and settle onto the ground in one piece as the aircraft lost power.

Ryan killed the soldier in the spider hole with a burst from his M-134 minigun, the electric Gatling gun we had mounted on all the Scout birds for self-protection, and then went over to check on Joiner and Hyden. Neither of them were wounded, however their Loach was in deep elephant grass and there was nowhere to land and pick them up.

With Ryan circling low overhead in his Loach, McGurk providing gun cover with his Cobra and the Boss standing by to help out in his Huey, Joiner and Hyden were frantically removing their gear out of the downed aircraft and piling it on top, including their personal weapons, grenades and any sensitive materials. They didn't know if more bad guys might emerge from more hiding places at any moment.

With so little room around the downed aircraft, Major Curtin couldn't get in with his Huey and directed Ryan to try and rescue them with his little Scout bird. The OH-6 Loach has just enough room for two people to squeeze in the back, however now with two guys up front, plus their minigun system, plus Joiner and Hyden, the aircraft would be severely overloaded and possibly unable to fly out of there.

Ryan zoomed in low, came to a quick stop over the downed bird and then very gently rested the tips of his landing gear on top of the rotor blades of the downed bird. Now with Ryan's Loach stable, Joiner and Hyden threw their stuff in the back and climbed in.

Ryan started pulling in the power to take off. He totally maxed it out to get airborne and then plunged down the hillside to gain speed. They had to find some place to land quickly as, sure enough, his little Scout bird was overloaded and straining to stay in the air.

They made it to an old abandoned airstrip just a few minutes away in the bottom of the valley. Aloui airstrip had been built by the French back in the '50s. Now pock marked with bomb craters and overgrown with vegetation, the strip was not useable for fixed wing aircraft but still had some open areas sufficient to land helicopters. Ryan landed safely and Joiner and Hyden transferred to the Boss's Huey. Mike Ryan had saved the day!

While Major Curtin came in to pick them up, he was calling back to base to get crews, riggers and aircraft to come in and sling load out the downed bird with a Huey. He didn't want to have to destroy it in place and hoped to be able to get a team back in there to haul it out, which is what they did. The

CO got called on the carpet for that escapade. It wouldn't be the last time he got chewed out for our antics.

The rest of us continued our reconnaissance flights, calling in dozens of spot reports as we found more evidence of enemy activity; trails, footprints, bicycle tracks, fighting positions, bunkers and hooches. There was definitely a lot of enemy activity in the area.

Eddy Joiner's Scout bird being sling-loaded home after being shot down trying to grapple-hook an enemy Chicom 12.7mm Anti-Aircraft Gun.

On the evening of 8 May, we all assembled in the mess hall for another operational brief. This one was definitely different. The place was packed and included a lot of new faces. Several map boards had been erected on easels. The Boss looked serious.

We leaped to our feet as "Attention" was called and we knew someone of high rank had entered. The Squadron Commander, Lieutenant Colonel Bill DeLoach walked in and took a seat up front accompanied by Brigadier General James Smith, the Assistant Division Commander (ADC) for the 101st Division. Known on the radio as "Hawkeye", he seemed to be everywhere and lived up to the name.

"At Ease, Gentlemen," someone commanded. The rest of us took our seats and the briefing started.

"Holy cow, this is really serious," I thought.

"Gentlemen, day after tomorrow on the morning of 10 May, Operation Apache Snow will get underway to take control of the A Shau Valley." Major Curtin began.

"Intelligence and our own reconnaissance operations indicate significant enemy presence in the valley."

"The 101st Division intends to take control of the valley to deny the enemy any further capability to conduct combat operations from there," he explained.

"To do that, there will be a massive air assault operation, airlifting approximately 10 Battalions of 3rd Brigade infantry, ARVN and 9th Marine forces into multiple landing zones in the valley supported by Air Force, Navy and Marine tactical air support, artillery, aerial rocket artillery and us," he said as he paused and looked across the room to make sure he had our attention. No doubt about that!

"This may be the largest air assault operation of the Vietnam War. Pay close attention to the following briefs by Captain Dowdy and others as this has to be orchestrated to the minute and even second and failure is not an option," he emphasized.

It quickly became obvious that a lot of detailed planning had been going on for quite some time to launch an operation of this magnitude.

Mike leaned over and whispered to me "Wow. This is just like out of a World War II movie or something."

After the initial brief of the Operations Order outlining the overall concept for the operation, the Squadron Commander and General Smith took their leave and we spent the next two hours going over the details for our part in Apache Snow.

The five-part sequence of an Operations Order (OPORD) is memorized by all soldiers; Situation, Mission, Execution, Support and Command and Signal. We carefully reviewed each of the five parts to understand the planning of the operation and our role in it.

General Creighton Abrams had taken over command of all US forces in Vietnam from General Westmoreland, who was now the Army's Chief of Staff back in Washington DC. General Abrams and his staff at Military Assistance Command Vietnam (MACV) suspected that the North Vietnamese Army was again building up forces and supplies in the area of the A Shau Valley, after being devastated a year earlier during the Tet Offensive of 1968.

Reconnaissance indicated that as many as a thousand enemy trucks a day were moving south on Route 922 parallel to us and just across the border in Laos, which had prompted Operation Dewey Canyon north of the A Shau a month earlier with the 3rd Marine Division and their 9th Marine Regiment.

The 9th Marines fought several intense battles with well-equipped NVA forces capturing tons of weapons, ammunition and supplies and destroying many enemy structures, including a fully equipped field hospital with eight buildings.

As a follow-up to Operation Dewey Canyon, Army Corps Commander Lieutenant General Richard G. Stilwell tasked Major General Melvin Zais, Commander of the 101st Airborne

Division (Airmobile) to plan and conduct an operation to find, fix and destroy enemy forces, supplies and equipment in the A Shau Valley.

General Stillwell would augment the 101st Division with additional forces; the 9th Marine Regiment, two Army of Vietnam (ARVN) Infantry Battalions and the US 3/5 Mechanized Infantry Battalion.

General Zais met with all the Commanders and tasked his own 3rd Brigade, commanded by Colonel Joseph B. Conmy Jr., to conduct a reconnaissance in force with three Battalions in the western center of the valley near Hill 937 adjacent to the Laotian border.

Colonel Conmy planned to have the Battalions reinforce one another to concentrate combat power whenever they found major enemy resistance. Their assigned helicopters could rapidly move forces about the battlefield.

The two ARVN Battalions would be airlifted in, north and south of the 3rd Brigade, to conduct reconnaissance in force and block enemy escape routes to the south and west.

The 9th Marines would be airlifted into the far north of the A Shau to also conduct reconnaissance and block enemy escape routes to the north and west.

The 3/5 Mechanized Infantry with their tanks and tracked vehicles were to clear and open the final portion of the road that had been under construction from Camp Eagle near Hue, west through the hills and mountains to the heart of the A Shau.

The 3rd Brigade would employ three Battalions to aggressively conduct reconnaissance in force operations in the west center of the A Shau, north of the Aloui airstrip.

1/506th in the south would recon northwest along the Laotian border.

3/187th Airborne Infantry in the middle would recon north of Aloui towards Hill 937, Dong Ap Bia.

2/501st in the north would recon southeast towards the Laotian border.

It would be a three-pronged pincer type reconnaissance; 1/506th Battalion on the left, 3/187 Battalion in the middle, and 2/501st Battalion on the right.

3/1 ARVN Battalion would provide a blocking force across the middle of the valley south of Aloui airstrip at Ta Bat.

1/1 ARVN Battalion would provide a blocking force in the north near Tiger Mountain.

9th Marines would provide additional blocking forces north of 1/1 ARVNs.

One Company (approx. 130 soldiers), B Company 3/187th was to be held back as Brigade Reserve.

There were six landing zones (LZs) identified to airlift all the forces into their respective locations. Another 30 or so alternate LZs were targeted to keep the enemy guessing as to which ones we would actually be using.

The plan called for 70 minutes of preparation fires. In first was TAC air (Air Force, Navy and Marine fighter jets) for 50 minutes, dropping hundreds of bombs at all the identified landing zones. The fighters would peel off at H hour -20 minutes, when the artillery would take over for 18 minutes of bombardment, followed by us at H hour -02 minutes doing a quick one-minute recon of the LZs and then at H hour -01minute Aerial Rocket Artillery (ARA) Cobras doing a last one-minute pounding of the LZs, as the Hueys carrying the troops were on their final approach to the landing zones at H-hour.

Whew! Timed to the minute and second like the Boss had said. What could go wrong?

The following day we still had missions to fly in the valley and then spent more hours back at home base updating our map books, organizing our gear, reviewing our tasks, prepping our aircraft and getting ready for the big day. I don't think any of us got much sleep that night.

May 10 (Day 1)

Up at zero-dark-thirty on 10 May. I had showered and shaved the night before, so I quickly donned my jungle fatigues and after a cup of coffee and a quick trip to the shitter, met Mike Talton back at the hooch, grabbed our gear and headed to the flight line.

We were pretty loaded down. Besides our chicken plates, dog tags, P-38 can openers and survival vests, we had a couple of boxes of C-Rations, a cooler of water, map books and knee boards with pencils and grease pens.

And Mike never went anywhere without his Thompson sub-machine gun, so we packed that too. Good man to have along in a fight.

The armament guys had loaded up our rocket pods, Gatling gun and grenade launcher for us. Our crew chief had done all the maintenance work during the night. All we had to do was load our stuff, do a thorough preflight inspection to make sure everything was in order and we would be good to go.

Our crank time was at 0650 hours to get our ships up and running. Radio check in at 0655. Launch at 0700. H-hour with troops in the landing zone (LZ #2) was set at 0801.

The Air Force was already out there doing the initial bombing of possible landing zones. There were some 30 LZs that had been identified, however only six would be used on this day. We would bomb and put in artillery on nearly all of them so the enemy wouldn't get a clue as to which ones we would actually be using.

Nearly 2,000 soldiers of the 1/506th, 2/501st and 3/187th Airborne Infantry Battalions were being organized out at Firebase Blaze to load aboard 65 UH-1 Hueys to combat assault in waves out to the landing zones.

Nearly every helicopter in the 101st Division was going to be used to move and support the troops.

The troop-carrying helicopters from the 101st Aviation Battalion with their call signs: Thunder, Comancheros, Kingsmen, and Black Widows.

More troop-carrying Hueys and escorting Cobra gunships from the 158th Aviation Battalion: Ghost Riders, Lancers, Phoenix and Redskins.

Huge cargo helicopters from the 159th Aviation Battalion to carry troops, supplies and large equipment like artillery cannons, call signs: Pachyderms, Varsity, Playtex and Hurricanes.

4/77th Aerial Rocket Artillery (ARA) Cobras: Dragons, Toros and Griffin.

A and C Troops, 2/17th Air Cavalry with their Hueys, Cobras and Scouts: Assault and Condor.

20th TASS USAF Forward Air Controllers (FACs) with their 0-1 Bird Dogs and 0-2 Skymasters: Bilk and Speedy.

326th Medical Battalion Hueys to conduct medical evacuations (Medevacs) day and night, in all weather conditions and under fire; the heroes of Eagle Dustoff.

Well over a hundred helicopters of all types and sizes plus Air Force fixed wing FAC controllers and TAC air fighters to support this massive effort.

The TAC air bombing was followed by nearly an hour of artillery preparation from the firebases surrounding the valley to the east. Thousands of rounds of 105mm, 155mm and 8inch high explosives would fill the air and shake the ground, hopefully causing lots of grief and confusion for the enemy.

As the artillery fire was lifted and shifted we were to immediately fly in, do a quick recon of the landing zone to make sure it was clear of bad guys, and then get out of the way because we only had seconds before the "Dragons" would be firing up the LZ right behind us and the troop-carrying Hueys coming in for landing behind their fire.

The "Dragons" were Cobras of A Battery, 4/77 Aerial Rocket Artillery (ARA) Battalion. They were under the command and control of the Artillery Commander. When they provide close air support to the ground troops they are directly employed by the Artillery Forward Observer who is with the Infantry. They were simply known as "ARA", and we considered them our friendly archrivals.

We in the Air Cavalry were usually first on the field of battle conducting reconnaissance to find and fix the enemy and dealing with them within our means. Our motto was "Out Front".

If we needed help, we could call in artillery or tactical air support from the Air Force, Navy or Marines. Or we could call ARA.

The ARA would usually come in at a high altitude, 2,000 feet (which we considered the Stratosphere for a helicopter), fire their rockets at targets we marked for them, break off their runs at 1,000 feet so as not to get too close to the action (that's where we usually started our runs), then return back to base as the heroes saving the day.

It was "friendly competition".

Time now was 0755. "Lancer" Hueys from Bravo Company 158th Aviation Battalion were in the air carrying troops of D Company, 3/187th Airborne Infantry from Firebase Blaze just a few minutes away. Artillery was lifting and we were zooming in to Landing Zone #2 to see the results of all the explosions and mayhem.

Al Goodspeed in his Scout bird was the first in, flying low over the landing zone with Mike and I above and behind, guns and rockets cocked and ready to pounce if he received fire.

He just had time to call us that things were quiet when all hell broke loose. The ARA Cobras didn't see us still in the LZ and cut loose with their rockets.

"HOLY SHIT, WHAT'S HAPPENING?" Speed screamed, as shrapnel from the exploding rockets started tearing through the fuselage of his Loach.

"ARA, WE'RE STILL IN THE LZ!" I started yelling over the radio net, as the smoke trails of rockets zipped by close overhead and warheads were exploding all around us.

"DON'T YOU SEE US?" (expletives deleted) I screamed as both Speed and I broke left, trying to survive the mayhem.

"Enough of that," came over the radio from the CO, Major Curtin. Swearing over the radio was NEVER tolerated and I would be counseled for that later.

"Cover the Slicks inbound" he directed, as we circled around to the east and I tried to regain my composure.

I could see the Lancers and their Hueys or "Slicks" as we called them as they were devoid of rocket pods and cannons. They did have two machine guns, one on either side, manned by the Crew Chief and Door Gunner, often hanging by straps or mounted on a pedestal so they could be easily handled.

It was a large formation of ten or more aircraft. They had lifted off from Firebase Blaze at 0750 fully loaded with troops of 3/187th Infantry and were cresting the rise on the east side of the valley above LZ Rendezvous, headed our way.

We joined alongside the formation, directing them inbound to the LZ. They were escorted by their own D/158 Cobra Gunships that were darting ahead firing more rockets on either side of the landing zone as ARA had peeled off and were circling overhead.

158th Aviation Battalion Hueys Over the A Shau

Landing zone #2, designated for the 3/187th Airborne Infantry Battalion, was a small LZ in the saddle or low area of a ridge northeast of Hill 937. The landing zone could only accommodate two ships at a time, so the large formation of Hueys started splitting up as pairs and made their approach to the landing zone two at a time.

The two-ship formation of Hueys flared in unison with their tails pointed towards the ground, trying to slow down. Like a choreographed ballet movement, they slowed simultaneously from nearly 100 miles per hour to a stop, hovering a few feet above the ground, as the troops jumped out and took up defensive positions. Then, just as they had arrived, they nosed over like racecars taking off from the starting line to gain speed and rose in a single movement as the next pair came in right behind them.

The first insertion of troops was over in seconds. The faster the better as every Huey crew and infantryman knew; each second stationary in an LZ was a second closer to death.

Repeated again and again, it only took a few minutes to land D Company and the Hueys were already headed back to Blaze for more.

D Company "Rakkasans" were on the ground at 0801. A and C Companies were already in the air just a few minutes away. They landed in the LZ at 0820 followed by the Mortar Section and remaining elements of 3/187th Battalion at 0856; nearly 500 soldiers in all.

The 1/506th Airborne Infantry Battalion had already landed all their troops in Landing Zone #1 at 0730. They had been supported by our sister unit, C Troop, 2/17th Air Cavalry, the "Condors".

The 2/501st Battalion would be inserted next northeast of us at 1001 hours, followed by the two ARVN Battalions south and north at 1020 and 1300 hours respectively.

It was a huge operation with each landing zone requiring the same scenario of tactical air bombing, followed by artillery preparation, followed by Air Cavalry recon, followed by ARA fire prep, followed by tight formations of helicopters landing in unison, trying not to run into each other while getting troops on the ground as fast as possible.

Miraculously, no aircraft were lost during these initial air assaults. One big CH-47 Chinook cargo helicopter hauling an artillery piece was shot down while landing at a firebase on Tiger Mountain later in the day, however, no one was injured and the aircraft was later recovered.

The largest air assault operation of the war up until then was a huge success! There were well over 100 aircraft involved. In addition to the 65 troop-carrying Hueys, there were the Gunships and Scouts of the 2/17th Air Cavalry, Cobras with the 4/77th ARA, Cargo helicopters of the 159th, Medevac helicopters with the 326th, Forward Air Controller aircraft with the 20th TASS and Air Force, Navy and Marine fighter jets. The whole operation had gone brilliantly and the enemy was deceived for the moment.

Now we in Alpha Troop, 2/17 Air Cav focused on supporting the 3rd Brigade and more specifically, the 3/187th Airborne Infantry Battalion.

Lieutenant Colonel (LTC) Weldon Honeycutt, call sign "Blackjack", was the Commander of the Battalion and flew overhead in a command and control (C&C) bird, directing the action and coordinating the operation of his three Companies.

He landed in LZ #2 at 1046 to join his soldiers and establish his command post.

D Company was first in, reconned southeast and secured an area of higher ground towards Hill 937. The Battalion Headquarters and Mortar Section followed D Company and established a Command Post within D Company's perimeter. Mortar positions were dug and a small landing zone cleared.

This location would prove to be critical, as Lieutenant Colonel Honeycutt would direct operations from there over the next 10 days.

A Company had reached higher ground 500 meters to the northeast and then reconned northwest all the way down to the river, which was the boundary between South Vietnam and Laos.

C Company was securing LZ #2 for additional forces.

Honeycutt requested and received B Company that was being held as the Brigade reserve. B Company landed in the LZ at 1600 and 3/187th was complete with a force of nearly 600 soldiers.

Honeycutt ordered B Company to begin a reconnaissance southeast through D Company's location and continue up even higher ground towards Hill 937. He wanted to establish his command post up there the next day.

We in the Air Cav had set up a round-robin affair, rotating teams out and back from Firebase Blaze to rearm and refuel while keeping one or two Pink teams of a Cobra and a Loach on station at all times.

We were finding lots of enemy activity on the higher ground above our troops; Hill 900, 916 and 937 and the connecting ridgelines. The whole area was steep terrain covered in heavy jungle, tall trees and thick bamboo, making identification of friend and foe difficult from the start.

The cardinal sin for Gunship Pilots is to mistakenly hurt our own. We always made it an absolute priority to identify where the friendlies were first, before unleashing our firepower.

We had identified where all the Battalion elements were and set up our target runs to avoid hitting any friendlies if our rockets, grenades or bullets went long or short as we engaged enemy targets.

I made it a practice to personally identify the friendlies in addition to the Scout bird when we were in close contact situations, sometimes even "Danger Close" when firing within 50 meters of friendly troops. In those cases, we usually didn't fire rockets or grenades because of the exploding shrapnel. I would fire the mini-gun in a locked position at a "low-rate" of 2000 rounds per minute and "walk" the stream of bullets in close to the friendlies, sometimes into the trees over their heads in case enemy snipers were hiding up there.

As B Company continued up the high ground they ran into heavy enemy resistance from small arms fire and rocket propelled grenades, suffering three wounded.

We leaped into action and attacked the ridgeline in front of them and Hill 937, while they called in artillery, mortar and ARA fire. The skirmish was over quickly. The enemy retreated to their concealed fighting places. B Company established a night defensive position (NDP). The wounded were Medevaced out by helicopter as darkness fell and we returned to home base.

I lay awake that night thinking about the infantry soldiers still out there in the jungle manning their positions. I racked my brain as to how I could do a better job helping them and defeating the enemy. It would become a nightly ritual for my entire tour. The guys carrying a rucksack and rifle deserved everything I could give them and more.

May 11 (Day 2)

We were up at zero-dark thirty again and headed to the A Shau. Two teams of us headed directly to 3/187th's location while another two landed at Blaze to standby and replace us when we got low on fuel or ran out of ammo.

The night had been relatively calm for the troops. At 0600 they set off a "Fireball" where everyone points their weapons outward from their positions and lets loose for a few seconds in case the enemy is creeping up on them. We did the same thing at our big bases with automatic weapons, machine guns and artillery, calling it a "Mad Minute".

We arrived on station shortly after their Fireball and almost immediately discovered and engaged bad guys running around between fighting positions up on the higher ground.

All three of the Battalion's companies were on the move. A Company to the northeast, B Company to the southeast towards Hill 937 and C Company south and east, with D Company securing the Headquarters Command Post (CP) and night defensive positions (NDPs).

A, B and C Companies were finding lots of enemy activity including enemy dead from artillery, air strikes and us. And we discovered small telephone poles with communications wire going from east to west up and over Hill 937, which was further evidence of a sizeable force that was well entrenched up there.

Late in the afternoon as B Company continued through the heavy jungle climbing up the ridge towards Hill 937, a lone sniper took them under fire apparently trying to draw them into an ambush.

A few minutes later the enemy ambush was sprung and they came under heavy fire. Three B Company soldiers were killed and two more wounded. Lieutenant Colonel Honeycutt ordered the B Company Commander to drive on attacking the enemy before retrieving the wounded, calling all of us in for support; Air Cav, ARA, artillery and air strikes.

Then the unthinkable happened. An ARA Gunship mistakenly turned into the friendlies on a gun run and hit directly into the Battalion Command Post killing one soldier and injuring 35 others, including Honeycutt himself. Though wounded, Honeycutt continued to direct and provide support for his battalion.

B Company's wounded and KIA were Medevaced by Eagle Dustoff at 1845 and many other aircraft provided Medevac support for the Headquarters' wounded. All those requiring evacuation were out by 1930. Honeycutt refused evacuation and remained with his soldiers.

All Companies set up their night defensive positions and all was quiet.

May 12 (Day 3)

We were getting into a routine now. Up at zero-dark thirty and out to the battlefield by sun up. Rotating our teams in and out of the Battalions' area of operations (AO). Communicating with the Ground Commanders, Forward Air Controllers, Artillery, Medevacs and our own Headquarters.

Providing reconnaissance and close air support. Rearming and refueling as necessary, sometimes "hot".

When the Air Force (God Bless them) comes in and drops their bombs, they head back to Da Nang, Thailand or Guam or somewhere else far away and taxi up to their parking spot directed in by their Crew Chief. The Crew Chief then helps them take off their seat belts and descend a ladder to the waiting crew vehicle. In air-conditioned comfort, they're driven to the Officers Club for a chicken salad sandwich and a glass of iced tea, while ordnance crews rearm and refuel their airplane. They may do this once or even twice a day.

The Navy (God Bless them too, except on Army/Navy Game Day) comes in, drops their bombs and then heads back to the Carrier well offshore. Once on deck, they are greeted by a brown-shirted Plane Captain and escorted to their air-conditioned wardroom for a chicken salad sandwich – toasted please– and a glass of sweetened iced tea while the aircraft is moved below decks for ordnance loading. They usually only do this once a day.

The Army (Thank God for the infinite wisdom of the Green Machine) thinks all that is a waste of time. The Army prepositions your fuel and ammo just minutes from the fighting at what's called a Forward Arming and Refueling Point (FARP, like fart with a P). And you're expected to carry your own C-Rations (canned dog food) and water to eat and drink whenever you can get around to it. Only sissies eat chicken salad sandwiches!

And there is usually NO Plane Captain, Crew Chief or even Ordnance people ready to greet you as you land at a FARP. You're expected to do it all yourself.

Hot rearming and refueling is where we land out there at a firebase next to our fuel and ammunition and get out and load the Cobra ourselves, without shutting down!

We bring the engine down to flight idle and with the rotors still spinning, lock down the controls so it won't take off without us, undo our seatbelts, remove our helmets and chicken plates and then get busy reloading the aircraft as fast as we can to get back in the action quickly.

When we arrive "on station" we are fully loaded with rockets, grenades and bullets and about two hours of fuel on board. If there's a lot of action right away, as is happening here in the A Shau, we may run out of all our ammo in just a few minutes and still have an hour or more of fuel. In that case, we head back to the nearest FARP and then load rockets on board as fast as we can and be airborne again in minutes.

The safety guys would go nuts seeing this in action today but it was what we had to do at the time. People were dying and we needed to get back into the action fast.

Rearming our Cobra near the A Shau. Mike Talton on the left with the submachine gun on his hip and Lew Jennings on the right with the rocket across his shoulders. Two Alpha Troop Armorers in front lending a hand.

We arrived on station as the sun came up. Again, all was mostly quiet for the ground troops during the night. I was off supporting the other Maneuver Battalions, when Honeycutt called for engineers to be flown out to B Company's location to cut a new landing zone out of the tall jungle and trees to evacuate more wounded.

Our own Blue Platoon with their Hueys were on standby to provide support to any of the 3rd Brigade units. Mark Stevens and Dave Goodman (Goody-Two-Shoes) volunteered to fly their Hueys out to do the job. Each Huey had a Pilot and Copilot up front and a Crew Chief and Door Gunner manning M-60 machine guns in the back.

Mark and Goody landed at a newly constructed firebase in the middle of the Valley called Currahee. They were briefed by a Lieutenant Colonel on the mission and location of the drop zone and loaded the necessary equipment and engineers on board.

None of us Scouts or Guns were apparently available to escort them in or provide covering fire if they got into trouble.

Disaster loomed ahead. Here is what happened in Mark Stevens' own words:

"Jackie Wilson was my Copilot and I believe it was Crew Chief Joe Morgan and Door Gunner Larry Lyles in the back."

"We emptied everything not nailed down in the aircraft and rigged long rappelling lines to lower the engineers and equipment into the drop zone as there was no place to land yet. Both aircraft were loaded with the engineer equipment and personnel and I was named Flight Lead."

"I was briefed by a Lieutenant Colonel on the mission. He was out of 3rd Brigade Headquarters. We were to support Honeycutt's Battalion. His call sign was Blackjack. We were to report to him as we approached the area."

"I was given coordinates to the drop zone location and we departed for the 10-minute trip north. I located the DZ and had Goodie orbit off to the south while I went in for the initial drop."

"Once situated over the trees, about 200 to 250 feet above the ground, the lines were thrown out and the engineers lowered chain saws and other equipment and then began their descent, one out each side of the aircraft at a time."

"About then I caught a black object flying by in my peripheral vision. The next thing I knew our aircraft rocked upward into the air, ass end first. A rocket-propelled grenade just missed us!"

"We still had guys on the ropes and keeping the aircraft steady so as not to drag them through the trees was paramount in my mind. I asked the crew if they knew what that was and someone said they thought it was an RPG."

"I no sooner got that info and another one came at us again! If anyone says you can't see the bullet that will kill you, I beg to differ. This RPG hit closer to the ship but still missed. I knew the next one would nail us if we didn't move and the guy lobbing the RPG's was getting better with each one."

"I told the engineer Captain on board I needed to get the hell out of there pronto! He agreed."

"The guys in the back checked for the engineers still on the lines and the highest one was almost down."

"I told the crew to cut the lines with machetes we kept in the back of the seats and they did, punching holes in the ship's deck as they hacked thru the lines. I didn't much care, we knew we needed to boogie before the next RPG connected."

"I nosed the ship over just as the third round hit the trees where we were, or it seemed like that to all of us on board."

"I told Goodie I was going back to Currahee as I had no more lines and he was to follow."

"We got back there and I was met by the Lieutenant Colonel. I explained the situation and said the place needed some serious prepping fires before that should be tried again."

"Apparently you guys were off doing something else and I was told that there were no Gunship assets and the mission still had to be completed."

"I said I had no more lines, but that excuse fell on deaf ears as new lines were immediately presented to me."

"I also need to add here I was low on fuel, but thought I could make it work if we could get in and out quickly. There wasn't a FARP anywhere nearby so I needed to have enough fuel to get to Blaze, as I recall."

"With new gear on board, we saddled up again and headed back to the DZ up by Hill 937, or Dong Ap Bia, as it was called on the map. I had Goodie do the same as last time and orbit to the south. I knew the way in and out and felt I could get in, get over the spot and then get out quick, leaving little time for my NVA friend to bag his Huey."

"I settled in over the trees and the guys in back threw out the lines. They started zipping down when we all heard the aircraft being stitched with AK 47 rounds. We had the last of the folks on the lines and couldn't move, so we were once again a great target."

"We heard the ground fire again and within seconds the cyclic began to get heavy and hard to move. It didn't take much thought to know the hydraulics were going fast."

"All the engineers were off the lines and on the ground. I had the aircraft stabilized. I figured I was home free when all of a sudden, we were slammed with an RPG. It hit just aft of the transmission near the tail boom mounts. We immediately flipped upside down and went inverted into the trees."

"As the aircraft was doing its best to spin and come apart, I could see the blades smashing into the trees. I can honestly say that I never saw my life flashing before me. In fact, I found myself trying to still control the ship even though logically, I knew it was impossible to do."

"We hit the ground upside down. I looked over at Jackie and asked if he was all right. I already knew he was alive because he had hit the floor microphone switch as we descended through the trees and I could hear him praying to

God. I credit Jackie for getting the attention of the Almighty and that saved us."

"We were both hanging from the straps upside down and when I let the seatbelt lock loose, I promptly fell into the greenhouse overhead (green plastic windows built in for shade)."

"Later I realized I had lost my .38 pistol when I did this, no great loss in the scheme of things, but it still would have been nice to have with me. Never again did I put the holster between my legs and have the weapon loose."

"More important, I later found I also lost my 'lucky hat'!"

"I managed to get my butt out of the aircraft and that's when I noticed it was on fire! I started up the hill pretty much on autopilot when I realized I needed to check on others."

"I found Jackie under a rotor blade that had caught him in his slide down the hill after his egress."

"I then helped Lyles who had been thrown from the aircraft, in spite of the fact he had on a seat belt and was tethered by a body harness. Imagine the G force that took! As the impact tossed him out, his right arm bicep caught on the door lock and the muscle was pretty much ripped off, along with breaking his arm."

"I took stock of all the folks and their injuries and felt very lucky we were in as good a shape as we were."

"I loved that Huey. It crashed through the trees inverted, breaking up all the way down and we all survived. And we were well enough that if we could manage to get out of there, we would have a great war story."

"The engineer Captain who had flown out with us was unharmed but shook up. Jackie had sprained his leg or ankle. Joe Morgan seemed okay even though he had not been strapped in. To this day, I am still amazed that he was only held in place by his own sheer willpower and physical strength as his only place to hold on to was the back of my seat. And Lyles, though in pain, would certainly live to tell his story."

"Once I had everyone moved away from the burning aircraft, I noticed an E-5 Sergeant worming his way down the slope towards us."

"I will never forget that welcome sight. He was a redhead, covered in filth, wearing a scruffy growth of beard and was chewing tobacco. His pants were torn along the front to the point where I could see his balls."

"He looked at me and said; 'Gawd damned Sir, I wouldn't do what you do for all the money in the world!'

"I looked at him and busted up laughing. This guy was telling ME that!"

"Sarge, I will do this little crash scene three more times for you today, if you can get me out of here each time I crash."

"That's when I figured out it's *different strokes for different folks*."

"He led and helped us up the hill to their defensive positions. When I had everyone settled in foxholes, I went to find the officer in charge. I was told he was dead so I spoke to the Senior NCO, who was the unit's First Sergeant. I asked if I could use his radio to call for some assistance. Silly me, whatever made me think that would happen."

"About this time the machine gun ammo in the aircraft started cooking off and the hill erupted in a demonstration of firepower I cannot begin to describe. All those grunts thought the NVA were charging up the hill as the aircraft rounds cooked off and they responded in kind. About this time the

First Shirt got up and began stomping around, shouting 'cease fire, cease fire'! He gave them all a taste of what I would call a 'highly charged verbal assault'. Even I had never heard some of those words. They sure worked though."

"I couldn't dig a hole deep enough, fast enough. I had no weapon, no steel pot and I was out in the open. Yup, I was definitely scared."

"I tried to make radio contact with our Troop via Blackjack's C&C and was told under no uncertain terms it wasn't going to happen. There was too much going on and assets were needed elsewhere and besides there was no LZ for an extraction or time to bring in more help. I would have to do what I could for the crew for the time being and just work with the First Sergeant and settle in."

"I don't take no for an answer very well, at least not the first few times. It was time for action."

"I asked the First Sergeant for a steel pot and a weapon. I was given a dead man's helmet and his M-16 rifle and flak jacket."

"I then asked the engineer Captain if he still wanted to make an LZ. He didn't seem too keen on it but I told him I would get him out of there before the day was up if he would show me how to use the C-4 plastic explosive he had brought to blow trees down to make an LZ."

"After a quick lesson, he handed me the bag of explosives and detonator cord. I took the bag and headed back down the hill to where I thought it would be the easiest access to the unit and began wiring up the C-4 to trees."

"I honestly don't remember what happened to the Captain after I left him, I seem to recall he was helping with the chain saw elsewhere, as I didn't see him again till several hours later."

"As I was working my way down the hill my NVA friend with the RPG must have seen me and began shooting at me again. I couldn't believe it, what's up with this guy? He already bagged the Huey, give me a break!"

"I was able to contact a Cobra from some unit and asked for some help if they could find the guy. He wanted to know where I was and where I thought Charlie was. I gave him my coordinates as best as I could figure them and the RPG position as best as I could tell. A pair of Cobras made one pass each prior to bringing in the heat."

"On the second pass, they started shooting 40mm grenades. Again, I learned something that day."

"If you have never been on the ground and seen a Cobra beating down in line with your position and shooting straight at you, you haven't lived! I now knew how the NVA had to feel. I thought for sure I was a dead man."

"Imagine my surprise as the Cobra passed over and I was still alive to see the second one inbound looking exactly like the first. After the two passes I never heard from Charlie again, so either they got him or he figured I wasn't worth his skin."

"After a number of hours, I managed to get an LZ blown that was big enough for my taste. If I was flying, I knew I could easily navigate my way into it and back out in a Huey."

"I managed to get a Medevac on the radio and I walked them in. The Pilot said he couldn't land and refused to do so. You think I wasn't pissed? I know what you need to land a Huey and he had it. I guess that we Cav guys had different standards!"

"The good news was that a Loach that was in the area, possibly part of the Cobras that had helped me earlier, (I never knew), offered to help. I asked him to stand by as I needed to get the wounded and the dead bodies into the area to move them out. He told me he would take only the wounded."

"I managed to get all the Grunts and those who had been on my aircraft who were wounded out first and then my guys who were not wounded. That Pilot and his Observer were great. He made multiple trips. He had to be Cav!"

"Once all the folks that needed to get taken out had been evaced, he told me he had to get back for fuel but would try and return for the dead. I asked if he could take out two more right then and he agreed to do so."

"I bid goodbye to the First Sergeant and threw a dead body in the back, or should I say, half a body because the guy wrapped in the poncho had been hit dead in his backpack by an RPG and it had blown him diagonally in half. It was the Commanding Officer. I tossed him in the back and clambered over him."

"As the Loach backed out of the LZ, the rotor wash caused the poncho to fly back and that vision I have carried ever since. It took me years to eat meat again after that!"

"The Loach dropped me at Firebase Eagles Nest. When I got out, to my total surprise, my legs completely gave out on me. I fell to the deck like a bag of wet rags. Everything worked but my legs. The Observer got out and helped me get to the side of the landing pad where I sat on some rocket boxes."

"I later figured out that I had been running on adrenalin for so long, that when I was finally clear, the 'coming off it effect' manifested itself by a complete loss of strength in my legs. It took about 5 to 10 minutes for me to get back to normal."

"In the meantime, a Huey from the Troop showed up, I think Keith was flying it and brought me back to our main base at Camp Eagle. I was sent to the Infirmary to fix some scratches and bruises and sent back to the unit."

"Regarding my lucky hat. The loss of it was catastrophic for me. Don't ask me why, I am not superstitious, but for some reason I had made it my good luck charm. It had 'New Hampshire Forever', embroidered in the back and had been with me for the past six months thru several hairy situations. I foolishly felt it got me through a whole bunch of those 'moments of sheer terror' from the old Dutchmasters, B Troop, 7/1st Air Cav in the Delta to some more while at Camp Evans and Eagle. I knew that without that hat I was gonna die!"

"A day or two later, once cleared back on flight status, I was assigned another aircraft and we had a mission. I am not ashamed to tell you, I was flat-assed scared to go. Petrified might be a better description!"

"But as you know you can't show fear or be scared, John Wayne, Mom, Apple Pie, The Flag and all that. But I can tell you that I had to 'force' myself to go on that mission. I literally had to will every step to the flight line. I can still see my boots taking one step at a time as I willed them to take one after another. I can still see the little puffs of dust as each step hit the dirt and the shine disappear as the dust covered my boots."

"I had a new hat made up too but it just wasn't the same. All the way to the staging area I prayed that no mission would be called up. And I prayed the whole time we were waiting to be called up at the staging area. I almost made it too because it was the end of the day and we were headed home, when we were called up for Blues in contact."

"I was beside myself. I knew it would be the same though, every day from now on and I didn't want to go thru this for the rest of the tour. I kept talking to myself; what the hell is the matter with you Stevens? You are not a chicken, why do you feel like this? It was only a stupid hat!"

"Was I learning another thing about myself? Was I Chicken? No, I can't be. But maybe I am!"

"I remember firing up the aircraft and we headed out, me dreading the thought of it. NO HAT, I'm gonna die!"

"Well as you know, I didn't die! In fact, what happened was another life lesson, as a matter of fact, two lessons."

"The first lesson was, you can't let your fear overwhelm you. Life is what it is and what will happen will happen. Integrity and honor are what it is all about."

"And the second lesson was, there is no such thing as a good luck charm."

"Incidentally, once we got into the mission I forgot all about my fear and it never raised its ugly specter again."

"When I was formally awarded the Silver Star for that combat action, I was totally blown away. I never knew about it until I received it. Jackie told me he had put me in for it. In fact, he said he had put me in for the Medal of Honor! I don't know if he really did or not, I was certainly honored regardless."

"I never thought what I did was anything special. I was only doing what came naturally. Hell, I wanted out and I couldn't leave my crew, so I did what I had to do to get us out."

"None of it would have worked without the engineer Captain to show me what to do with the C-4, or the Cobras who zapped the NVA, or the Loach that did more than his share."

"And old Goodie-Two Shoes never had to go in and he was most appreciative. He thanked me later!"

That was Mark's harrowing story on this 12th day of May, Day 3 of the battle for Hamburger Hill. The LZ that he created became critical for supplying Honeycutt's Battalion and providing adequate access for medical evacuations. Mark would go on to save many more lives during his tour.

Day 3 continued with us battling bad guys on the higher ground at every opportunity.

We helped Bilk 37, a Forward Air Controller, locate and mark enemy targets for eight airstrikes that day. The airstrikes included Napalm, 500-pound and 1,000-pound delayed fuse high explosive bombs that were great at destroying bunkers. The USAF "Gunfighters" out of Da Nang with their F-4 Phantom Jets were especially accurate on their bombing runs, flying low and slow to make sure they put bombs on target.

Thunder 44, an LOH assigned to support the Battalion and being flown by Eric "Crazy" Rairdon, had been transferring wounded from the upper LZ that Mark created to the lower LZ for further evacuation. Time and again he would be cited throughout the battle for his heroism in rescuing wounded. He may have been the one that had rescued Mark earlier in the day.

Honeycutt was also Medevaced for a short period to treat the festering shrapnel wounds he had received in the friendly fire incident. He returned immediately to resume command.

All remained quiet for the battalion that night, however, the NVA had other plans for the Artillery base across the valley at Airborne.

May 13 (Day 4)

At 0330 hours, 13 May, all hell broke loose at Firebase Airborne up on the western ridge of the valley, that had been providing effective artillery support to Honeycutt's Battalion and other units with their 105 and 155mm cannons.

Sappers wearing nothing but a loin cloth or nude except for a bandana around their heads to keep the sweat out of their eyes, had slowly crept up the side of the steep mountain, somehow slithered through the tons of debris and fallen trees surrounding the firebase, disabled the trigger flares by tying them closed with string, disabled or turned around the Claymore mines that had been set out, cut through the wire and, with their satchel charges ready, entered the perimeter silently and unseen.

The first signal that Airborne was under attack was a burst of enemy automatic weapons and mortar fire at one end by NVA Infantry, while the sappers ran through the base in the glow of torched ammunition stores throwing satchel charges into the bunkers of our sleeping troops.

The attack lasted about 90 minutes with many of the Artillerymen fighting for their lives, firing their huge cannons at point blank range against the enemy infiltrators, using the rarely employed "Beehive" rounds that contained thousands of small flechettes, like nails, to inflict the most damage at close range.

When the battle was over, friendly casualties included 22 killed, 61 wounded and five Howitzers damaged or destroyed.

As dawn broke, our own Alpha Troop teams were up at Airborne searching the ridge and surrounding dense jungle terrain trying to find signs of the enemy who had inflicted so many casualties and covering Medevacs into and out of the firebase.

2nd Battalion, 501st Infantry would be diverted from their mission reconning the west side of the valley later in the day and airlifted into Airborne to provide security and hunt down the attackers.

Over at Hill 937 Eddy Joiner, call sign Assault 11 and Mike Talton, Assault 27 and myself, Assault 23 arrived on station. Eddy immediately saw enemy activity on the hill and adjacent ridgelines. We identified Honeycutt's Companies and Headquarters locations and then began engaging enemy targets. Bilk 37 arrived on station too and we helped him bring in effective air strikes throughout the day.

We in A Troop were maxed out, flying missions all over the valley supporting the 3rd Brigade. Major Curtin seemed to be everywhere, flying in his C&C Huey with rescue equipment on board in case we ran into more trouble on this day.

Things were getting intense as more enemy activity was identified near Hill 937 and Honeycutt's B and C Companies were running into more and more resistance, resulting in more of their guys getting killed and wounded.

We were into the hot refueling and rearming mode to get back and forth to the battle as quickly as possible.

No sooner had we arrived back to help 3/187th, when an Eagle Dustoff Medevac Helicopter, called in to evacuate more wounded, was hit by an RPG and crashed. They were hovering with their hoist basket down to rescue the wounded, when they were hit and plummeted down on top of the soldiers on the ground. Five were killed, including three of the Helicopter Crew, and three more wounded.

B, C and D Companies of the Battalion were all on the move again trying to make progress up the steep, jungle covered slopes towards Hill 937. For the third time they met fierce resistance, especially B Company.

By the end of Day 4, the Battalion had suffered four more soldiers killed and another 33 wounded.

All the wounded and KIA were evacuated by nightfall as the Companies set up ambushes at their night defensive positions. An unknown number of enemy were killed or wounded by the near continuous strikes of TAC air, Artillery, mortars, ARA and our own Scouts and Gunships as well as by the valiant fighting on the part of our ground troops.

The Battalion was now well aware they were facing a formidably large and well entrenched enemy force. Their total casualties since starting the operation were now nine killed and 83 wounded, including one killed and 36 wounded by friendly fire.

Honeycutt ordered an alert posture to make sure they would not be surprised by the enemy during the night, while still trying to afford some rest for the troops; 100 percent on alert until 2400 hours (midnight), 50% until 0300 hours, then 100 percent again until 0600 hours.

A strict STAND-TO was also ordered for 0500 hours daily, where every man and officer were to be in a fighting position; weapons at the ready and communications established with Headquarters.

The rest of the time the troops could try and get some individual rest as the situation permitted. That's how Army soldiers learn to fall asleep almost on command whenever the opportunity affords itself, even under the most trying conditions.

May 14 (Day 5)

Day 5 found us from Alpha Troop, 2/17th Air Cav once again out in the AO at dawn. Our teams spread out to support 3rd Brigade units from FB Airborne in the north, to Airstrip Aloui in the south and Honeycutt's 3/187th Battalion in the middle.

Lieutenant Colonel Honeycutt was determined to launch another attack towards Hill 937. It would again be a three-pronged attack; this time with D Company from the north and B and C Companies from the west.

First, D Company was to recover the dead and wounded from the Medevac helicopter crash the day before and move them to the upper LZ for evacuation and then attack north towards Hill 937. A Company was to assist D Company in moving the victims to the upper LZ and then secure the saddle command post.

We continued to provide reconnaissance and close air support throughout the day, attacking the enemy at every opportunity.

We were hot refueling and rearming almost continuously to provide support to the grunts in contact. I was firing hundreds of rockets while Mike Talton was firing hundreds of grenades and thousands of bullets from the mini-gun, as we rearmed again and again.

Bilk 37 was also on the scene, coordinating ten more airstrikes interspersed with ARA and artillery bombardments.

Hill 937 and adjacent ridgelines were now becoming visible as jungle canopy and trees were stripped away and the ground laid bare by the airstrikes and artillery barrages. The enemy fortifications of spider holes, trenches and bunkers were coming into view.

By mid-morning C Company had almost reached the top of the mountain, however was repulsed by heavy enemy fire, suffering more casualties, and had to withdraw back down the slope.

B Company had reached the top of the adjacent ridgeline discovering many enemy bodies, pieces of bodies, blood trails, blown bunkers and fighting positions. They too were meeting continued heavy resistance from enemy forces in fortified fighting positions.

Honeycutt ordered B Company to withdraw from the ridge top as their flank was exposed by C Company's withdrawal.

At the end of the day both Companies were ordered to set up night defensive positions, consolidate and report their unit strength.

B Company had lost 25 percent of its soldiers and C Company had lost nearly 50 percent.

In addition to providing close air support and fighting the bad guys, we were escorting a steady stream of Medevac helicopters from Eagle Dustoff coming in to the lower LZ, one at a time, to pick up the wounded. They were the Air Ambulances; unarmed Hueys with big red crosses painted on the nose. Their Pilots and crews were heroes to all of us.

There was only one way in and one way out of the lower landing zone and only room for one ship at a time. As they came in and out from the same direction, it didn't take long for the enemy to zero in on them. Consequently, they were under nearly constant fire as they continued to evacuate the wounded.

As the last of six Dustoff helicopters took off from the LZ, Dick Dato and I were covering them and witnessed a sight that brought us to tears as he relates what happened:

"The Dustoff was totally loaded as it lifted off from the landing zone. One last soldier on the ground apparently panicked and decided he wanted to leave on that last bird too. He grabbed onto the landing gear skid and held on for dear life as the bird rose from the landing zone." Dick recalls.

"The Dustoff crew saw him hanging on, however couldn't do anything to reach him or try to get him on board. I saw him hanging on too as we followed them out of the landing zone. He lost his grip a minute or so later and fell from about 300 feet back into the trees down the side of the mountain."

The Dustoff crews had dedicated their lives to saving others and all were devastated by this tragedy. We searched for days, however never found his body.

Late that afternoon the Brigade Commander landed at the Battalion Command Post to meet with Honeycutt and talk with the soldiers. After his departure, Honeycutt ordered his Companies to prepare for another assault of Hill 937 the following day. He also notified A Company that they would be relieving C Company for the assault, as they had suffered so many casualties. C Company would stay back to secure the blocking position at the Battalion Headquarters. The battle would continue in the morning.

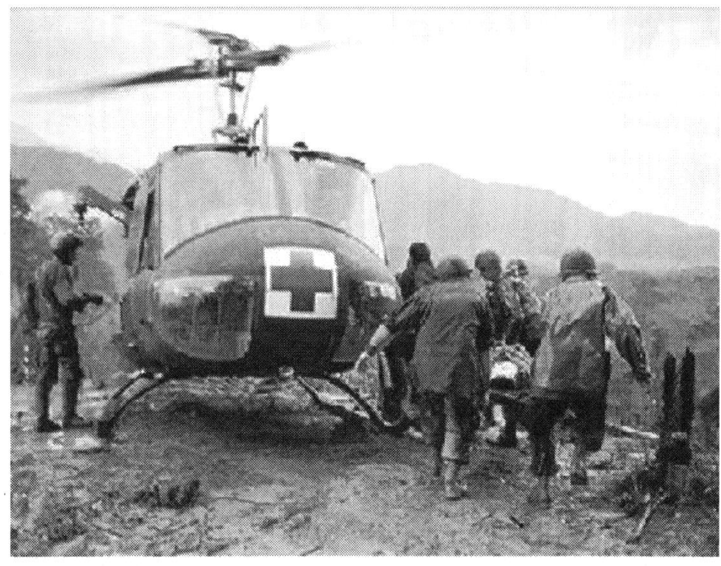

Dustoff *So That Others May Live*

May 15 (Day 6)

Our teams were out there again early, along with Bilk 37, who started bringing in airstrikes to try and soften up Hill 937 for the next assault by A and B Companies. We continued reconnaissance, providing as much enemy information to Honeycutt as possible as they prepared to launch the attack.

At 1200 hours A and B Companies began the assault nearly side by side. The NVA, which usually attacks at their time and place of choice, was remaining steadfast to defend this mountain, regardless of the cost.

Both Companies began receiving heavy fire from enemy fortified positions. The NVA were using automatic weapons, machine guns and rocket-propelled grenades. Our guys continued their advance using maximum firepower and creeping mortar and artillery fires in front of them. Our Pink Teams and ARA Cobras continued providing close air support

At 1400 both Companies were closing on the objective and were just 150 meters from the top of the hill when the unthinkable happened again. ARA Cobras mistakenly hit B Company soldiers, resulting in two killed and fourteen wounded. The wounded included the Company Commander, his Radio Operators and the First Sergeant.

At the same time, C Company and the Battalion Headquarters were hit by enemy mortar rounds wounding eight, including Honeycutt and his Operations Officer again.

By 1415 B Company was moving their wounded to the lower LZ and a new Captain, who had just come on board to be the Battalion Intelligence Officer, was given command of B Company.

By 1500 A Company, which had continued the attack, reported they were within 75 meters to the top of the hill.

Honeycutt called in the situation to higher Headquarters. He feared that while A Company might make it to the top, they would be understrength and alone as B Company's Command Group had been taken out by the ARA friendly fire incident and were pulling back to their defensive positions of the night before. He recommended the Battalion pull back all their forces and the Air Force resume bombing.

The momentum of the attack had been broken. A Company was ordered to withdraw.

Within minutes the enemy sensed what was happening and counter attacked, following A Company down the hill, trying to outflank them and attack from the sides and rear. A Company returned fire all around them and made it back to the lower LZ, where they consolidated defenses with B Company.

As evening fell and the Battalion set up their night defensive positions, things were really looking grim. A Company had lost nearly 20 percent of their people. B Company was in a bad way now, down nearly 50 percent and had lost their Command Group. C Company was also in bad shape at 50 percent strength. And the Battalion Commander and his Operations Officer were both wounded.

The Brigade Commander ordered the 1/506th Battalion, located a few kilometers south and led by Lieutenant Colonel J. M. Bowers, to immediately head north to reinforce Honeycutt's 3/187th.

Intelligence had identified the enemy forces fighting 3/187th as elements of the 29th NVA Regiment, "The Pride of Ho Chi Minh", with a force much larger than anyone had originally anticipated.

As Air Force "Spooky" and "Shadow" Gunships flew throughout the night raining down cannon fire on the enemy in support of 3/187th, plans were being prepared to attempt yet another attack of Hill 937. This time it would be a coordinated two-Battalion attack with eight Companies on May 17: Bowers' 1/506th Airborne Infantry with four Companies from the south and Honeycutt's 3/187th with what remained of his Companies from the north.

May 16 (Day 7)

The 3/187th focused on rest and resupply to get ready for the assault planned for the following day. D Company replaced B Company for the planned assault as they had suffered so many casualties the day before. B Company would provide security for the lower LZ.

Brigadier General Smith, the Assistant Division Commander, ordered LTC Honeycutt be evacuated to have the shrapnel removed that was near his spine. Honeycutt returned to be with his soldiers that evening.

The Corps Commander visited the Battalion for a first-hand brief on the situation. The News Media also started arriving, taking pictures of the devastation; crashed helicopters and wounded soldiers being tended to by fellow soldiers and Medics.

Our primary mission this day shifted to supporting 1/506th as they headed north to get into position to support 3/187th, to conduct the simultaneous two-Battalion assault the next day.

It was slow going for 1/506th. They were initially making good progress and then were slowed down by attacks from enemy trail watchers and snipers. Then as they started climbing to higher ground, they ran into the enemy's fortified defensive positions, receiving significant automatic weapons and RPG fire. Their casualties started mounting.

May 17 (Day 8)

The 1/506th Battalion would be assaulting Hill 937 from the south with three Companies abreast, while 3/187th would establish a blocking position on the north side and provide supporting fires. 3/187th was not to become "decisively engaged". They were to only apply pressure on the enemy while 1/506th hopefully made more progress towards Hill 937 from the south.

A new Aircraft Commander from our unit was first out to the AO. Mike Talton had somehow survived his time as my front seat Copilot and Bullet Catcher. He was now Assault 27!

Talton was first to arrive on station with his team and started identifying friendly locations and reporting on enemy activity, as Honeycutt's A and D Companies moved out to set up their blocking positions north of Hill 937 to support Bowers' 1/506th forthcoming attack from the south. The attack was scheduled to commence at 1000 hours.

I was out there too, flying with Keith Finley up front. Keith was another California boy like myself. He was a laid back, casual guy with a great sense of humor, yet totally professional. I liked him a lot. We would be rotating on station throughout the day with Talton and his team.

Mike Ryan, another California boy, was flying as my teammate in his Scout bird. He had come over with the unit from Fort Campbell as a Slick Pilot and was now flying Scouts. He had testicles the size of basketballs and nerves of steel – prerequisites for great Scout Pilots.

The plan called for the Air Force to drop 1,000 pound bombs with delayed fuses so they would go deep into the ground before exploding, thereby destroying the fortified positions on Hill 937. The bombings would be followed by Artillery using high explosive shells and CS teargas canisters, to force the enemy out of their fortified positions and into the open. Then we would come in to do a quick recon to assess the damage and employ additional supporting fire.

The attack was delayed until 1130 to allow 1/506th more time to get in position. Then the Air Force and Artillery preparations got underway.

Finley and I had relieved Talton's team as they headed back to refuel.

Bilk 35, an Air Force Forward Air Controller (FAC) flying in his little single-engine Bird Dog spotter plane, was doing a great job directing the fighters into targets on Hill 937. After watching the huge geysers of dirt created when the thousand pounders exploded and then the wispy white clouds of CS gas as the Artillery canisters hit, mixed with the gray of high explosive detonations, we raced in to take a look at the damage. "How could anyone survive that?" I thought – mistakenly!

"TAKING FIRE, TAKING FIRE!" Ryan yelled over the radio as he peeled off to the right. We could see enemy soldiers forced from their hiding places by the CS gas as Finley laid into them with the mini-gun to cover Ryan's escape. They started dropping like flies and diving for cover.

Ryan did a hard pedal-turn and covered us with the mini-gun on his Scout bird as we broke right and climbed to set up a rocket run. I gained about 500 feet in just a few seconds, turned back towards the target, got the bad guys in my sights and let loose with several pairs of rockets before peeling off again and calling in ARA. They came in right behind us letting loose dozens of more rockets.

We all pulled off as 1/506th began their attack from the south at 1130 hours, while the 3/187th provided supporting fire from the north.

The NVA had discovered our radio frequency and several times that morning transmitted Honeycutt's call sign over and over; "Blackjack, Blackjack, calling Blackjack". We could hear their accents though and knew to ignore them.

The enemy also tried to confuse us by randomly popping colored smoke grenades. Our troops used smoke grenades a lot to mark their positions for our gun runs and fighter bombings, and to bring in Supply and Medevac Helicopters. Our guys would call us and say they were popping yellow smoke but then we would see yellow smoke rising in two or three locations. The bad guys were on to us!

We immediately changed tactics for employing smoke. We asked our guys to pop smoke but NOT tell us the color. We then would identify the colors that appeared; "banana" for yellow, "goofy grape" for purple, etc. Our guys would confirm which color was theirs. If we saw other colors rising out of the jungle, we knew it was the bad guys and could go after them as they had marked their own locations!

We continued to engage the enemy with ARA, airstrikes and Artillery whenever we could, when not endangering our own forces.

The enemy was well entrenched and apparently being reinforced with fresh replacements from their sanctuaries just across the border in Laos. Many of the enemy dead had fresh uniforms, equipment and haircuts.

The fighting was vicious and at the end of the day1/506th was forced to pull back, as intense enemy fires kept them from reaching their objective. The 3/187th had been continually attacked at their blocking position as well.

The 3rd Brigade Commander, Colonel Conmy, decided that 1/506th was close enough to do a coordinated attack the following day. He felt they couldn't let up the pressure to allow the NVA to send in fresh troops from Laos so ordered both Battalions to prepare for full on attacks in the morning.

We had also received word late in the day that the 2nd Battalion, 1st ARVN Division just to the north of us near Tiger Mountain, had discovered enemy staging and supply areas. They had captured huge hauls of weapons, supplies and equipment including Russian-made trucks and bulldozers.

Overall, American and ARVN forces were taking a heavy toll on the enemy. If only we could take Hill 937. Dong Ap Bia was its name on the map. Local Vietnamese tribesmen knew it as "The Mountain of the Crouching Beast". Now it was becoming known by our soldiers and referred to by the press as "Hamburger Hill".

Thunder 44, Piloted by Eric Reardon lands the Commanding Officer of 3/187th Airborne Infantry Battalion, Lieutenant Colonel Weldon Honeycutt, on Hamburger Hill.

May 18 (Day 9)

It was another max effort by our unit, Alpha Troop, 2/17th Air Cav, providing hunter-killer teams in support of the 3rd Brigade.

Mike Talton, Assault 27 was partnered with "Uncle" Bob Larsen, Assault 14 in the Scout bird. Bob was a Hollywood-looking guy from Michigan with jet-black hair and an easy smile. For some unknown reason, I thought of him as family and got into the habit of calling him "Uncle Bob", even on the radio. He and Talton were in the A Shau early, watching FAC Bilk 14 directing airstrikes on Hill 900, 916 and 937.

Airstrikes were to continue until 0830 followed by Artillery registration (marking the targets) until 0900, CS gas Artillery until 0905, and regular Artillery bombardment until 0925.

1/506th and 3/187th were to be in position to move out and begin attacking from the south and north precisely at 0926.

But things weren't going well, right from the start.

The airstrikes were late and didn't finish until 0914.

The CS gas canisters weren't fired by Artillery until 0940 then landed short, right in the middle of A Company, 3/187th location. Although not causing any casualties, the gas disrupted A Company's preparation for the impending attack.

"Hawkeye" General Jim Smith, the 101st ADC called off the CS gas bombardment himself and started the high-explosive Artillery prep at 1010 hours continuing until 1025.

Honeycutt's D and A Companies had donned their gas masks and assaulted the hill under cover by the Artillery. They had made it to within 200 meters of the hilltop when they started receiving heavy fire from their flank where

1/506th was supposed to be, but they had been slowed down and were still too far away, leaving that flank open.

As the Artillery bombardment ended and D Company got within 100 meters of the hilltop, enemy fire became overwhelming with automatic weapons, Claymore mines, hand grenades and RPGs raining down on them and deadly sniper fire coming from the treetops. D Company was taking heavy casualties. At 1142 the Company Commander was hit and the 2nd Platoon Leader took over.

Honeycutt's A Company was also taking heavy casualties. C Company was busy hauling ammunition up the hill to D Company and taking the wounded back with them to the lower LZ, being guarded by the remaining elements of B Company.

Bowers' 1/506th Battalion was meeting heavy resistance on the other side of the hill as well and it was becoming increasingly difficult to bring in supporting fire from Artillery, TAC air, ARA and our own Gunships, as the enemy and friendly forces were battling within 20 meters of one another.

Talton and Larsen's team had been attacking the enemy whenever and wherever they could.

Bilk 35 was also on station now trying to direct more bomb runs on the enemy locations while keeping our troops out of danger, which was becoming an impossible task.

Once again, the unthinkable happened when a Gunship mistakenly attacked friendly solders of the Battalion, killing one soldier and injuring five more. Honeycutt, frustrated and furious, ordered all ARA Cobras to leave the area. He would direct any supporting fires himself.

As if that wasn't enough, one of our own became a casualty.

"Uncle Bob" Larsen, Assault 14, was flying low and fast in his little bird trying to spot the enemy locations where the ground troops were receiving the most fire. He spotted them below the tall trees in their bunkers and spider holes and circled around to drop a white phosphorous grenade to mark their position. Enemy snipers took a bead on him and fired a shot right through the front Plexiglas bubble into his cockpit. The bullet hit his tail rotor pedal, went through his foot, hit the fire extinguisher under his seat which exploded, sending hot shards of shrapnel into his legs. Screaming in pain, he managed to set the helicopter on the ground in one piece near B Company. They were carrying their dead and wounded down the hill, however, stopped to help Bob and secure the helicopter. After being treated by combat medics, he flew the helicopter out and over to LZ Rendezvous where he was Medevaced.

Geez, what more could go wrong?

Mother Nature answered with a violent thunderstorm and torrential rain that brought the battle to a halt. With visibility in the driving rain down to a few meters and the ground turned to mud, friendly forces couldn't make any headway. The Companies were ordered to pull back and recover their dead and wounded. Hamburger Hill would not be conquered on this day.

General Zais, Commander of the 101st Division, now considered halting Apache Snow altogether, pulling out the troops and letting the Air Force take over to bombard the area. That would mean giving up the battle and letting the NVA achieve victory. He decided that was not an option and to continue the operation in earnest with the solid backing of General Stillwell and General Abrams.

General Zais, his ADC General Smith, 3rd Brigade Commander Colonel Conmy and ARVN Division Commander General Truong planned for a four-Battalion coordinated attack in two days. That would be four times the number of troops attacking Hill 937 than back on Day 1.

What Colonel Conmy didn't reveal to Colonel Honeycutt was his decision to replace the beleaguered 3/187th with a fresh Battalion; Lieutenant Colonel Gene Sherron's 2/501st. He felt that Honeycutt and his soldiers, ever the warriors, had fought magnificently, however the Battalion was no longer an effective fighting force; 320 killed or wounded and two of its four Company Commanders now casualties, including eight of twelve Platoon Leaders.

As the dead and wounded were being recovered and the troops consolidating at their defensive positions, the Division Commander, Lucky Eagle arrived at Honeycutt's Command Post. He briefed the plans for the pending attack of four Battalions; 1/506th, 2/501st and two ARVN battalions.

Honeycutt could not believe what he was hearing. After all the heroic efforts of his soldiers, they were to be left out of the final battle for Hamburger Hill.

We don't know exactly what was said between these two battle-seasoned soldiers however, we do know that Honeycutt forcefully made his case that his men had fought valiantly and should be allowed to continue the fight. He desperately wanted to be part of the action and emphasized to General Zais that he only needed one more Company for reinforcement to be combat ready again.

General Zais relented and agreed to provide a Company from 2/501st to Honeycutt. Lieutenant Colonel Sherron coordinated the support to Honeycutt by providing his own A Company, 2/501st which was helicoptered into the lower LZ before nightfall.

May 19 (Day 10)

The two Battalions, 1/506th and 3/187th were back in their defensive positions on lower terrain to the south and north of the three-hill ridge. The dead and wounded had been recovered and evacuated. The soldiers were being fed and resupplied. Preparations were underway for the next assault.

With the troops pulled back from the higher ground, we were free to attack at will with airstrikes, Artillery, ARA and our own Gunships. We spent the entire day cycling back and forth to rearm and refuel and hit the enemy locations again and again. Thousands of bombs, Artillery rounds, ARA and our own rockets, grenades and gunfire had pounded the enemy locations all day and into the night.

Nearly all of us from A Troop were out there raising mayhem today!

I was out there with Eddy Joiner as my Scout team member.

Lenny Constantine, Assault 24 was out there with Tom Michel, Assault 12.

Bruce McNeel, Assault 25 was flying a Cobra with Dick Dato in the front seat and Mike Ryan, Assault 18, flying the little Scout bird.

Mike Talton, Assault 27 was out there again. I think he had Don McGurk as his front seat and Roger Barnard, Assault 17 flying Scout for him.

Keith Finley was out there again too, flying front seat for Don McGillicuddy, Assault 29, and their Loach.

Our first order of business that morning had been to evacuate Uncle Bob. His wounds had been attended to by B Company combat medics and, although still severely wounded, managed to fly the Scout bird out himself. He landed at a nearby firebase and was Medevaced by Eagle Dustoff to 18th Surgical at Camp Evans. He was later flown out for treatment and surgery in Japan. We wouldn't see him again for months.

The 2/501st Battalion was combat assaulted into a landing zone to the north west of Hill 937. They met little resistance and conducted a reconnaissance in force to their attack positions.

General Truong's 2nd Battalion, 3rd ARVN Regiment was helicoptered into Firebase Currahee by CH-47 Chinooks and then conducted a combat assault by Hueys into their attack positions to the south east.

According to the official after-action report of the 101st Division, this is how the ground forces were organized for battle the night of 19 May:

The 2/501st to the northeast still had a mile of rough uphill terrain to cover before reaching the top of Hill 937.

The ARVN Battalions, a kilometer to the southeast had an easier approach with lighter resistance.

The 1/506th was to the southwest and facing steep terrain and heavy resistance.

The 3/187th to the northwest was closest to Hill 937 and facing the enemy's heaviest defenses.

Huge expanses of Hill 937 were now laid bare by the incessant bombing and with all units in position, H-hour was set for 1000 hours the following morning.

May 20 (Day 11)

We were up and at 'em before dawn and on our way to the A Shau for the big day.

Honeycutt's Battalion already had their stand-to at 0530 and a Fireball to boot.

FAC Speedy 11, a twin engine 0-2 Cessna Skymaster, was on station directing multiple airstrikes with high explosive bombs and napalm canisters.

Ed Bobilya, Assault 21, who had been my mentor down south with C Troop, 7/1st Air Cav was first on station with Roger Barnard flying the little bird. They were reconning just to the west and at 0640 were already reporting enemy activity to the ground units.

The rest of us set up our rotations so we could provide continuous cover and support throughout the area as the ground units prepared for H-hour.

Newsmen started arriving at Honeycutt's Command Post location at 0830.

Massive Artillery barrages started at 0906 as we and the Air Force FAC pulled back off station to watch the show.

Promptly at 1000 hours the Artillery barrage ceased and all four Battalions started attacking towards Hamburger Hill.

3/187th, for the first time, was meeting light resistance and by 1020 were just 125 meters from reaching the crest. As they reached the top of the hill though, the enemy was waiting for them and opened up with automatic weapons, machine guns, RPGs and hand grenades. The fighting intensified all around them over the next hour with the enemy also firing 60mm mortars from distant areas.

Honeycutt ordered that his soldiers keep their fires low as 2/3 ARVN forces were coming up to the hilltop from the opposite direction. He also ordered our Pink teams to find and engage the enemy's attacking mortars on the distant ridgelines.

2/3 ARVN coming from the opposite direction were also starting to meet with heavier enemy resistance as they neared the hilltop. Honeycutt had requested they keep marking their most forward positions with purple smoke to keep the friendly forces on either side and in front of them apprised of their location, to preclude friendly fire incidents. He had also requested the same with yellow smoke from the most forward elements of 1/506th.

We were all over the place trying to identify and engage bad guys, while protecting our own Ground Forces and keeping the Ground Commanders informed as best we could regarding the constantly changing situation. And while the enemy was inflicting casualties on our friendly forces, especially 1/506th fighting near hills 900 and 916 towards hill 937, all were making headway.

The first elements to reach the top of the mountain were Honeycutt's C Company, 3/187th although they were still receiving heavy close-in fire from surrounding enemy fire positions. The fighting continued as the rest of the Battalion consolidated their efforts behind C Company and more ammo was being brought forward. Thunder 44, Honeycutt's Loach zoomed in and kicked out loads of ammo right over the troops in another courageous act, for which he was noted.

Fighting continued throughout the day with us providing close air support and our crews displaying exceptional expertise and courage. One act in particular bears repeating.

Lenny Constantine, Assault 24 in his Cobra saw friendly lead elements at the edge of the hilltop hesitating to proceed any further or recover their wounded for fear they would be exposed to more enemy fire from a machine gun emplacement above them.

They didn't realize that Lenny had just busted a bunker wide open with close-in rocket fire, killing the guys manning the machine gun. In an act of enormous courage, he hovered down in front of the bunker, landed, and had his front seat train the Gatling gun and grenade launcher on the smoking ruins to show the grunts they were safe, while he opened his canopy and waved them forward. They recovered their wounded and seized the high ground as Lenny waved once again and took off to find and attack more enemy locations.

The battle was a great success by military standards. It was estimated the enemy had lost well over a thousand soldiers and many more were wounded. One captured prisoner admitted his unit had been decimated with 80 percent casualties.

The official after-action report stated: "This multi-Battalion combined operation was a classic campaign which found the enemy, fixed his location, and methodically and devastatingly destroyed him in place. The effect of this was to destroy the combat effectiveness of not only the Maneuver Battalions of the 29th NVA Regiment, but also its Central Headquarters."

The 101st Division Summary further stated, "Through intense close-in fighting the 101st Airborne troopers contributed another gallant victory to the Vietnamese War effort by almost completely eliminating one North Vietnamese Regiment and putting the (A Shau) Valley under Free World control for the first time since 1965."

Official enemy losses were reported as 1,038 killed. Friendly losses were 109 killed and 673 wounded. We had won the battle, however, unbeknownst to us, in the eye of public opinion, we had lost the war.

On May 19, Associated Press reporter Jay Sharbutt had filed a story of Operation Apache Snow and the battle for Hill 937 calling it a "meat grinder" and questioned why soldiers had to attack the same hill so many times instead of the Air Force just bombing it. Sharbutt's story was carried by newspapers throughout the USA.

Sharbutt followed that up with another story of the capture of "Hamburger Hill" and the agonizing 11 assaults by Lieutenant Colonel Honeycutt and soldiers of the 1/387th, which prompted Senator Kennedy to denounce the battle as "senseless and irresponsible....madness."

Life Magazine in their June 27, 1969 issue published photos of 241 US servicemen who had been killed during a week in Vietnam. An accompanying article described the premonitions some had before their deaths including one written by a soldier on Hamburger Hill: "You may not be able to read this. I am writing in a hurry. I see death coming up the hill."

While only five out of the 241 pictured had been killed on Hamburger Hill, many Americans believed all those featured had died in that battle.

By then Hamburger Hill had been abandoned and was already being reoccupied by the NVA. The American public was outraged. President Nixon informed General Abrams he didn't want to see any more battles like that one. And, unbeknownst to us doing the fighting, the objective of the war apparently was not to win, it was to appease.

President Nixon convinced South Vietnam's President Thieu that they needed to take over the war effort calling it "Vietnamization" and announced the first US troop withdrawals from the war effort. Secret peace talks got underway while we continued the fight in the A Shau and elsewhere throughout Vietnam.

I didn't know about any of that and I probably wouldn't have cared.

Whether it was Iron Raven, Hawkeye, Blackjack or many others who called for support, we in the Air Cav were always there to answer the call.

They didn't care if the person answering the call was 19 or 90 years old, Warrant Officer or Colonel. They needed a cool, calm professional answering their call for help. And if they called us, they knew within seconds that they had the right guy:

A guy who would help them find their way when they were lost and disoriented in ten-foot tall elephant grass.

A guy who would help them define their fields of fire to provide overlapping cover for their night defensive positions.

A guy who would adjust artillery on target when they couldn't see more than a few feet.

A guy who would coordinate fighter bombing runs right on target with the FAC.

A guy who would shoot the snipers out of the trees over their heads.

A guy who would blow bunkers, reaping havoc in front of them with point blank rocket runs.

A guy who would risk his life escorting "Dustoff" in for their dead and wounded.

A guy who would go in knowing he would probably be shot down and when crashed inverted, would construct an LZ, under fire, to evacuate the dead and wounded.

A guy who would continually fly low and slow to identify enemy positions until he was shot through the legs, forced to land, bind his wounds with the help of combat medics and then fly himself out again in the face of certain death.

And finally, a guy who would land his Cobra in the middle of an enemy bunker complex facing the smoking ruins of enemy bunkers and machine emplacements he had personally destroyed to signal the troops that it was okay to move forward and recover their dead and wounded.

I, and my brothers in Alpha Troop were always glad to be that guy. Like our fellow Army Helicopter Pilots, we couldn't do enough for the troops and were honored to serve.

Hamburger Hill After Apache Snow

Top, Scout Pilot Eddy Joiner, Assault 11. Below, Mark Stevens, Assault 43, receives the Silver Star for his actions on Hamburger Hill.

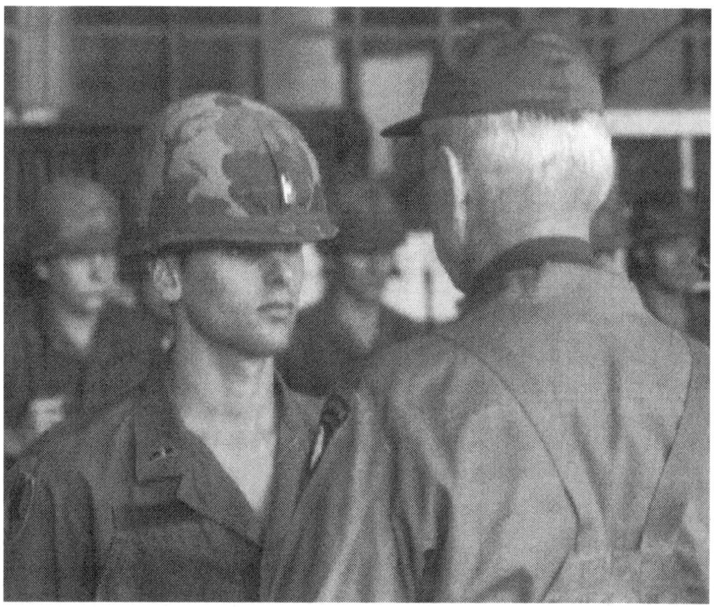

CHAPTER FIFTEEN

MONTGOMERY RENDEZVOUS

Hamburger Hill was finally taken on May 20, 1969 and Lieutenant Colonel Honeycutt's 3/187th Battalion was air lifted out the next day, 21 May.

The drama wasn't over though as the enemy continued attacking with mortar fire as the helicopters came in to extract the troops. Honeycutt was airborne in a Loach, directing gunships and artillery fire until late afternoon when the last troops left at 1500 hours. The Battalion was deployed to the coastal plain for a much-needed rest.

The fighting wasn't over for us in Alpha Troop either as we continued our mission of finding, fixing and destroying enemy forces and their supplies and equipment in the northern A Shau Valley for several more weeks in an operation called Montgomery Rendezvous.

The 3rd Brigade was still out there too. The road from Camp Eagle had been completed by the 326th Engineers and 3/5th Mechanized Infantry, LZ Rendezvous and Firebase

Currahee were still up and running in the bottom of the valley and the 1/506th and 2/501st Airborne Infantry Battalions were conducting reconnaissance-in-force missions to root out enemy locations.

We roamed the area searching for the NVA that were infiltrating from Laos. They had suffered terrible losses inflicted by the 9th Marines in Operation Dewey Canyon and then by the Army's 101st Division and 1st ARVN Division in Operation Apache Snow. Yet here they were again, starting to appear in the A Shau just days after the battle for Hamburger Hill.

Our teams discovered a large rope bridge in the western mountains spanning a deep canyon between two ridges. The bridge had been strategically positioned far down the sides of the canyon, making it nearly impossible to get to and destroy with fighter jets or artillery. We were having trouble trying to destroy it with rocket fire from our Gunships, as there was no way out at the end of a rocket run to turn left or right and escape enemy fires. And over-flying the target at low altitude invited disaster.

Len Constantine finally saved the day. He carefully maneuvered his Cobra way up high and almost slowed to a stop before beginning his gun run, carefully aiming the gun sight and pulling in just enough power to streamline the aircraft. Firing off several pairs of rockets that were dead on target, even at long range, allowed him adequate time to maneuver without crashing into the sides of the canyon. He did the same thing two more times while his Scout bird provided covering fire with his mini-gun. The bridge finally collapsed and crashed to the bottom of the canyon. There was a lot of hollering and congratulations over the radio. "Yay Lenny!"

We weren't congratulating ourselves a week later though when we lost one of our own back on Hamburger Hill.

We had abandoned the hill earlier as there was no one left to fight, however, just a few days later our Scouts started seeing evidence that the enemy was reoccupying some of the bunkers and fortified positions on the hill.

Dick Dato recalls how it all started.

"I was flying with Don McGurk in a Cobra. Our Pink Team had just completed a mission a little north of Hamburger Hill near Tiger Mountain and we were on our way back to Firebase Blaze to rearm and refuel, when Don mentioned he wanted to swing by Hamburger Hill and get some pictures," Dick remembers.

"When we arrived and flew low over the scene of the battle that had a taken place earlier, our Scout saw NVA soldiers out in the open around a campfire waving to us, like they were friendlies. We actually fell for the deception, took a bunch of photos, then called in the report of seeing the soldiers as we headed to Blaze. We were immediately told there were no friendlies on Hamburger Hill and to get back there ASAP! We refueled and headed back but alas, they were gone or at least in hiding."

"As we continued checking things out, Don thought he saw movement at one of the bunkers. We finally laced it with fire and sure enough, on our next pass saw a tripod-mounted machine gun lying on its side next to the bunker."

"Our Scout came in low and saw at least two enemy soldiers hiding in the back of the bunker. That's when we called in for a snatch mission to get the bad guys and recover the machine gun. Major Curtin decided to do a mini-air assault and land the Blues (our 40-man infantry platoon) on the ridge to check it out," Dick concluded.

Captain Lou Herrick had taken over command of the Blues from Keith Reed just a few days earlier on June 1st. Lou had led the Lift Platoon of Hueys prior to that. Today, June 6th would mark his first mission on the ground leading the Blues.

Mark Stevens and the rest of our Huey Pilots airlifted Lou and the Blues into a landing zone on a ridge just to the west and below Hamburger Hill. Don McGurk and Dick Dato were flying a Cobra overhead and Tom Michel was scouting low in his Loach.

The Blues started their reconnaissance patrol heading up the ridge towards the hill. As they approached a line of old bunkers, all hell broke loose when enemy soldiers, concealed in the bunkers and nearby fighting positions, launched a coordinated ambush. Point man Sp5 Norman Brown was killed instantly. A bullet grazed Lou's head, wounding him in the ear. He ordered the Platoon to pull back, deploy and return fire as McGurk and Dato fired rockets and grenades and Michel fired his minigun from the Scout bird at the enemy positions. McGurk, Dato and Michel quickly ran out of ammo and I (Assault 23) was called in to relieve them on station.

When I arrived a few minutes later, Lou and the Platoon were pinned down by the enemy's continued fire from the fortified positions on the higher ground. We came in hot and smoked the positions with our rockets, grenades and minigun as Lou led his men forward to recover Brown's body.

I could see the enemy soldiers firing from the bunkers and trenches and continued to engage them at near point-blank range. Their bunkers were small and well protected. I needed to be accurate with the rockets and put them right through the small 3 by 3-foot openings in the bunkers to blow them up from the inside out.

On each pass, I would shoot a couple of pairs of rockets while Keith Finley in the front seat fired hundreds of rounds from our turret mounted minigun to protect us as we broke left or right to set up another run. Our Scout, Mike Ryan would follow behind in his little bird shooting underneath us with his minigun. A great wingman, Ryan saved my bacon many times as I tried to do the same for him.

The battle was fierce and we quickly ran out of ammunition, however I continued to make fake gun runs at the enemy to keep their heads down while Lou and his soldiers recovered Brown's body and withdrew back to the landing zone for extraction. Another team quickly showed up to replace us and continue covering the Blues as we headed to the nearest firebase to rearm.

The Hueys were already in the air and the Blues were successfully extracted and flown back to home base at Camp Eagle. The rest of us continued to attack enemy positions on the hill with Artillery and our own rockets, grenades and minigun fire from the helicopters.

I saw Lou later back at home base after he and the other soldiers in his platoon had been treated for their wounds. He thanked me profusely for the close air support work and especially the fake gun runs, even when out of ammo, to help protect the troops. He said he would put me in for a Silver Star, however, that was not to be. Lou could not forgive himself for Brown's death and several days later asked to be relieved of command. Don McGurk would take over from Lou as leader of the Blues.

The rest of us in the Weapons and Scout Platoons continued to roam the A Shau with our hunter-killer teams of a single Cobra and single Loach, trying to locate the NVA who were continuing to infiltrate the valley.

A few days later on 9 June the enemy attacked Firebase Currahee, located in the middle of the valley below Hamburger Hill, and ambushed a convoy on the newly constructed road, Highway 547, from Camp Eagle to the A Shau.

Eddy Joiner and I were flying out of Firebase Blaze headed to the valley, when I got the call the convoy was under attack. In just a few minutes we were overhead. Things looked grim for our guys on the ground.

A North Vietnamese soldier, in an apparent suicide maneuver, had stepped out into the road and fired point blank at tanks leading the convoy. The lead tank returned fire killing the enemy soldier instantly. The rest of the convoy stopped as the tanks deployed in a 'Herringbone' formation, each pivoting in place to a 45-degree angle to fire outward. That's exactly what the enemy wanted them to do.

With the entire convoy now at a standstill, they became sitting ducks as hidden enemy fighters on the high ground on both sides of the highway launched their ambush. They damaged or destroyed nearly every vehicle in the convoy, killing or wounding many of the occupants.

When we arrived overhead many of the vehicles were on fire, some blown clear off the highway, and guys on the ground were screaming for help. We immediately started reconning the hills on both sides of the highway looking for the bad guys, while the friendlies on the ground repeatedly warned us that we were receiving fire as well.

We discovered some fighting positions and fired on a few enemy soldiers we detected however, in typical NVA hit and run tactics, most of the enemy forces had melted into the surrounding jungle to fight another day.

All that week we continued to discover enemy soldiers and engineers reoccupying the high ground around Hamburger Hill and reconstructing the bunkers, spider holes and fighting positions.

For three days in a row after, I had attacked a small enemy engineer unit, complete with bulldozer, working on a hilltop just to the west of Dong Ap Bia.

Each night I would lay awake on my bunk back at the hooch thinking of ways I could try to outsmart them and attack them again without getting shot down.

Each day I would come in low level from a different direction, pop up to see if I could catch them by surprise, and come in hot blasting at the hilltop.

It turns out Lenny Constantine had been doing the same thing with his team and adjusted Artillery barrages on the site as well.

We were definitely becoming a thorn in their side.

On the fourth day, June 10th, Dick Dato was flying back seat on his first mission as a new Cobra Aircraft Commander with his mentor, Bruce McNeel, in the front seat. Lenny and I had told them about the enemy activity in the area and they set up for another attack on the same hilltop. The bad guys were waiting for them this time with automatic weapons and rocket-propelled grenades (RPGs).

On their very first run they took a direct hit from an RPG which severed the tail boom and put them into a violent spin as they plummeted towards the ground. The aircraft hit a tree, stopping the spin, however, then dropped another hundred feet or so straight down, slamming into the ground with such force that the airframe was crushed and both of them were severely injured and knocked unconscious.

Eddy Joiner was flying the Scout bird and called the May Day over the radio alerting all of us that Dato and McNeel had crashed. The Boss was on the scene in minutes and a Medevac Helicopter, "Eagle Dustoff", was on the way.

Lenny arrived on the scene in his Cobra and with the help of the Scouts kept the bad guys at bay while the Medevac was coming in for the pickup. Lenny remembers all he could see of the wreckage was the top of Dato's head where the canopy had been busted through. McNeel was slumped over and unconscious in the front seat.

What transpired next was the stuff of legends.

Dick Dato regained consciousness and somehow managed to climb out of the back seat. Even though blinded by severe facial injuries he felt his way along the crushed fuselage around the front of the aircraft to the opposite side where McNeel still sat unconscious in the front seat also with severe facial injuries.

Dick is a big, strong guy over six feet tall and nearly 200 pounds of solid muscle. He is also famous for his no nonsense "can do" attitude. Even with his injuries, he reached into the damaged front cockpit, undid McNeel's seat belt and shoulder harness and then lifted him out and laid him down on the ground beside the aircraft. They huddled there, somewhat protected from enemy fire, while the rest of us blasted the hill and covered the Medevac Helicopter that was lowering a basket down to recover them.

Lenny recalls that he would never forget the sight of Dick Dato holding Bruce McNeel in his arms, staring towards the sky hoping help would arrive.

Dick was trying to see the rescue Huey hovering over him, however he was so severely injured and blinded that he couldn't see the basket coming down to them on the hoist wire. The Eagle Dustoff crew carefully nudged him with the basket, which he managed to grab, as they lowered it to the ground.

He then placed McNeel in the basket and waited on his knees, his head hanging down, as the basket was hoisted up to the rescue helicopter. Once McNeel was safely aboard, the basket was lowered again and gently nudged against him so he could feel it, then he climbed into it and was hoisted to safety. Safety was a relative term as all the while the bad guys were trying to shoot the Medevac down while we were blasting their positions.

Two more bunks in the hooch were empty that night as we packed up Dick and Bruce's stuff to be shipped back to the States. Their time in Vietnam was over. I hoped and prayed Dick Dato and Bruce McNeel would be able to recover from their wounds.

For years, I felt guilty that somehow it was my fault they were ambushed. I should have been the one attacking the hilltop again.

Three days later we would lose Scout Pilot Mike Ryan. He would be wounded in a horrific crash over on the west side of the valley, near where Lenny Constantine had blown up the bridge.

"It was Friday, the 13th," Ryan recalls. "I knew something bad was going to happen."

Circling in low in his Scout bird with his Observer, Bob Bickle, they spotted an enemy hooch structure below the triple canopy jungle. Don McGurk and Mike Talton were flying the Cobra, providing cover overhead. It was Talton's final ride as a Copilot before being promoted to Aircraft Commander.

Ryan started receiving fire and broke off while Bickle threw out a white phosphorous grenade to mark the enemy location. McGurk dove in to attack the structure with rockets while Ryan circled around to cover them in his Loach.

As McGurk broke off his run, Ryan continued the attack, firing the minigun. Then when he tried to break left, the controls wouldn't respond! They continued their dive straight into the mountainside down through the trees and thick jungle.

As McGurk and Talton lined up for another rocket run, they looked around to see where Ryan was. "Crap, I lost him!" Talton yelled into the microphone as McGurk took his finger off the firing button, which would have launched another flurry of rockets.

"He just disappeared," Talton explained as they strained to see Ryan's Scout bird. "They were gone in an instant, literally swallowed by the jungle."

"I kept trying to fly the Loach as we crashed down through the trees," Ryan recalls, "but it was no use as our controls had been shot away and the collective I was holding in my left hand had broken off and wasn't connected to anything."

"We finally hit the ground and rolled onto our left side. The whole front of the cockpit had been ripped away. I was hanging in my harness in the right seat. Bickle was trapped under the airframe in the left seat."

"My left leg hurt like hell. Turns out it was broken, as my ankle had been violently twisted in the crash. I had also taken a bullet in the calf and another bullet had grazed my thigh after ricocheting off the .38 pistol I kept strapped between my legs to protect the family jewels. Thank God for that!"

"I unbuckled my harness and fell on top of Bickle," Ryan continued. "His left arm was stuck under the door frame. There wasn't much left of the aircraft so I crawled out and simply lifted the whole damn thing up and he got his arm out. I unbuckled him and he fell out on the ground with me. We crawled over and huddled under a tree and popped a smoke grenade so the guys overhead could see our position."

"We started hearing Vietnamese voices nearby and figured we were going to be discovered any minute. Bickle and I made a pact that we wouldn't be captured alive and counted the bullets we had on hand for our pistols."

"Then we saw 20 or so enemy soldiers, but they were running away! Apparently, McGurk was diving at them from overhead and scaring them off."

"Then we saw the Huey hovering over us above the trees. It was the Boss (Major Curtin). His crew chief, Duane Acord, was peering down at us and dropping a line with a 4 by 4 attached."

Major Curtin always carried emergency rescue gear aboard his Huey in the event we were shot down, so he could try and rescue us. The Army hadn't devised standardized rescue gear yet and it was left to each unit to devise their own methods. In this case, it was a single 60 to 120-foot line with a 4 inch by 4 inch by 4 foot square post tied to it in the middle. The idea was to lower it to the person on the ground and, if they were able, they could sit on it with the line between their legs and hold on as the aircraft lifted them out of the jungle.

"Bickle and I sat on the 4 by 4 facing each other with the line between us. Acord had sent down another piece of rope 10 feet long or so. We tied ourselves together and held on for dear life. As the Boss and his Pilot, Keith Nichols, tried to lift us out of the jungle, we swung back and forth crashing into trees hoping the Huey had enough power to get us out of there!"

"We got a little banged up but they were able to do it and after we cleared the trees they flew us, dangling below the helicopter at the end of the line, over to the old Aloui Airstrip nearby where we landed and then helped us into the Huey. Curtin then flew us all the way back to the 22nd Surgical Hospital at Phu Bai."

"They performed emergency surgery on my leg and transferred me down to the 6th Convalescent Center at Nha Trang," Ryan recalled. "The medical folks kept asking me if I wanted to go home. I told them I just wanted to go back to the unit. After almost three months at Nha Trang they allowed me to go back north to rejoin the Troop," Ryan concluded.

We had lost two of our best Scout Pilots. Bob Larsen was recovering in Japan after being shot down and wounded at Hamburger Hill and Mike Ryan was recovering down at Nha Trang. At the time, we didn't know whether either one of them would be returning to the unit.

A new replacement Scout Pilot arrived about then. His name was Dick Melick.

"I arrived at the unit and the CO told me I would be a Scout Pilot," Dick remembers. "I was a Huey Pilot but the Boss needed Scout Pilots, so I was assigned to Eddy Joiner to mentor and train me as a Scout flying the OH-6 Loach," he continued.

"Eddy told me about the Scout crashes. There had been nearly one a week lately."

"Goodspeed had been shot down on his first mission into the A Shau Valley, although he survived and was flying again. His Observer had been severely wounded though and apparently had lost his leg."

"A week later Bob Larsen had been shot down near Hamburger Hill and wounded when a bullet went through his foot, exploded the fire extinguisher under his seat and he took shrapnel in his legs. He had been evacuated to Japan."

"And now Mike Ryan had been wounded and evacuated too!"

"We're going back out to the A Shau," Eddy told me as I got ready for my first mission. I didn't know he was also known as "The Mad Bomber" because of his passion for constructing home-made explosive devices to blow things up."

"Here, carry this in your lap," Eddy instructed. "We're going to use it to blow up a bridge today!"

"He had taken an empty 5-gallon gas can, filled it with a jellied gasoline concoction similar to napalm and had taped a white phosphorous grenade on top. He intended for us to drop it onto a hanging bridge they had discovered earlier out there in the mountains."

"It seemed awfully dangerous to me," Melick recalls, "however I was a newbie and Ed 'The Mad Bomber' was my mentor."

What Ed didn't mention to Melick was his failed attempt to blow up the bridge a day or two before. He had constructed a gasoline bomb and actually landed on the bridge, balancing the helicopter skids on the bridge while holding power to keep the weight off while his Observer pulled the pin, dropped the bomb and they took off. The bomb blew, however the structure was so wet from recent rains that it didn't catch on fire and remained intact. This would be the second attempt.

"I could barely fit in the tiny Loach helicopter and trying to manhandle the heavy 5-gallon jerry can bomb at the same was no easy task," Melick continued.

"We flew out to the west side of the A Shau Valley. Ed explained that one of the Gunship Pilots was able to destroy a bridge out there a week earlier but this one was in a deep crevasse and well camouflaged and the only way to get to it was to fly in and hover right over it."

"We did just that and Ed instructed me to pop the handle on the white phosphorous grenade and I would have about two seconds to throw the whole thing out onto the bridge."

"I did as he told me but had a tough time lifting the jerry can clear of the aircraft, dropping it as the seconds ticked away. The thing blew up just below us about one second after I dropped it, showering the bridge with gasoline and setting everything on fire. It scared the shit out of me!"

"Eddy was just laughing and hooting and hollering. Job well done!" he said as a compliment.

"We sent in our spot reports of more enemy build-up on that side of the valley and our successful destruction of the suspension bridge," Melick continued. "I would end up being signed off and flying as a Scout in a little over a week instead of the usual two months and would fly over 130 hours a month as a Scout Pilot."

Dick Melick would become a great Scout Pilot for the Troop. He would later take over our Aircraft Maintenance

Operations to keep the birds flying and end up as the unit Operations Officer, running the Tactical Operations Center.

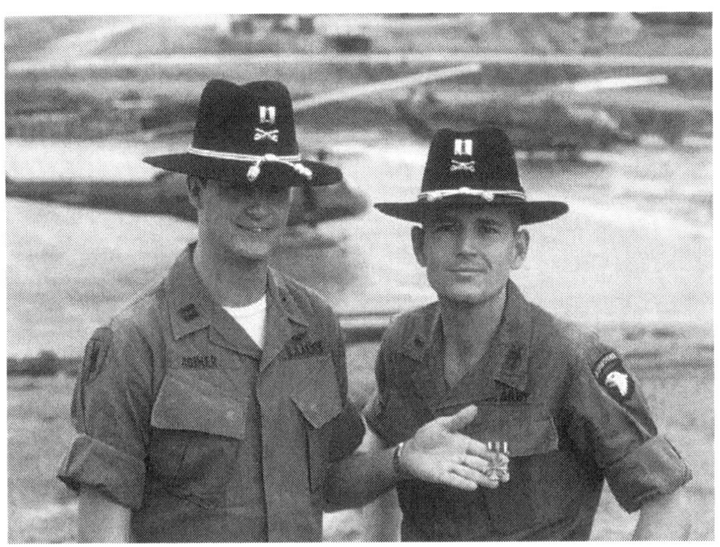

Eddy "Mad Bomber" Joiner congratulates his "Assistant Mad Bomber" Dick Melick on receiving the Distinguished Flying Cross for destroying the bridge with an "incendiary device".

In the meantime, with all the new enemy activity being reported by our Air Cavalry Teams, enemy skirmishes with the two Airborne Infantry Battalions still out there, Firebase Currahee being attacked and the 3/5th Mech convoy ambushed, the Brass finally decided enough was enough. Time to bring in the heavies. A B-52 "Arc Light'" Air Strike was requested.

B-52's, introduced in the 1950's, had been built as Strategic Nuclear-weapons carrying Bombers for the Air Force's Strategic Air Command (SAC).

General Westmoreland lobbied to get B-52 support in Vietnam as a Tactical Bomber, dropping conventional "Iron

Bombs". SAC relented and two Bomber Wings with their B-52s were modified to carry high explosive bombs and deployed to Andersen Air Force Base in Guam to support Ground Commanders in Vietnam with massive tactical bombing capability.

A total of 72 B-52 Bombers were modified for Tactical Air support. In 1967, the B-52's were moved to Thailand to provide quicker response times and eliminate the aerial refueling required by the 2,500-mile flights from Guam.

Each B-52 could carry a massive 60,000 pounds of ordnance with 108 bombs; eighty-four 500-pounders internally, and another twenty-four 750-pound bombs on external wing racks.

They typically flew in formations of three or more dropping their bombs from 30,000 feet. We were warned well in advance whenever an Arc Light was inbound and to stay well clear of the ensuing carnage.

Mike Talton and Al Goodspeed were standing by to witness the Arc Light a few days later. They were circling over the A Shau Valley, well clear of the intended target area around Don Ap Bia. They were to go in after the Arc Light to do a "BDA" or Bomb Damage Assessment.

Mike Talton relates what happened.

"Speed and I and were tasked to stand by along the eastern ridge of the Valley, directly across the Valley floor from Hamburger Hill. An Arc Light was scheduled to walk bombs across the top of the Hill and Speed and I were to zoom into the smoke and perform a BDA to assess the results of the strike."

"As we flew north looking west or to our left at the Hill, mushrooms started to grow out of the trees south of the Hill, three lines of mushrooms, straight lines running from south to north."

"The mushrooms started as small blooms just visible above the tree lines that had survived the Battle for Hamburger Hill back in May, and then grew rapidly as dirty brown, black and grey miniature atomic-bomb-like clouds, rolling and boiling and interlaced with flashes of red. As we watched them grow and extend their line northward, down into gullies and up over ridges, heading for the Hill, it occurred to us that we had visuals but no audibles, no sound. Everything was silent, except for the sounds of our helicopter."

"Then our Cobra literally rolled over onto its right side away from the lines of mushroom clouds, as if pushed by a huge unseen hand, and at that instant we were 'hit' by the sounds of deep, rolling thunder that went on and on. At some point, the visuals and audibles seemed to synch up so that we saw the bomb explosions and heard the loud booms somewhat simultaneously, even though what we were hearing and seeing was lagging due to the time it took for the sounds to travel across the Valley and from the Hill to our over-watch position along the eastern ridge line."

"It appeared there were three B-52's running in a 'V' formation high over our heads, so high that we never saw them, not even contrails. We knew they were in a 'V' of three because of the strikes of their bombs when we saw the first 'mushrooms' bloom."

"The three bomb lines ran over the top of the Hill and onward to the north for some distance. Don't know how many bombs they dropped or if they were all of the same weight and fuse type, but the explosions occurred rapidly, joined together by an invisible force that kept the three lines parallel and straight, at least from our perspective."

"Speed took off in his little Scout bird on a beeline for the Hill as soon as the last boom 'boomed'. Don't remember if he aimed for the crest or if he started his recon from the south along the same bomb run used by the High Flyers."

"The massive destruction of the Arc Light was incredible to behold. Huge bomb craters, blown bunkers, destroyed fighting positions, collapsed trenches and tunnels. We didn't see any bodies. I think if there were any enemy left, they had been blown to smithereens or buried deep in their own underground fortresses."

"From then on, I wished we had Arc Light on call like TAC Air, Artillery or ARA," Mike concluded.

The B-52 *Stratofortress,* as it was officially designated, became known throughout the Air Force simply as the *BUFF* – Big, Ugly, Fat, Fucker!

General William Westmoreland considered B-52s essential to U.S. efforts in Vietnam. From June 1965 until August 1973, when operations ceased, the BUFFs flew 124,532 sorties, successfully dropping their bomb loads on targets.

Thirty-One B-52s were lost, eighteen shot down by the enemy (all over North Vietnam), and the other thirteen lost to operational problems.

B-52 tail gunners, believe it or not, were also credited with three air-to-air combat kills, shooting down MIGs with their Quad-50's, earning the B-52 the distinction as the largest aircraft ever credited with air-to-air combat kills.

We loved the BUFFs and became forever indebted to the B-52 drivers and crews for their efforts helping those of us down in the trenches.

That night back at home base, we hoisted a few to the Air Force as we enjoyed the taste of sweet revenge seeing Hamburger Hill blown to bits once again.

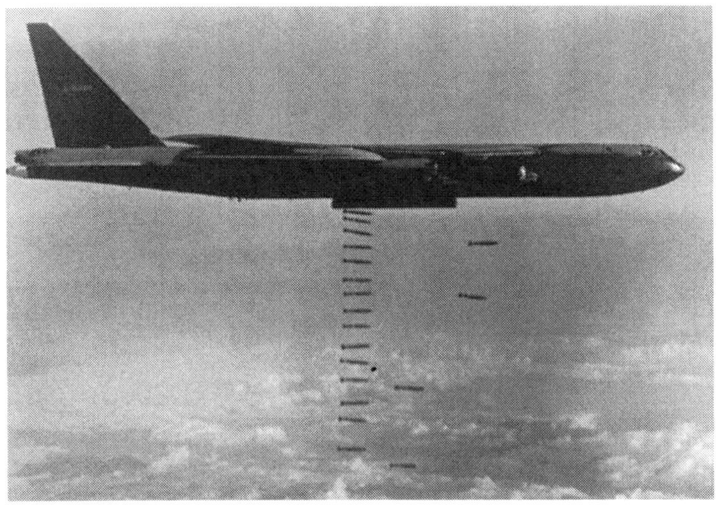

B-52 BUFF Arc Light

Eddy "Mad Bomber" Joiner, Assault 11

CHAPTER SIXTEEN

MONSOON

The summer Monsoon season roared in on July 11, my 23rd birthday, when Typhoon Tess came within 50 miles of Camp Eagle with lots of rain and wind and setting records for rainfall that month.

The weather was really cramping our style and wreaking havoc with our support to the troops in the field. The heavy rains and winds were keeping us from flying for days on end.

We tried to keep busy and stay dry, whiling away the hours in our hooches reading, playing cards, cleaning our gear, studying our flight manuals (or other technical publications like Playboy Magazine), or just trying to get some sleep. The problem was, we were being constantly interrupted by Captain Roy "Bud" Dowdy, the Executive Officer or XO of our unit.

Executive Officers are the second-in-command guys in most military organizations. Their primary responsibility is to take care of all the administrative and housekeeping chores in the unit so the Commanding Officer can concentrate on leading and commanding. That automatically makes the Executive Officer a pain in the ass. The better he is at his job, the more painful it is for the rest of us. And Bud Dowdy was a very good XO!

The last two days Dowdy had been on a rant about sand bags. Our hooches were surrounded by stacks of sand bags up to about four feet high, to protect the occupants from enemy fire, especially shrapnel, from incoming mortars and rockets.

It seemed like every time we got into a good card game or deep into the latest edition of Playboy Magazine, Dowdy would come barging in and roust us out into the pouring rain to fill and stack more sand bags. I think he just had a hard-on for us lazy Warrant Officer Pilots.

After two days of this never-ending harassment, the CO came to our hooch asking for volunteers to do a reconnaissance mission of the nearby Perfume River. I couldn't raise my hand fast enough as I leaped up from my bunk and was already putting on my gear and heading for the door.

Hunched over into the wind and rain and wearing a poncho to keep me dry, I ran to the hooch next door to get Stan Shearin as my Copilot. Stan was a tall, lanky, good-looking guy with an easy smile. What I really liked about him was his size. He would fill up the entire front cockpit and was the perfect Bullet Catcher.

We headed up to see Sergeant Saunders at the Operations Bunker to get our Mission Brief. Al Goodspeed was already there and would be our Scout for the mission.

The Perfume River was just a few kilometers (klicks for short) from our base at Camp Eagle. We were to fly out and conduct a reconnaissance of the river to make sure the enemy wasn't taking advantage of the rotten weather to creep up on our Base Defenses.

The whole operation shouldn't take more than an hour to perform unless we ran into trouble. And I wasn't in any hurry to see the XO again anytime soon.

Our CO, Major Tom Curtin, was going to join us on the mission, flying his Huey. I think he was tired of hanging around home base the past few days and just wanted to get out into the fresh air with us. He didn't have to fill sand bags for the XO, so I don't think he really cared when he got back.

The weather was pretty crummy with low ceilings and limited visibility in the fog and rain. We followed the CO's Huey and Al Goodspeed in his Loach with me dragging up the rear in our Cobra. We hadn't been flying five minutes though when the CO called, "23 and 16, Assault 6. I'm heading back to base. This weather is too lousy to be out here although you can continue the mission if you're up for it."

"16, 23, you up for it?" I queried Speed. "23, 16, roger, let's do it," he replied.

"6 this is 23, we'll continue the mission, over," I called to the Boss as he headed back to Camp Eagle.

"16, 23, let's drop down low on the river and take it nice and slow in this visibility," I called to Speed.

The visibility was really terrible. I could hardly see a thing in front of us with the rain pounding on the front windshield. I pushed right pedal and crabbed the helicopter to look out the side as we flew along at less than 50 knots. The visibility while crabbing that way was much better.

"Stan, keep a close eye on where we're at on the Tactical Map in case we need to make any calls or reports," I directed.

He spread out the map in front of him to follow along. It covered the whole front windshield as I strained to keep an eye on Speed as he weaved back and forth low over the water in front of us.

We hadn't been flying another two minutes when BAM! We smashed headlong into a huge tree angled out over the river. The collision was violent and threw us forward into our shoulder harnesses as the helicopter came to a sudden stop and started to fall sideways into the water below.

I could see branches flying all around us and getting stuck into the rocket pods as we fell sideways out of the tree. I pulled pitch to slow the fall and eased the cyclic forward, trying to wish the helicopter into flying again. I was certain the landing gear was gone and had no idea of what other damage had been done as the helicopter barely recovered and started flying again just inches above the water.

"Stan, you okay?" I called on the intercom, as my stomach tried to recover from the sudden rush of adrenalin.

"Yeah, I'm okay. What the hell just happened?"

"We ran into a tree. Let me call Speed and get him back here to take a look at us to see what was damaged."

"16, 23. Turn around and fly back down the river. We've run into a tree and I need you to assess the damage," I called.

"23, 16. On my way. You guys okay?"

Before I could answer, the Boss called.

"23, this is 6. Did I hear you right? You ran into a tree?"

He was still on frequency. Damn, no getting around this one!

"6, 23. Roger that. We're assessing the damage now. I think the skids may have been torn off and the landing gear gone. I don't know if the turret with the mini-gun and grenade launcher is still there. I can see damage to the Wing Stores," I replied. "Otherwise, we're still airborne and heading back to base."

"Roger," the Boss replied. "I'll get the Maintenance Crews ready for your arrival."

Good grief! We're the only ones out here in this weather which means everyone in the unit is going to be there to witness my arrival. I'll be the laughing stock of Alpha Troop if not all of Camp Eagle!

Speed came up close in his Scout bird to take a look at the damage.

"Your skids are still attached and your gun turret is still there, however you have branches sticking out of your rocket pods and what looks like significant damage to your right wing," he described.

That was good news. I hadn't ripped off the turret and the landing gear was still attached, however it couldn't be trusted to hold the weight of the helicopter. And there was no way to jettison the rockets or pods so we'll just have to land with all the ordnance on board.

The next ten minutes were used to coordinate a plan over the radio with Home Base as we found our way back.

The plan was to fly up the ravine at our Base Camp to the foot of the maintenance ramp, then turn the Cobra around, facing back out towards the perimeter in case one or more of the rockets were to launch or explode accidentally.

Once turned around, I would not land but maintain a hover until the Maintenance Crews could position stacks of sandbags under each wing to keep the helicopter from rolling over if the landing gear failed.

Once the sandbags were in place and all Ground Crew clear, I would gently settle the helicopter on to its landing gear.

The plan worked like a charm to the cheers of hundreds of spectators as I humbly climbed out of my damaged Cobra. The poor thing was a sorry sight with branches and leaves sticking out of the rocket pods and a huge dent in the right wing where it impacted the tree. This was going to cost me more than a few paychecks.

The Armorers couldn't dislodge the tree branches jammed into the rocket pods so, for safety, they took the 19 and 7-shot pods off the wings and buried them in a pit with the rockets still in the tubes.

Next, they disassembled the wing and did a dye-penetrant check to see if the wing mount hard points on the fuselage had been damaged or cracked. If so, the whole helicopter would have to be shipped back to the States for repair and I would probably be on my way to prison at Leavenworth. Luckily for me, the hard points passed inspection.

The next problem was that we didn't have a wing in stock to replace the one I had severely damaged. To compound the situation, the Commanding General was taking advantage of the bad weather and coming to the unit to present medals to many of us for actions out in the A Shau. We didn't want him to see the damage and have to explain that one of our bonehead Pilots had run into a tree.

The Maintenance Crew hurriedly reattached the wing, put the Cobra in the Maintenance Hangar and covered the damaged wing with a tarp. The helicopter was now officially in the hangar for "routine" maintenance while I was ordered to go find a new wing.

There were only a few units in the Division that had Cobras. And of those, maybe one might have a wing they could give me. The price would be high for sure.

I called the 101st Assault Helicopter Battalion. No luck.

Then I called the 158th Assault Helicopter Battalion. No luck.

The only unit left that had lots of Cobras was our arch rivals, the 4/77th Aerial Rocket Artillery (ARA). I reluctantly gave them a call.

Lo and behold they had one on hand! And they were willing to discuss a trade! I headed right over to their Headquarters.

Word had gotten around. I was famous, or infamous, depending on your perspective. The 4/77th CO and Maintenance Officer were there to greet me. They seemed to be stifling a chuckle as they extended a handshake.

"Mr. Jennings! Glad to meet you. Heard you're looking for a wing for your Cobra. How did you lose it?" the CO asked, as they both burst out laughing.

"Never mind, we heard the story. How about we sit down and discuss how we're going to handle the transaction," he continued as we went inside.

Apparently, they had already come to a consensus on how the deal would go down. We hadn't even taken a seat yet when they both turned towards me, the Maintenance Officer announcing: "The cost is a case of prime Wild Turkey Kentucky Bourbon Whiskey, delivered!"

I couldn't believe my ears. "Deal!" I blurted, as we shook hands all around.

The case of Wild Turkey was on the next flight from the big BX (Base Exchange) at Da Nang, courtesy of the US Air

Force. It had cost me nearly a month's pay, however I had avoided a Court-Martial that day.

I would be awarded a medal instead, as I looked past the Commanding General's shoulder to the tarp-covered wing as he presented me the Distinguished Flying Cross for our actions when Speed had crashed back in May.

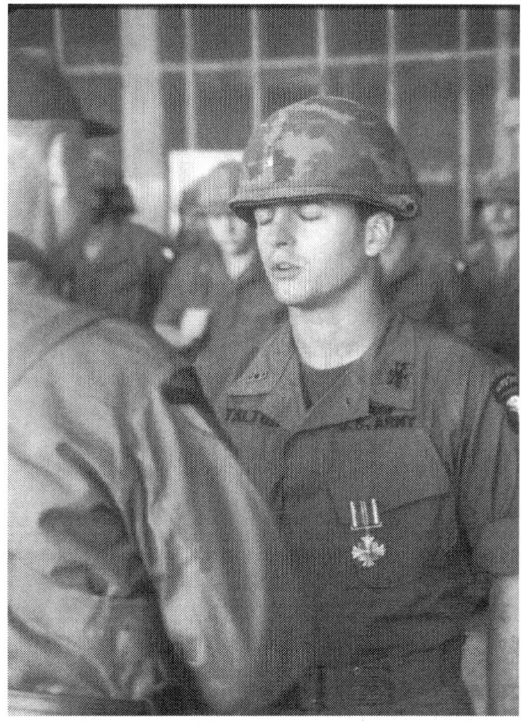

Mike Talton receives the Distinguished Flying Cross for Valor from Major General John M. Wright. His eyes are closed as he describes to the General that's how he reacts to enemy aircraft fire or GBOFs to survive.

CHAPTER SEVENTEEN

ASSAULT 27 DISAPPEARS

It was early September, 1969. During a lull in the action while resting at Firebase Rendezvous when another team had relieved us on station, I witnessed a sight I will never forget.

We had already refueled and rearmed and I was lying on the open ammo bay door of my Cobra taking a rest break with Mike Talton and Eddy Joiner.

There were many troops and Hueys awaiting deployment and a lot of activity going on.

Mike poked me awake and pointed in the direction of a Huey that was just taking off. "Look at that guy! What he's doing is really dangerous and going to get somebody killed," he grimaced.

The Huey was nosed over at a crazy angle, almost vertical, with a load of troops on board, doors open, their legs hanging out, totally not secured. I was amazed they didn't fall out.

"Holy cow, let's watch him to see what he's going to do," I said as the Huey gained speed and altitude and then turned back like he was going to land.

"Let's go over and have a talk with him when he gets down," I said. Pious experts that all Pilots tend to be, we criticized each other mercilessly.

We watched him approach and just as he was slowing down to come to a hover or land, it appeared he was losing control and started heading right towards us!

Maybe he was experiencing hydraulic failure or something. In a Huey, when you lose hydraulic pressure the controls become almost like concrete and very hard to move. If you can control the helicopter at all, you want to get some airspeed and do a running landing. If you try to come to a stop and lose translational lift, the helicopter becomes uncontrollable, and that's apparently what was happening now.

We all got to our feet and started running as the Huey was rapidly approaching us just five feet or so off the ground.

All of a sudden, it pitched straight up, seeming to climb for the sky! The troops and all manner of supplies and equipment started spilling out of the helicopter as it climbed with the nose pointed straight up.

At about a hundred feet, it stopped in midair and came back down tail first, crashed, and rolled into a muddy ravine just yards from us and caught on fire.

"HOLY SHIT!" Joiner exclaimed. "Let's get 'em out of there!" as he and Talton started running to the wreckage while I got the fire extinguisher out of my Cobra.

They jumped down into the ravine and immediately sank waist deep in mud and who knows what other stuff. The aircraft was on its side, the front windshield was blown and the Pilot was still in his harness. The Copilot was missing.

Joiner and Talton pulled themselves up over the nose of the aircraft to reach the Pilot. He was definitely wounded and incoherent. He had a hole in his forehead like a pen or pencil had stabbed him. Mike later theorized he had hit his forehead on the "Chinese Hat" microphone button on the top of the cyclic. At that moment, he didn't seem to care about the head wound and was screaming about the pain in his thumb.

I was futilely trying to put out the fire when a soldier nearly knocked me down with a huge fire extinguisher on wheels he had dragged over from the FARP area. He took over fighting the fire while I went forward to help Joiner and Talton with the injured Pilot.

More folks had run over to help by then. Someone had a poncho we used as a stretcher to put the Pilot onto. As I knelt over him, he continued to complain about his hand as the wound in his forehead continued to bleed. Then a huge CH-47 Chinook helicopter landed near us after dropping off fuel bladders at the FARP and volunteered to take all the dead or injured to hospital facilities at Camp Evans.

We searched for and found the Copilot standing on the other side of the ravine unhurt, but in shock.

We located the rest of the passengers. All were injured, however miraculously none had been killed. We quickly loaded everyone aboard the Chinook, which headed to medical facilities in minutes.

To this day I can still see the helicopter going straight up, in slow motion, as the soldiers and their equipment are spilling out both sides and falling to the ground.

I later recommended Eddy Joiner and Mike Talton for Soldiers Medals. These medals are awarded to soldiers displaying conspicuous courage, saving the lives of others in a non-combat situation.

It was September 15th and I was standing by at LZ Rendezvous for another mission, when I received the terrible news that my roommate and dear friend, Mike Talton, had gone down in his Cobra somewhere in the northern A Shau. He and John Bacic were flying as part of a Pink Team on a reconnaissance mission with Mike Ryan, Assault 18, as their scout. Our beloved Major Tom Curtin had turned over command of our unit to Major Tom Trombley, who was also with them in the Command and Control Huey. His call sign as the Commander was Assault 6.

They had simply disappeared and a frantic search was on. What the heck had happened? Here's Mike Talton to tell us in his own words.

"We had been tasked to conduct a recon northwest of the A Shau Valley to identify NVA forces coming over the border from Laos. We knew they were traveling across the border at night and that they were using multiple crossing points through the mountain valleys and over the Xe Pon River, bringing men and equipment to the fight in the area south of the DMZ. Even though we had fought the NVA repeatedly during the spring and summer, they were still very active in the mountains and valleys of NW South Vietnam. Our job, as always, was to find them and stop them wherever and whenever we could."

"Assault 6 decided to fly with a single Pink Team on the recon mission up the A Shau Valley and points to the northwest, anticipating that we would require an 'On-Station' swap out of the Team once we got involved with the reconnaissance. It was a big area and would require a lot of flight time to run the border and then follow any active routes that we discovered. More flight time than we could provide in a single fuel load."

"With the load of rockets, minigun ammo and 40mm grenades that we carried in our Cobra, we had to limit our fuel to about 1.5 hours of flight time. Out of those 90 minutes, we had to carve out the time it would take to get to and then back from the mission area. Since the area we wanted to recon started at a point about 10 minutes away, even by the most direct route across the mountains, we would only have 60 to 70 minutes to spend searching for the bad guys before we had to head back for refueling."

"Our Standard Operating Procedure (SOP) required we land with enough fuel in the tanks to keep the engine churning. That would almost certainly guarantee that a second, and maybe even a third Pink Team would be called out to complete the recon mission."

"We were staging out of LZ Rendezvous, a Support Base plowed out of the flat terrain snuggled up to the eastern wall of the A Shau Valley, across the Valley and to the southeast of Hamburger Hill. Rendezvous was a forward staging area where we could pre-position helicopters and soldiers and some limited supplies like food and water."

"While the Rendezvous location allowed us to cut 30 minutes of flight time out of our reaction times to calls for air support, it required we preposition to Rendezvous from our home base at Camp Eagle in the mornings and recover back to Eagle when the sun went down. We didn't leave helicopters in the Valley at night, as they would become primary targets for the NVA."

"Rendezvous was where we often sat waiting our turn at bat. If time permitted, we would sometimes have a C-ration lunch between missions after warming up the 'entrée' can in the hot exhaust tube of our L13 engines. We Snake drivers would kick back in our cockpit seats, canopy doors open, with the 27-inch wide '540' rotor blades pulled into a position where their shadows could provide us shade and welcome relief from the typically hot sun."

"Combat troops (Airborne Infantry) sometimes waited at Rendezvous as well. They would ride into battle in the Hueys, with their legs hanging over the edges of the cabin decking, their weapons pointed toward the jungle beneath them, their eyes looking and watching and their pulses beating faster, waiting for something to happen."

"The CO, Tom Trombley, briefed the mission with us, as we marked our maps with the info and climbed into our respective helicopters. After we completed our run-up checks and confirmed that our three-ship team had radio communications on the three frequencies we would be using for the mission, Assault 6's C&C bird took off to the west and then turned north as he climbed into the sky above the A Shau. Assault 18 followed him in his OH-6A Scout, westbound initially and then northbound and climbing. I followed my Scout, skimming the toes of the heavy Snake along the dusty surface of Rendezvous' mostly flat surface. Once I accelerated through transitional lift and starting to fly for real, I rolled into a right-hand turn and adjusted my route of flight so that I could join up as number 3 in a loose trail formation, following the others. I keyed my VHF radio and transmitted a call to Assault 6 to advise both him and Assault 18 that we were off and running."

"Ahead of us and at higher altitudes, we saw our Scout and C&C bird established on a northerly, heading up the Valley, generally following highway 548, en route to our intended mission Area of Operations."

"The skies were clear and blue and it was a great September day for flying in the skies of South Vietnam!"

"Though we had a full load of ordnance with 350 40mm grenades for the grenade launcher, 4000 rounds of 7.62mm bullets for the minigun and 52 2.75 inch rockets with 17 pound warheads, and were carrying 1.5 hours of JP4 in the two internal fuel tanks, the Cobra was running smoothly and climbing steadily as we flew on to catch up to our Scout bird."

"Since our primary responsibility as part of the Pink Team was to provide gun cover for the Scout, we wanted to be in a reasonably close overwatch position on him at all times, hopefully as a visible deterrent to any bad guys on the ground who might be anxious to bag themselves a seemingly vulnerable helicopter, and as a very real armed response in case the deterrent idea failed to work. At the moment, because he took off before we did, the Scout was further ahead of us than we liked, so we were hustling to catch up."

"About five minutes after takeoff, as we reached an altitude about even with the Scout bird, though still behind and slightly to the right of him, I increased the collective for a bit more power and thrust, and pressed slightly forward on the cyclic to stop our climb and to increase our airspeed to 100 knots or so. As I made the control changes, I automatically applied a bit of left tail rotor control pedal to compensate for the increase in collective pitch and power."

"Nothing happened. There was no response to my pedal input. The pedal moved forward as I pushed it with my left foot, but the nose of the Cobra continued to drift off to the right because of the increase in collective, just the opposite of what should have happened when I pressed the pedal."

"I instinctively applied more pressure on the left pedal and watched as the nose failed to respond. In fact, it moved further to the right. We were now in a slight sideslip with the nose cocked off to the right of our flight path and the fuselage rolled slightly to the left, in the direction of flight due to the earlier cyclic input, not much, but enough to tell me that we were now in the *Twilight Zone*."

"I realized that my tail rotor pedals were no longer controlling the pitch of the tail rotor blades. I had lost the ability to directly control the yaw attitude of my Cobra. I could not make the Cobra's nose point in a direction of my choosing. Now it would point wherever the laws of aerodynamics and physics dictated and my Copilot and I would be along for the ride."

"I removed both feet from the pedals and as if to confirm my light bulb moment of inspiration, I tapped the left pedal with the toe of my left boot. It effortlessly glided forward to its stop, while the right pedal, mechanically linked to the left pedal, glided rearward. When the pedals reached the limits of their respective travels, they struck their physical stops and bounced back to travel all the way in their opposite directions until they again reached the mechanical limits of travel and again began another glide. Not good!"

"I placed my feet back on the pedals and confirmed by feel that there was no perceivable resistance to any pressure I placed on the pedals. They were now free spirits, serving only as foot rests. As anyone who has flown Cobras before would suspect, my front seat Copilot's pedals were just as useless as mine, although at that instance he did not yet know it (as he was busy with other tasks, leaving me to fly the aircraft)."

"Somehow, control for the tail rotor way back behind us, some 35 feet away, was severed or broken or disconnected or who knew what!"

"Total loss of tail rotor control during flight is one of those events that qualifies as a genuine, five-star, highlighted-in-red Emergency. The Cobra's Operator's Manual addresses such an event in the section devoted to Emergency Procedures. It explains that depending on several variables, including airspeed and altitude, the best course of action might be a full autorotation to a 'suitable' landing spot, while attempting to decelerate and cushion the landing prior to impact."

"Ideally you want to land as slowly and softly as possible."

"The problem with tail rotor failures involving complete loss of control is that at the moment you are trying to cushion the impact, you will be increasing the amount of collective pitch in the main rotor system. This, in turn, will increase the amount of torque being exerted through the transmission on the fuselage and without a controllable tail rotor to counter the torque, the fuselage is going to spin in a direction opposite to the direction that the main rotor is spinning. To the right in all Bell helicopters, including this one."

"The result is that the soft impact idea suddenly becomes a soon-to-be-forgotten memory as the spinning helicopter does just about whatever it wants to do, including impacting the world with a lot of noise, dust and flying debris, but hopefully no fire."

"The Emergency Procedures further advise that since the crew cannot exert physical direct control over the tail rotor during the autorotation, care should be taken to delay application of collective pitch for as long as practicable, to keep the helicopter from spinning to the right uncontrollably due to torque effects of the main rotor system on the fuselage."

"A complete loss of control over the tail rotor is one of those emergencies that Pilots read about, talk about and theorize about, but back then in 1969 there was no practical way to practice and refine these theories. Only those who actually experienced the event, and lived to tell about it, knew for sure what worked and what didn't."

"In the brief course of a few seconds our great September day was becoming a bit cloudy. The good news was that our Cobra was still 'churning and burning' and as far as I could tell, nothing was flying off of it."

"Knowing that the first rule of flying is to fly the aircraft, I decided to do just that, making a mental note to keep the airspeed above 80 knots in an attempt to keep the fuselage streamlined into the air and pointing more or less in the direction I wanted to travel. I planned to minimize all control inputs as much as possible to keep things stable for as long as possible, meaning no turns, no changes in altitude and no changes in airspeed and for sure, no increases in collective pitch control."

"I keyed the microphone switch on the cyclic to call our Scout and C&C to alert them to our problem. Although I initially heard a tone in my earphones as if the radio was keying for transmission, the sound bled off to nothingness, silence, no radio, like it ran out of steam or power. I released the switch and then pressed it forward again and again. Still nothing. I switched to the UHF radio and repeated my attempt to make a call, but it didn't work either. Neither did our FM radio. All our communications were gone."

"I sensed that something really bad must have happened to cause the tail rotor failure and a complete loss of radio communications at the same time."

"It was time to advise my Copilot, John Bacic, that the price of poker had just gone up."

"I quickly explained about the pedals and the radios and naturally had him check on things from his seat up front. He tried his radio control panel for all three radios and his floor and cyclic microphone switches. Nothing worked for him either. I showed him what happened when I kicked the pedals. He wasn't impressed, but those pedals swishing back and forth without the aircraft responding did get his undivided attention."

"Up ahead our team flew on, blithely unaware that they were leaving us in their proverbial dust and that we might possibly disappear into the jungle below without a trace."

"Since we couldn't communicate with anyone by radio and our current direction of flight was taking us away from friendly forces, I decided to turn around and head back to Rendezvous. My plan was to fly back down the A Shau valley until we got close enough to Rendezvous, then execute an autorotation to the ground. If we could reach a point where we were in sight of the base camp, chances were that friendly forces could give us a hand in case things didn't go well."

"It wasn't much of a plan, as plans go, but it turns out that it didn't matter anyway. Our faithful steed had a different idea and was just waiting for the appropriate moment to demonstrate it to John and me."

"I decided to make a 180° turn to the right, thinking that a right turn would cause the relative wind to act on the fuselage in such a way as to mitigate any tendency for a right-hand spin. As I started a gentle right bank using cyclic control input only, the helicopter properly rolled to the right and started a turn of sorts. I deliberately did not increase the collective pitch control as the turn began, thinking that I didn't want to increase the torque since I couldn't counter it with the tail rotor."

"Initially things looked OK. The helicopter was beginning to turn and we were essentially maintaining altitude, but the airspeed was decaying. We had inadvertently slowed from 100 knots to 80."

"In the turn, without adding power by way of collective pitch, we were maintaining altitude but sacrificing airspeed to do it. In the few nano-seconds it took for me to realize our predicament, the helicopter reached the point that it no longer wished to be a helicopter and decided to be a spinning top instead."

"In the literal blink of an eye, we started to spin to the right. The spin was a surprise but not totally unexpected, after all, we had read about it and talked about it and now we were getting to experience it."

"The rate of spin increased quickly due to a variety of forces at work, not the least of which might have been an instinctive and unintentional increase of collective pitch when the spinning helicopter, now no longer our friend, began to lose altitude and airspeed simultaneously. We were heading down to the jungle below, that much was certain, but the spin was now rapid enough that the world outside of our cockpit was a blur, colored in greens, browns and blues, but still a blur without clear visual references as to our height above the trees and ground."

"Perhaps my brain was spinning as quickly as our helicopter but for reasons not now remembered, I decided that we might be able to fly ourselves out of the spin if we could gain airspeed. Seems logical, right? Losing airspeed contributed to the spin; regaining airspeed might stop the spin or at least, slow it enough that we could see visual references outside of the cockpit."

"Why didn't I enter autorotation, reducing the collective to full down position and chopping the throttle to slow or stop the spin? That was the recommended response to a total loss of tail rotor control, but that was BEFORE you started to spin. Now that we were well established in a Disney Land E-ticket ride of a spin, would the sudden change in torque and other forces cause the main rotor to fail at the mast or at the transmission or who knows where? At the time, the uncertainties of what might happen persuaded us to try the 'fly it out of the spin' idea. John and I even discussed it briefly or maybe I discussed it and he politely listened."

"Retrospectively, trying to fly out of a fully developed spin was a mistake. The autorotation now seems to have been the better idea. In fact, it was the only good idea, but at the time I didn't have the advantage of 20-20 hindsight."

"As we spun down to the inevitable crash, John and I tightened our lap belts, locked our shoulder harnesses, tightened our SPH-4 flight helmet chinstraps and lowered our helmet visors."

"John keyed his intercom switch and advised me that when we crashed he didn't want the rotor blades to come through his cockpit and chop his head off, something that we had both heard about happening as the result of Cobras crashing in the jungles of Vietnam. He said he was unlocking his shoulder harness and putting his head down between his knees, or as close to that position as he could manage, given he was wearing his helmet and his chicken plate. He was a slim guy so he had the flexibility to reduce his 'vertical signature' in the front seat. He had already stowed the flex sight for the XM-28 turret. He was now ready to crash!"

"I still had the cyclic and collective in my hands and my feet were resting on the tail rotor pedals, but I was no longer flying other than to keep the fuselage more or less level. A cardinal and possibly mortal sin was for the Aircraft Commander to give up his command while his bird was still in the air, but we were both just passengers now."

"Moments later the inevitable impact occurred and it was violent to say the least. We were over the tall-treed jungle on the valley floor and struck the trees first. We didn't see them at the time of impact but we felt the tremendous jolts and heard the loud sounds of the helicopter chopping wood. We bounced off of the armor-plated sides of our seats as we were slammed around inside of our respective cockpits. Legs and arms flailed and heads whipped back and forth as the crash continued and the Cobra slammed down through the jungle. Along the way our rotation slowed or stopped and I actually saw a snap shot of tree trunks through the right front canopy. Then we flipped upside down and there was nothingness."

"John was yelling something. The turbine jet engine was screaming somewhere in the darkness behind me. We were motionless."

"Get out! Get out!" John was yelling at me. "It's going to catch fire! It's going to blow up! Mike, get out!"

"I was hanging upside down with my arms dangling. Our crashing had come to a stop. We were completely inverted, presumably resting on what remained of the fuselage, including the vertical fin at the end of the tail boom miraculously still attached to the main fuselage plus the transmission cowling and the cockpit framework."

"Apparently we did not hit the ground itself with great force. The effort spent chopping wood had consumed much of our impact energy. As a result, we escaped being crushed flat by the 9000 plus pounds of helicopter, fuel, weapons and unexpended ordnance that had come to rest above, with us hanging upside down underneath."

"I had been knocked unconscious sometime during the crash sequence when my head, still in my helmet, had been thrown back until it contacted the right rear armored plate of my seat. The force of the helmet striking the ceramic armor fractured the helmet and a portion of the blow transferred to my skull and I went to sleep, missing the final moments of our crash."

"John's shouting brought me back from wherever I had gone. I realized that he was not in the helicopter. His voice was coming to me from my right, but when I looked, he was not visible. The only thing I could see was a wall of dirt and debris. The Plexiglas of my canopy door was shattered and gone."

"The smell of fuel was strong. JP4 was draining out of the tanks somewhere and its familiar aroma filled my nose."

"The engine was still doing what it was supposed to do, with the battery and the fuel and the throttle still in their 'go' positions. As far as it was concerned, I still wanted it to churn and burn and it was doing its best to perform as requested. In retrospect, it is amazing that it stayed in its mounts and that all of its associated subsystems were still functioning as well as they apparently were."

"Sluggishly I struggled with the problem of how to do what John was urgently commanding me to do. I fumbled for my seat belt–shoulder harness buckle, trying to locate by feel the oversized knob at the end of the metal lever that would release my restraints, so that I could exit the aircraft."

"I found the seat belt lever, pulled it and fell several feet onto my head and shoulders into a creek bed full of running water and JP4 fuel. We had come to rest upside down in a creek bed that was banked on each side by steeply inclined walls of dirt and jungle growth. Whatever fuel we were losing was floating past the wreckage, past my cockpit, past my now soaked olive drab (OD) Nomex uniform. Fortunately, God kept blowing out the devil's matches and we had no fire."

"I didn't know if John could see me from wherever he was, presumably up on the bank to my right, but regardless, he was still yelling at me to get out of the Cobra. As I started to respond to him, I remembered the engine and felt the need to shut it down before I crawled out of the shattered cockpit."

"I looked up at my cockpit, trying to see and identify the switches that I needed to move in order to cut off the electricity and fuel to the engine's ignition and fuel control systems. I couldn't recognize anything by sight as my tinted visor was still down in front of my face and it was dark up in the portion of the cockpit where the switches were."

"I fumbled and searched by touch for the battery toggle switch and the fuel switch. I thought I found them and I moved each of them to what I thought was the OFF position.

Then I rolled off the throttle at last, telling the engine that I no longer needed it."

"I learned days later that I actually hadn't done any of those things. The rescuers found the battery and fuel were still on, the throttle was not fully closed, and the engine had been left running for a long time."

"Finally, I crawled out of the wreckage through what used to be my cockpit door, only this time I didn't have to open it. Once I had cleared the helicopter and started up the sloping bank, I could see John standing up on the bank urging me on. He appeared unharmed. Somehow, he had escaped being decapitated. Whether or not one or both of the blades swept through his cockpit on the way down, I forgot to ask and to this day, I do not know. He was alive and seemingly full of energy. He wanted me to get my butt up the bank so we could put some distance between us and the Cobra, still fully armed and nearly full of fuel. I scrambled to comply with his wishes."

"Once we had moved to the east of our crash site and were taking a breather at the base of a tall tree, we began to assess our predicament."

"Nearly everything that I had brought with me when we took off from Rendezvous was still back at the crash site. My M2 fully automatic .30 caliber WWII era carbine that I had cut down so that it was a machine pistol with no butt stock or forearm, my small OD canvas survival bag with its few cans of C-rations and extra M2 carbine magazines and boxes of .38 caliber ammo for my pistol, my 35mm camera, and as I looked down at the empty holster slung around my waist, I noticed my S&W .38 caliber revolver was missing too. Even my combat tactical map and survival knife were gone. Everything was back there in the wreckage."

"John's personal inventory was a little better than mine, mainly because he had successfully traded something to someone for an Air Force issue SRU-21P survival vest."

"When the Air Force issued vests to their Pilots, the multitude of zippered and Velcro-closed pockets scattered around the aramid mesh vest were filled to the bursting point with wonderful things a Pilot needs when he is trying to escape and evade after being shot down in a combat zone; a compass and map and first aid kits and matches and a signal mirror and emergency flares and an AN/ARC-90 survival radio, for instance."

"Unfortunately, John's version did not include many of those essential items and instead of bulging, the pockets of his vest were sadly very flat, at least most of them. He had a few miscellaneous items but no survival radio that would have allowed us to communicate on the UHF emergency guard frequency with our C&C bird and our Scout."

"John did have two important pieces of survival gear however, a 'Signal Kit, Foliage Penetrating' also known as the A/P-25 S-1 Signal Kit, Personal Distress or simply signal flares, and his Smith & Wesson .38 caliber revolver."

"If you are going to war, it's always a good idea to have a weapon. John had his .38. I had nothing, but I did have John."

"After we decided that we were indeed alive and except for a swollen lump on the back of my head, one battered knee and a small cut along my jaw line where the buckle of my helmet's chin strap had taken a hunk out of my skin, we were in good shape for the shape we were in."

"Then John realized that he was beginning to feel some pain in his face, from his lower jaw to be more precise. It was then that we discovered that his jaw was broken. He had kept his head, but had cracked his jawbone. As the shock of the crash progressively wore-off, the effect of the jaw injury progressed as well, but John didn't complain, he just stopped talking except to mumble through his clenched teeth."

"Faintly, we began to hear what seemed to be helicopters. The sound of rotor blades cutting through the air became more distinct, even at our level at the base of the tall trees with their overhead canopy. Our C&C and Scout birds must be flying back down the valley trying to figure out what had happened to us."

"We decided that one of us needed to climb a tree to the top of the canopy so that we could see the helicopters and signal them. If our crashed Cobra had caught on fire like we thought it was going to do, the ensuing fire, smoke and explosions would have been a perfect signal beacon for anyone interested in rescuing us, but it had not and I need to thank God more often for that fact."

"As I was starting up the tree, I thought to ask John how much .38 caliber ammunition he had in his vest. He looked up at me and shrugged. Opening the cylinder of his revolver he looked at it and then held it up so that I could see it as well. The open cylinder and the look on his face answered my question."

"We had six rounds. No more in the vest. Another of those flat pockets in John's vest where the Air Force jocks carried full boxes of ammo. I don't remember if I suggested to him that he save two of the rounds for us. At least he didn't have an empty chamber like the gunslingers of old used to have in their Colt Single Action Army revolvers. I think I told him to pick his shots if we suddenly came under ground attack. All four of them. He didn't laugh."

"So up the tree I went, leaving John to maintain our perimeter defense with his six rounds. I carried John's signal flares with me."

"For the record, the signal flare kit consisted of one metal, black finished, handheld launcher similar to a large fountain pen with seven red pyrotechnic flares, each of which would screw into one end of the launcher so that the operator, me, could pull back and then release the spring-loaded firing pin. The flare would then launch like a miniature red rocket, flying in the direction selected by the operator, again me, when I pointed the launcher. Certainly, at night, but even during daylight, the flares were supposed to provide a bright signal to anyone paying attention that someone at the opposite end of the rocket's flight path was in need of help."

"Fortunately, my selected tree had many branches growing closely enough together that I could move upward from one to another without any serious risk that I was going to fall out of the tree and leave John to fend for himself with only six cartridges and no flares."

"At last I climbed above the dense foliage. I was on top of the world! Not really, but I was on top of my tree. Orienting myself to the visual references surrounding me, I looked off to the north up the A Shau Valley and sure enough, there they were. Two helicopters, one UH-1 and one OH-6, flying in trail with the Scout in the lead and heading almost directly at me. I think I waved. They were too far away to see me. Even if they were closer, I was only a small white face on top of a body wearing an olive drab Nomex uniform, swinging in the top of a very green tree and surrounded by many, many more green trees."

"Watching my Scout bird grow larger and larger as he flew closer and closer, I saw that he was going to pass me off to the east. I pulled John's flares and launcher out of my pocket and quickly screwed one of the metal bodied flares into the launcher, making sure that the firing pin was set back against its spring in its safety notch, just enough rearward that it would not contact the flare's primer as I tightened the connection. I kept one eye on my Scout and one eye on the flare launcher as I completed my task."

"With the flare screwed in all the way and with my thumb on the firing pin release knob, I pointed the flare toward the Scout. I could see the Pilot and his Observer now, the Pilot through the right cockpit doorway since he was flying without doors installed, and the Observer through the left side windscreen. Both of them were looking down and around, their heads moving back and forth as they visually searched for us. I was reminded that they had no idea where we were and that they were retracing our previous flight path, the one we had taken after departing Rendezvous."

"I started to release the firing pin on the launcher, but stopped. I needed to aim the flare so that its little rocket motor would drive it across the flight path of the Scout. Having never fired one of the flares before, as this was Air Force standard issue and I was an Army Pilot, I wasn't sure what to expect when the flare launched and flew. How big would the visual signature be, I wondered, with no way of knowing until I fired the first flare. So be it. Launch that sucker!"

"With a bang, the flare launched and flew true, straight and normal, I guess. It went where I had pointed and it glowed red as it went right across the nose of the Scout, only neither of the guys saw it. They were still looking down and the flare crossed their flight path above their line of sight. At least I thought that is what happened, because as I waited for a reaction to my flare, I was surprised and disappointed that there was no reaction. None at all."

"One flare down and six to go. John and I now had exactly the same number of rounds left to fight the fight in case any of the bad guys, who had probably been watching us corkscrew into the jungle, decided to come find us before our friends did."

"I unscrewed the spent flare case and inserted a new one, working as quickly as I could while maintaining my perch in the top of the tree. Fortunately, I had fired the first flare while the Scout bird was still short of our position, but if I didn't hurry, he might fly past me before I could fire another flare. At the time, I wasn't even thinking about the C&C bird. I was totally focused on my Scout as he was supposed to be the eyes of the Pink Team."

"Again, I was ready to release the firing pin when I suddenly realized that if the Scout saw the red projectile flying past his cockpit, he might think it was a tracer and instinctively have the Observer return fire with his M60 machine gun or maybe he would turn into the direction from which the tracer came and light it up with his mini-gun. Neither possibility was encouraging, but neither was the thought of being lost in the jungle, missing in action, spending the night in the boonies, especially with John and his broken jaw."

"I launched another flare into the air, aimed a little lower than the first one but still across the front of the Scout bird as it continued toward our position. Same results, which is to say, no results. Neither crewmember indicated that they saw the flare fly by their nose."

"A couple more flares fired at different heights relative to the Scout's altitude and line of flight failed to signal anything except maybe my frustration, but I still had flares left and I knew I wouldn't get any points for saving them."

"Again, I hurriedly removed an empty flare casing and installed a new one."

"Again, I aimed the flare at the Scout, except this time I aimed the flare AT the Scout, directly at the Pilot as he sat in his seat doing his job trying to find us."

"I added a touch of lead to account for his velocity. I didn't actually want to hit him but I figured that even if I did, there wouldn't be enough energy to harm him, especially since he was wearing his helmet and chicken plate."

"With fingers mentally crossed, I fired and the flare flew directly at the Scout bird. I couldn't tell exactly, due to the range and angle, where the flare ended up. Whether it flew through the rear compartment of the Scout or maybe hit the fuselage or not, I couldn't see. For sure though it did not hit the Pilot. He did nothing to indicate that the flare came anywhere near him or that he saw it."

"The Scout flew past us heading further south and I considered firing another flare in case the C&C bird might see it, but I didn't. He was still to our north flying toward us and I would have been firing it toward his nose or straight up into the air. While the flare would be visible to me, I doubted it would be visible to Assault 6 or his crew."

"Suddenly a burst of automatic weapons fire ripped off over to our east. It did not sound like US fire, in fact, it sounded like an AK-47. I didn't see tracers but the sound seemed like the weapon was oriented to the north or northwest, and given that we were in a jungle and that the sound was clear and sharp, it seemed like the weapon was pointed upward. Don't know why, but that is the impression I had as I listened to the burst; only one, then silence. Maybe a single 30 round magazine. Don't know the who or the why or the target, but at the time, I remember wishing that I had my M2 with its 30 round banana magazines and that John had more than six cartridges. A dozen fragmentation grenades would have been nice as well!"

"I looked to the south and saw the Scout turning to his right. He was making a 180° turn and coming back!"

"Somewhere along the way, one of the crew apparently saw our crash site. Suddenly, I could see them both gesturing and pointing at an area over to our west, about where I thought we had left our Cobra."

"I came out of that tree like it was a greased pole without limbs. Telling John that the Scout had spotted our wreckage, I helped him to his feet and the two of us hurriedly made our way through the underbrush to the crash site. When we arrived, and stepped out of the trees, the Scout was hovering overhead already. The crew saw us. We saw them. John and I waved. They waved. We were suddenly happy campers."

"It occurred to me days later that before John and I walked out of the jungle, the Scout crew must have thought we were still in the wreckage since it was belly up to them and the cockpits were obscured from their view. I wished I had a recording of the radio traffic before and after their discovery that we were still among the living."

"The Observer signaled us to move to the west. Turns out we had crashed just to the east of Highway 548 which was a dirt road that ran north to south through the A Shau valley, hooking up to the Ho Chi Minh trail as it came into South Vietnam from Laos. They wanted us to reach the road so that they could land and pick us up."

"Following the Scout as he continued to hover over our heads as we moved away from the crash site, we eventually reached the edge of the jungle. When we broke out of the brush onto Highway 548, as predicted, the Scout landed so that we could climb on board. I indicated that I wanted the left front seat, the Observer's position, and he got out and climbed into the back of the OH-6 along with John. I strapped into the front seat and seconds later we were airborne. As we climbed to altitude and started a turn to the east, I advised Assault18 that we had had automatic weapons fire to the east of our crash site. He adjusted his flight path to avoid the area I was indicating by pointing through his windscreen."

"I don't remember the specific radio conversation with Assault 6 as we flew out of the valley that day, or the cockpit chatter during the 30-minute flight back to the 18th Surgical Hospital at Camp Evans where our Scout dropped John and me off. I do know that we were both grateful for the rescue and disappointed that we had left a relatively new AH-1G Cobra upside down in the A Shau Valley."

"As a side note, at the time we crashed that day, our Cobra was the first and only air-conditioned Cobra received by A Troop. It was a totally new helicopter, fresh from Bell Textron and having that air conditioner was like winning the lottery."

"Riding in that air-conditioned Cobra was a wonderful relief from the heat and humidity of South East Asia. The AC could get so cold that, with the 100% humidity, it would spit tiny snow balls at you from the air ducts along the edges of our instrument panels, a feature that we liked to show off to our fellow aviators in their non-air conditioned UH-1s, OH-6s, and AH-1s as we flew alongside them and profiled with our visors down and big grins on our faces, complaining that we were afraid we were going to get frostbite."

"Oh, did I mention that the AC blew cold air through our seat cushions? Yes, a whole new meaning to the term 'frosted balls'."

"Now I had gone and demolished the primo bird in our fleet of Snakes. Not a way to win friends but fortunately they were a forgiving bunch of Aviation Brothers."

"Someone once said that any landing that you could walk away from was a good landing, especially if it was a crash landing. Maybe so or maybe not."

"Regardless, it turned out to be a hell of a September day."

"Post Script: Several days later I learned that John was Medevaced out of country due to his jaw injury. We never flew together again. Considering how things worked out, he probably thought that was a good thing. I heard years later that he had left the Service and had become a Minister. I wondered if our experience on the floor of the A Shau Valley had anything to do with his 'conversion' from a life-loving, sometimes-rowdy, always joking Army Helicopter Pilot to a man of the Lord."

"Oh, remember my M2 carbine, S&W revolver, camera etc.? Well, the Pilot of Assault 6's UH-1, I think it was Ed Bobilya, found all of that stuff in the creek under my cockpit when he and the Old Man landed to take a look at the aircraft before they blew everything in place. All of my personal items had fallen out of the cockpit and into the water. Being the kind, thoughtful Aviator Brother that he was, he recovered everything and then cleaned it, including my Pentax Spotmatic 35mm SLR camera. When I returned to the Troop after a short stay at the 18th Surg, he presented me with the items explaining that he was sorry but the film in the camera was lost to the water, but that the shutter seemed to have dried out OK. Even my guns were clean and oiled. Wherever he is today, I hope God has blessed him for his kindness way back then."

"By the way, he was the guy who actually shut down the engine of my Cobra. Throttle closed, fuel off, battery off. I am sure that engine was happy to finally go to sleep. It had given its all to keep us in the air that day, but it couldn't do it by itself." Mike concluded.

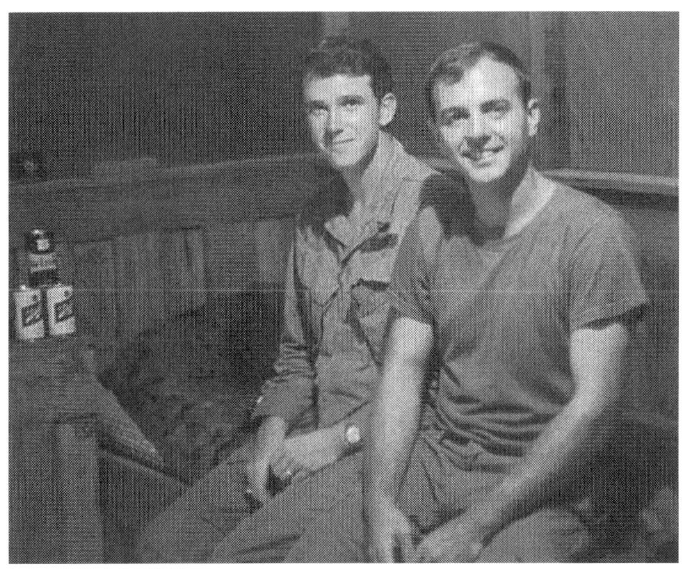

David Walls and Mike Talton, Assault 27.

Lew Jennings, Assault 23, Takin' A Break while Mike Ryan, Assault 18, makes coffee!

CHAPTER EIGHTEEN

MAI LOC

As the monsoon season dragged on into winter, A Troop left the A Shau on 29 September to begin conducting operations up near the demilitarized zone or DMZ at a Special Forces camp called Mai Loc. We staged our Loaches and Cobras there, as well as our Hueys and the Blue Platoon of Infantry. It was a dirt strip with a small Special Forces camp enclosed with rows of concertina wire.

Our missions varied from day to day at Mai Loc. Reconnaissance missions out on the Khe Sanh plain to the Laotian border. Search missions of the craggy cliffs, caves and mountainous terrain along the DMZ. And Ready Reaction Force for downed aircraft.

We had limited logistical support at Mai Loc and used more extensive support facilities at the former Marine base at Quang Tri about 20 minutes away for rearming, refueling and maintenance.

It was the fall of 1969. General Westmoreland was back in Washington D.C. as the Army Chief of Staff. General Creighton Abrams had replaced Westmoreland as

Commander, Military Assistance Command Vietnam (MACV).

The Marines had been moved south and most of the famous bases and sights of past bloody battles in northern I Corps had been abandoned; Khe Sanh, Vandergrift, Rockpile, Carol and others.

Lyndon Johnson was gone. The bombing of North Vietnam had been halted. Nixon was President. US force reduction had started. Peace talks were underway in Paris.

That did not for a second deter the NVA from continuing to build up their forces and prepare for further offensive operations in the south.

Now it was our turn to detect and try to stop their infiltration across the DMZ from the north and Laos from the west, as the III Marine Amphibious Forces and Army's 1st Cavalry Division had done the year before.

We were a relatively tiny force with a huge mission and little support. "If you ain't Cav you ain't shit," as the saying goes. "Out Front" was our motto and here we were, out front again. Just as we liked it.

Captain Don McGurk had taken over command of the Blues from Lou Herrick several months earlier. Calm, reserved and focused would describe Don. He was a true professional and courageous beyond belief.

It was 9 October 1969. We had been up at Mai Loc just a week or two. Don and the Blues were camped with an Infantry Battalion from the 3rd Brigade of the 101st Airborne inside a temporary perimeter they had established across the dirt runway from the Special Forces camp. The Blues had received a mission to conduct a search and destroy patrol in the mountainous area of the DMZ. The troops gathered for the

Mission Brief while the helicopter crews manned the Hueys that would be used to insert them in a landing zone just south of the DMZ, at the base of the mountains.

The Hueys cranked up, the troops loaded aboard, our Cobras were ready along with our Scout birds, as we all checked in on the radio and took off as one in a formation of 11; six Hueys, two Cobras, two Scouts and our new Boss, Major Tom Trombley, in the Command and Control (C&C) Huey. Trombley had taken over the Command of the Troop from Curtin back in late July.

We in the Cobras and Scouts flew out in front of the formation. It took just 15 minutes or so to get to the landing zone. The Scouts went in first to check for any enemy activity in the immediate vicinity of the LZ and mark it with colored smoke grenades for the inbound Hueys as the two Cobras circled on either side in a race track pattern to cover insertion of the troops.

The LZ was cold and the troops established a hasty defense as they exited the Hueys and the aircraft departed the area. The Cobras and Scouts continued aerial reconnaissance of the surrounding area as Don and his Platoon Sergeant led the patrol towards the base of the mountain to begin their reconnaissance mission.

"We came upon an area of high cliffs with several cave entrances, maybe four or five at the base of the cliffs," Don McGurk recalled.

"From the base, there was a slope of about 50 or 60 yards, covered in large boulders and various upright and felled trees. At the bottom of the slope was a path and adjacent to that was a dry creek bed or ravine," he explained.

"I left two Squads in the ravine to cover our approach to the caves and led the remainder of the Blues up the slope to the first cave entrance on the left. When we arrived at that entrance we stepped in and looked around but did not explore back into the cave. I left two men at the cave entrance to cover our backs as the rest of us moved along the base to look into the remainder of the cave entrances."

"About the third cave down, all hell broke loose. The Squads in the ravine were firing up to the cave entrances, tree branches were breaking and rounds were zinging off boulders."

"My RTO (Radio Telephone Operator) was crouched next to me. The PRC-47 radio crackled with the sounds of the guys calling and warning us the NVA were coming out of cave entrances behind us."

"I ordered all the men with me to move down the slope immediately to the ravine while I radioed for air support," he continued. "The enemy had gotten up on the cliffs and were lobbing hand grenades down on us as we moved. Luckily the shrapnel from the exploding grenades was deflected by the many rather large boulders on the slope."

"After getting to the ravine I was told that one of the two men left at the first cave entrance was KIA. I called again for air support, however no one responded to my call. I later found out that all the aircraft were back at Quang Tri refueling and no one had relieved the Pink Teams on station to provide continuous coverage."

"I took my RTO and one other trooper and climbed back up the slope to the two troopers at the first cave entrance to see what was going on for myself and support my troopers. It was true, Leon Trecinski had been killed. We each grabbed an arm or a leg and carried him down to the ravine. By the time we were all back in the ravine and preparing for some type of enemy attack, the aircraft had returned, fired up the area and got the bad guys off our backs. Leon was airlifted out and the remainder of us were then extracted and returned to Base Camp."

Lew here again. We all felt the pain of Leon's death and resolved to do a better job for our heroes carrying a rucksack and a rifle, as Don continued his story.

"Less than a week later I received orders to return to the caves with the Blues and an additional aircraft full of engineers," he related. "Higher Headquarters wanted the engineers to blow the cave entrances."

"We went back, all was quiet and the majority of the Blues remained in the ravine to cover the engineers moving up to the entrances. They placed their explosives, returned to the ravine and detonated the dynamite or C-4. After the smoke cleared there was nothing, no sign of any damage at all."

"The engineers went to go back up the slope and about halfway, there was a delayed reaction from the explosions as very large chunks of rock started falling from the cliff and rolling down the slope. Those engineers moved pretty fast down that slope back to the ravine. They agreed with me there was not much more we could do here and we called for extraction. We had no more dealings with those caves but we all had lasting memories of the NVA tossing grenades down on us and losing Leon."

As usual, Don was on the last bird out of the LZ.

We continued to fly out of Mai Loc the rest of October. It was wet and rainy with low clouds across the Khe Sanh plain. The higher ground to the south and the mountains of the DMZ to the north were nearly always obscured by clouds. We ran into small pockets of enemy troops, usually engineers out improving roads and trails. No major enemy activity though, as they seemed to be hindered by the bad weather as much as we were.

Mike Talton was up to his usual antics, from one near disaster to the next. As if his tail rotor failure in the A Shau wasn't enough excitement to last a lifetime.

This time he was flying a reconnaissance mission, boring holes in the sky without much of a care in the world, when he noticed that one of his 17- pound high-explosive warheads had come unscrewed from its rocket motor and was precariously hanging out of its tube in the rocket pod.

Mike related the story to me.

"To the casual Observer, it might not seem to be very important that the warhead was hanging out there almost free and clear, but not quite. To a steely-eyed, icy-nerved, combat-seasoned Cobra Pilot such as myself, that hanging warhead was a serious problem."

"Because it was in the number one tube, it meant that it and its soul mate in the number one tube over in the inboard rocket pod, attached to the left wing, would be the first rockets fired if I had to fire rockets using the inboard pods," he continued to explain.

"As soon as the right-hand rocket motor ignited and flew out of the number one tube, it would push the warhead out of the tube, maybe, and then it would be trapped inside the tube with all of its hot exhaust gases and flames heating up and eventually melting through the thin cylindrical wall of the rocket tube."

"Call me a pessimist or label me a paranoiac, it seemed to me that there was a good chance that the motor would succeed in burning its way into the surrounding tubes, all six of them, each of which held a rocket motor just like the one that would be setting the world on fire. Of course, I could then jettison the inboard pods, both of them, but call me Mr. Negative, because in my mind's eye I could see a color video of that burning pod doing a slow tumble in flight and somehow talking one or more of those adjacent rockets, complete with their warheads still screwed into their motor bodies, into igniting and giving me an E-Ticket Ride to the Pearly Gates."

"Even if the rocket motor was successful in pushing the tipped warhead out of the tube without causing a catastrophe in the process," he continued, "the motor would then become an unbalanced, self-propelled spear that had an open tube facing into its relative wind. Where it would go after flying out of the tube would be anybody's guess, but my guess was that it would fly up into the main rotor blades and then we were going to have a really bad day. No glass half full for me!"

"Sure, I could just not use the inboard tubes in case we got into a fire fight," he admitted, "but a Cobra Pilot has a really hard time convincing himself to carry 38 rockets to the fight and then not use them. Besides, who could predict that we wouldn't need those 38 rockets (make that 37 rockets, since one had decided to check out of the net)!"

"Looking at that hanging warhead again, I decided to shake it loose and then take my chances that the motor without a warhead would find its way out beyond rotor blades, IF I had to shoot it."

"I called my Scout up off of his tree top recon, briefly told him to take up a trail position on me and to stay at an altitude above the range of most ground fired weapons and then began a series of WAMs (wild-ass-maneuvers) in an attempt to shake the warhead loose. I tried rapidly induced cyclic dives, standing the Cobra on its nose, followed by rapid cyclic climbs, standing it on its tail. The warhead stubbornly stayed in place. If it moved at all, I didn't see it happen."

"Next I tried steeply nose low attitudes combined with quick up and down pumps of the collective in an attempt to cause a vertical vibration that might shake it loose. Still nothing, except that I think my front seat Copilot was getting a little airsick."

"Finally, I surrendered. The warhead had bonded to the rocket pod tube. They were now one. It was time for some drastic action."

"For those wondering why we didn't just land and remove the warhead by hand, or even screw it back into the rocket motor after landing, since a 17-pound warhead sticks out of the tube far enough to grip and turn it, the easy answer is that we were in the Land of the Bad Guys. There were no friendlies within thousands of meters, make that miles and miles for those of you who don't do metric, except for the Copilot in my front seat and the two guys in the Scout bird. If we landed and then the NVA decided to pop up out of the ground or jump out of the jungle or maybe even lob a few mortar rounds over to us, my front seat and I could become permanent residents of South Vietnam soil and our poor burnt out Cobra would become a permanent monument to a bad decision that I would likely reconsider as I sat at the feet of

Saint Peter, explaining why as an Army Aviator I deserved special dispensation."

"Landing to fix it was not an option," Mike emphasized.

"Time for outside of the box thinking, or out of the cockpit as it were. I gave control of the Cobra to my front seat, telling him to slow the aircraft to 40-45 knots indicated airspeed as specified by the Operator's Manual for opening a cockpit door in flight."

"He didn't argue when I explained that I planned to exit my cockpit and attempt to dislodge the warhead with a well-placed kick. I confirmed to him that I had to unplug my helmet and would not be able to communicate while outside the cockpit. Fortunately, he and I were friends, so I was fairly confident he would hold the helicopter steady, maintaining straight and level flight, resisting any temptation to wiggle the cyclic or bounce the collective just for grins."

"With our Scout following behind us (hopefully with his map across his lap in case someone needed to mark the spot where I impacted) and both aircraft above 1500 feet ground level to avoid enemy small arms fire, I unstrapped my shoulder harness and lap belt, opened my cockpit door and with an admonishment to my Copilot to remain cool, unplugged my helmet and carefully worked my way out of the cockpit. Piece of cake, I thought. Same as being on the ground, except that we weren't."

"Moments later I was standing outside in the wind with one foot on the little right-side fuselage step and the other on the step located on the front of the right skid tube. I hung onto the fuselage at the rear of my now empty cockpit and dared not look down at the ground far below."

"Exhilarating. Yeah, that's what it was! Exhilarating!"

"After studying the warhead for what was probably a few seconds but what may have seemed like hours to my Copilot, I decided that I had to stand on the small step at the front of the skid tube and use my other leg to reach for the warhead until I could touch it with the toe of my boot, maintaining all the while a one-handed death grip on the cockpit framework. I had never thought much about the advantages of being eight feet tall, but at that moment, five feet eleven inches seemed like a woefully short height when hanging onto the side of a flying helicopter with one leg stretched out to its physical limits."

"Reaching, reaching, stretching, stretching. There at last, as the tip of my jungle boot slid for the briefest of moments under the tip of the warhead right at the fuze, I flexed my foot and raised my toe and lo and behold, the warhead moved. It actually moved. It moved upward, until I could level it and then coax it out, very slowly, just enough to help gain its freedom. Away it fell as I recovered my leg and foot to the relative safety of the fuselage step beneath my cockpit door."

"I watched the warhead fall, its OD color fading from view during the last moments of its terminal flight to earth, blending into the greenish-brown terrain below me. If only there had been something for it to fall into. Even if it wasn't armed and couldn't blow anything up, it would have been a nice surprise for an NVA soldier to have it come crashing through the roof of his hidden bunker. Heck, maybe it did!"

"After I crawled back into my cockpit, I plugged my helmet into the intercom and advised my Copilot that I was back and the mission was a success. I closed my canopy and strapped into my seat. Then took the controls, advised our Scout that we were good to go, checked the time and our fuel and declared the mission complete, for that fuel load at least."

Mike "Warhead" Talton, Assault 27, Aviator extraordinaire! On call for rocket warhead removal anytime, anywhere, at any altitude and the purveyor of heart attacks for his Copilots. He became a legend among us in Alpha Troop!

As we were winding up operations out of Mai Loc in November, a very interesting and mysterious mission came in for the Blues.

One of our Scouts on a first light early morning recon discovered what seemed to be the lost wreckage of a Marine OV-10 Bronco twin-turboprop airplane on the very top of a mountain. The clouds had parted at sunrise at just the right moment to reveal the crash site. The Blues were called in to investigate, identify and recover any remains of the Pilot and Copilot.

This peak was covered in clouds most of the day except for a couple of hours right after sunrise, which might explain why it had not been found for the past one to two years.

Don McGurk relates the story.

"I was called in to Battalion Operations and briefed that the long-lost aircraft should have two Pilots and sensitive radio gear in the back. The S3 (Operations Officer) and CO of the Battalion wanted me to take my Blues onto the mountaintop and retrieve what we could. I asked to recon the area first with one of our Scouts, which we did the next morning. I returned to brief the S3 and told him there was no practical LZ up there. Also, even if we did get there, I could not realistically get everyone out in case of enemy activity."

"I suggested a plan to have myself and three others rappel into the area to complete the mission. If there was enemy activity, the Huey could fly in with the rope ladders extended and we could hook ourselves onto the ladders and be extracted. They accepted the plan and we executed it the next day."

"My RTO and Chief Warrant Officer Tom June, who was acting as an Assistant Platoon Leader and who eventually took over the Blues when I left around the end of November 1969 and one other trooper volunteered for the mission with me."

"Mark Stevens was the Huey Pilot and did an extraordinary job of hovering on that mountaintop while we rappelled in. My RTO and I took care of searching the aircraft while Tom and the other trooper did a recon of the surrounding area and provided security."

"We found only one body in the airplane. His weapon was missing as well as the emergency kit, so we can only assume that the other Pilot lived and tried to escape and evade back to friendly lines. He was still listed as MIA (Missing in Action) at this time."

"We placed the one Pilot in a body bag and put the equipment in the other bag. Mark flew back in with the Huey for our extraction, just as clouds were starting to form and obscure the mountaintop again. My RTO climbed the ladder first, I went up second and Tom and the other trooper hooked themselves onto the ladder with D-Rings, along with the two bags. Mark somehow managed to get us through the clouds to the valley below, landed and got everyone inside the Huey and then departed to return to Base Camp. He and his Copilot and crew did a super job of getting us off that mountain. At least we had recovered one fallen Marine for God, Country and his folks back home."

We wrapped up operations at Mai Loc by mid-November and Alpha Troop headed back south to Camp Eagle for more missions in the A Shau Valley and surrounding area. We would return a short time later to operate out of nearby Quang Tri.

The Special Forces Camp at Mai Loc came under attack six months later, resulting in 20 KIA. US Special Forces left the Camp in August 1970 and it was eventually abandoned completely by the Vietnamese Army when the NVA crossed the DMZ, attacking Quang Tri city and the surrounding province in April 1972.

Don McGurk On Patrol

Marine Corps and Air Force OV-10 Broncos & Stairway to Heaven

CHAPTER NINETEEN

HEAVEN'S SWING

It was late in the afternoon on a gloomy November day when I received word to report to the Tactical Operations Center (TOC). I was resting on my bunk in the hooch I shared with Mike Talton. I had been up since 4 a.m. as I had already flown the first-light reconnaissance mission out to the A Shau and had returned earlier in the day.

It was 26 November 1969 and by now I had flown over 500 combat missions during my tour in Vietnam. Only a couple more months, a few hundred more missions and I would get to go home. Having flown the first light reconnaissance, I was supposed to have the rest of the day off. Something bad must have happened if I was being called up to the TOC.

I quickly donned my gear, pulling a heavy bulletproof vest we called a "chicken plate" down over my head and jungle fatigue shirt and cinched the body armor over my chest with Velcro straps.

Next was a survival vest containing some signal flares, signal mirror, first aid kit, strobe light, flashlight and a few survival items like matches and fishing line in case we got shot down or crashed.

Then I strapped on my trusty .38 caliber pistol; a revolver that wasn't good for much of anything except a false sense of security. I carried it in a "John Wayne" western style holster and belt. Before I would get in the aircraft, I would swivel the belt around so that the holster and pistol covered my crotch giving some "additional" protection.

Last was my "Ballistic" helmet, an experimental flying helmet that supposedly was strong enough to deflect small arms fire, bullets smaller than a fifty-caliber round.

I grabbed my water jug and a box of C-rations on the way out of the hooch. It's always above a hundred degrees in that enclosed Cobra Plexiglas canopy if there's any sunlight at all, so I carried lots of water even though it was cool and rainy today, remnants of the monsoon season in Vietnam.

And we'll probably miss chow tonight at the mess hall so the C's will come in handy. Hopefully I made a good choice, like beans and franks.

In my haste, I didn't have time to pick and choose. Please Lord, just so it isn't beef and potatoes or tuna or scrambled eggs. I didn't want to look.

My Copilot that day was Stan Shearin. He had been alerted to ready our aircraft for an urgent mission as I headed towards the Operations bunker.

Mark Stevens joined me from the Lift Platoon. The Slick Pilots were famous guys in their own right, flying UH-1 Huey workhorses that could carry up to 10 soldiers and did everything; haul troops, food, ammo, beer, wounded, body bags, Generals, Privates, and even celebrities like Bob Hope. Anything, everything, anytime, anywhere.

Mark and I entered the bunker together and stooped low under the corrugated steel roof as we made our way past the piles of stacked sandbags and towards the sounds of crackling radios. We emerged into a small room filled with stale cigarette smoke and surrounded by maps of our Area of Operations, Mission Status Boards showing who was up flying, where they were located, and what unit they were supporting, Aircraft Status Boards indicating what aircraft were available and which ones were down for maintenance or had been destroyed by enemy fire or accident, and the SITREP Board indicating the date, time and short summary of the latest Situation Reports sent in by our own reconnaissance teams. This was the heartbeat and communications center for the unit.

Dick Melick had been promoted to Captain and was now the Troop Operations Officer running the TOC. Staff Sergeant Sanders was the Operations Sergeant and Melick's right-hand man.

"The 75th Rangers have a team in trouble somewhere in the mountains out towards Blaze," Sergeant Sanders said, as he started in on our Mission Brief and pointed to one of the maps.

"You and Mr. Stevens are to go out and find the team," Sarge continued. "They have been in contact with the enemy for six days and have run out of food, water and ammo and are suffering from exposure in this monsoon weather. On top of that, they're lost and can't give us exact coordinates. You need to find them and get 'em out! Here's your Mission Sheet with their frequencies and call sign."

The 75th Rangers were a band of courageous guys, specially trained in clandestine operations to find and fix the enemy with small Long Range Reconnaissance Patrol Teams (LRRPs) or simply “Lerps”. L Company lived next door to us back at Camp Eagle and we trained with them in helicopter operations to drop them into the jungle or pluck them out of tight spots with the use of ropes; long 120-foot lines called simply “strings” with a McGuire Rig attached.

The McGuire Rig was invented by Sergeant Major Charles T. McGuire of Project Delta Special Operations fame. It was an 8-foot long cargo strap, doubled over to form a large loop with a quick-fit buckle at one end and a smaller loop at the top for a wrist strap. The Rig was lowered down to the waiting soldier who would step into the larger loop, grab the wrist strap and be lifted out by the helicopter and when clear, be landed nearby for loading inside the Huey.

It was a simple system, however could not be used for long distances or with wounded personnel without undue danger of them falling from the Rig.

Later, the Army would develop the STABO (Short Tactical Air Borne Operations) harness. That harness, worn outside the fatigue uniform, provided loops to attach snap links for quick hook up to rescue lines which had loops built in as well. The STABO harness allowed rapid extraction of troops while also freeing their hands and arms to provide self-protection. Wounded soldiers could be snapped onto the rescue lines without danger of falling off.

Mark and I looked at the Mission Sheet and then at each other. The Team’s call sign was “Coca Cola”. It was already late afternoon, darkness a few hours away and low clouds in the mountains. We had to find them and we had to do it quick.

Mark had already preflighted his bird as he was on standby that day. His Copilot, Crew Chief and Door Gunner were already up on the flight line waiting for him. My Cobra Gunship was all ready to go too, since I had returned from the earlier reconnaissance mission and Stan had the blades untied and ready for start. We were up and airborne in less than ten minutes.

We flew a loose trail formation, one behind the other up Highway 547, the winding dirt road carved in the mountains by Army engineers that wound its way from the coastal plains near Hue and the 101st Airborne Division's Base at Camp Eagle to the A Shau Valley some 40 miles distant. I was flying my AH-1 Cobra Gunship. Mark was flying his UH-1H Huey.

We flew low past Firebase Bastogne at an altitude less than 100 feet to avoid their artillery gunfire and continued out towards Firebase Blaze en route to our objective, a small valley to the south at the base of a ridgeline where we hoped to establish contact with the beleaguered team. We squeezed under some low clouds settling on the higher ridges and arrived at our destination a few minutes later.

"Coca Cola, Coca Cola, this is Assault 23," I called on our fox-mike (FM) radio that was on the same frequency that the Team was operating. Mark was listening in from his Huey as we circled in the punch bowl of the valley with the surrounding mountains obscured by mist and clouds.

"Coca Cola, Coca Cola, Assault 23," I called again as we strained to hear any word from the Team.

My Cobra had been topped off with fuel and loaded with rockets, minigun ammo and grenades ready to defend Mark and rescue our comrades. The problem was, I was so heavy that I had to fly in continuous circles because if I let my airspeed drop below 30 miles per hour, my over-loaded

Gunship would merely run out of power and settle to the ground. And maybe not in one piece! So around and around the punch bowl we flew in low, lazy circles trying to make contact with the LRRPs.

"Coco Cola, Coca Cola, this is Assault 23," I tried again and again. After about 15 minutes, Mark called over to me. "23 this is 43, let me try flying up these ravines that are surrounding us and see if I can make contact with the Team. I'll take it nice and slow and keep you posted."

Man, that was definitely a dangerous idea. Flying up into those blind canyons, into the clouds, no altitude to speak of and little airspeed in bad-guy country was a recipe for disaster. But Mark was right, we didn't have a choice; the weather was closing in and darkness would soon be upon us.

"Roger that. I'll wait down here in the valley for you," was all I could say.

Mark started up the first ravine and disappeared into the clouds within seconds. "Coco Cola, Coca Cola this is Assault 43," he called. No answer. "Coca Cola, Coca Cola, this is Assault 43." Again, no answer.

"I'm coming back down. You should see me in a minute," Mark said as he slowly appeared out of the mist and continued descending into the valley.

"I'll try that ridge line further to the west to see if they might be up there," he radioed and spun off in that direction, as I continued circling.

"Coca Cola, Coca Cola, this is Assault 43," I heard Mark transmitting as he disappeared in the distance.

All of a sudden, we heard, "Assault 43, this is Coca Cola." It was an urgent whisper but sounded like a scream in our headsets. "We're in bad trouble here and need immediate extraction!" You could almost taste the terror in that voice.

I heard Mark's unusually calm reply, "Coca Cola, Assault 43, can you give me your location and number of souls over?"

"Assault 43, Coca Cola, there's five of us and we are on top of a ridgeline; we don't know our exact location," the strained voice replied. "We need to be extracted immediately, we're out of ammo and still in contact."

"Coca Cola, 43, we need to know where you guys are at. Can you hear my rotor blades, over?" Mark responded. The Huey is notorious for the noise it makes, as any Vietnam Vet can attest.

"No, we can't hear you and we don't know where we are, except that we are on top of a ridgeline in the clouds."

"Okay," Mark replied. "We are down in the valley below you. Just find a ravine or a creek bed and follow it downhill in a northerly direction and we'll find you".

I knew exactly what Mark was thinking, as if he had all the answers and it would be a piece of cake, but that's exactly what the Team needed to hear to give them hope. Mark's advice would get them headed downhill and hopefully towards us, so we would have a better chance of finding them.

A few minutes later Coca Cola called back; "We've found a stream bed and are following it downhill. Are you guys still there?"

"Yup, we're still here," Mark replied. "Give me a long count, one to ten, and I'll home in on your signal," Mark instructed.

Army helicopters were equipped with a special electronic device in the cockpit made for situations just like this one. As the LRRP Team transmitted on their radio, Mark could turn his helicopter until the needle lined up on the homing instrument on his panel to let him know the direction to the team. He got a good lock on the signal and his nose was pointing right at one of the ravines ahead of him.

"23, I'm heading up into this ravine with the creek bed to see if I can make contact with them," Mark advised.

"Roger that," was again about all I could say as he slowly disappeared up the ravine and into the clouds. I wouldn't be there to cover him if he ran into trouble.

"Keep talking to me on VHF and I'll also monitor fox mike," I said. The VHF was our "Company" radio to talk to each other. We had three different radios going at any one time; FM to talk to the ground guys like Coca Cola, UHF or ultra-high frequency to talk to the air guys like Air Traffic Control, Air Force, or Navy, and VHF or very high frequency to talk to each other on a dedicated air-to-air frequency just for us.

"I'm heading up into the ravine. I can't see forward at all 'cause of the clouds, but I can see the tree tops through the chin bubble and will just keep hopping up the creek bed, tree top to tree top. If we find them, we'll drop the strings and bring 'em out two or three at a time."

Strings were those 60 to 120-foot ropes the Hueys carried on board to drop ammo and supplies into the jungle, rappel troops to the ground when there was not a prepared landing zone available, or rescue people when in tight spots; mostly our own aircrews when they got shot down or ground troops like the LRRPs of L Company, 75th Rangers in this case. They had McGuire Rigs attached to the ends.

Mark had a half load of fuel on board and could only handle two or three people at a time dangling from those long lines yet still have enough power to hover. We had terrible memories of a recent accident when too many LRRP's scrambled onto the lines during a combat rescue and literally dragged one of our Hueys out of the air with their own weight, causing the ship to crash and killed one of the courageous guys we were trying to rescue. We wouldn't let that happen today, if we could get to them before the enemy did or darkness that, combined with this lousy weather, would cause us to have to abort the mission completely.

"Assault 43, Assault 43," the excited voice called over the radio. "We can hear you, we can hear you," the Ranger said between gasps for air. "We're running down the creek bed towards the noise, looking for you!"

Mark's hunch had paid off!

A few minutes later, Mark's cool, collected voice came over the radio.

"I have you in sight and we're dropping strings. I can only take a few out at a time. Only two people this time out. I repeat, only two people on the strings this time. I'll shuttle two of you down the mountain and come back to get the others," he repeated.

"23, can you give me a long count? We're coming out." Mark radioed. He was so calm, it was unnerving. "I'll be on instruments, so let me know when you have a visual."

I couldn't believe what I just heard! I instantly knew what Mark was going to try and do. He had turned the Huey around, facing downhill, with the canyon walls on either side and two Rangers hooked onto his strings dangling far below. He would have to pull them straight up at least 200 feet, to clear the trees, using every last reserve of horsepower from the engine, while flying blind in the clouds with granite on both sides. Unbelievable!

He noted the exact heading that he thought would take them safely out. He had requested a long count from me on the FM radio to home in on my signal to bring him out to the valley. He then proceeded to do a blind instrument takeoff straight up into the clouds, so the Rangers dangling below would clear the treetops and not drag them all back into the streambed below.

I flew directly toward the ravine into which he had disappeared. It had seemed like hours since I had last seen him. I started counting slowly on the FM radio; "one, two, three, four, five, six, seven, eight, niner, ten, niner, eight, seven, six, five, four, three, two, one, long count over," straining to see if they would come into sight.

And there they were! Two bodies appeared above me dangling out of the clouds as if on an invisible swing from heaven. No aircraft, no ropes visible, just two bodies swinging below the clouds!

"43, you're clear!" I yelled. "You're clear! Come on down!"

With that, Mark's Huey descended like a butterfly from the overcast sky and fluttered to the ground, gently settling the Rangers in the elephant grass of the valley floor.

As the LRRPs extricated themselves from the strings, Mark called me. "I'll head back up for the rest of the Team, keep an eye-out, will you?" he called. And immediately disappeared into the mist once again.

Mark repeated the same operation all over again to get the remaining members of the Team out. It was as exciting and breathtaking as the first time, with the rangers swinging from the clouds on strings provided by Alpha Troop, 2nd Squadron, 17th Cavalry.

We were low on fuel and darkness was falling as we flew out of the valley through a dip in a ridgeline and headed towards the nearest refueling point at Firebase Bastogne just a few minutes away.

As soon as we landed and with the ships still running as we started hot refueling, one of the LRRPs jumped out of the Huey and ran around to the front to shake Mark's hand. He and the others still inside the Huey all turned towards my Cobra and gave me a big thumbs-up. Their smiles were like sparkling sunshine amid the dirt, grime and camouflage that covered their bodies. All of us had lumps in our throats. It had been a great day.

On January 25, 1970 Mark Stevens was awarded the Distinguished Flying Cross for his heroic actions and would forever remain a hero to me.

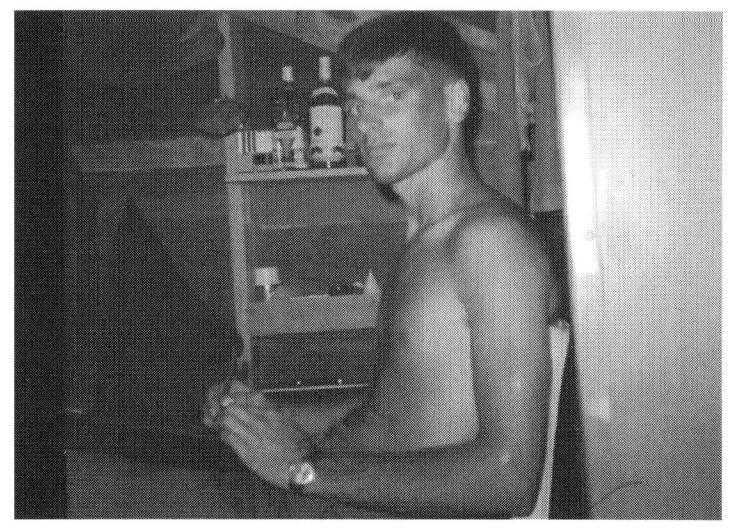

Mark Stevens, Assault 43 and Mark`s Huey below.

CHAPTER TWENTY

RECON RESCUE

It was a few days before Christmas on 22 December when our CO, Major Tom Trombley, burst into our hooch just before midnight.

"A Marine Corps Recon team on the eastern ridge out in the A Shau has been attacked by an unknown size enemy force and is in danger of being overrun. There's a low overcast cloud condition and no other aviation unit wants to challenge the weather to help them out. I need two volunteer Gun Pilots to help rescue those guys. Jennings, Talton, you are the most experienced Aircraft Commanders in the unit. What do you say? I need volunteers now!"

What do you say? "Yes, sir! Three bags full! Let's kick the tires and light the fires and head to the A Shau!" At least that's what I thought we said as we grabbed our gear and headed to the flight line.

I think Stan Shearin was my Copilot. I don't remember who was flying with Mike Talton. We checked in on the unit frequency as soon as we were up and running.

The CO was flying his Huey. The plan was for him to fly out first and climb up and through the overcast cloud layer. He would call when he was safely on top and then we would take off individually to join him. Once all of us were together above the clouds, we would be directed by radar out to the A Shau Valley and, when the radar folks told us we were over the center of the valley, would descend back down through the clouds and search for the Recon team.

What could go wrong with that?

The first problem was that none of us were well trained in "instrument flying" where you rely solely on your instruments to fly the aircraft. It would be required of us to safely fly in the clouds and darkness to the A Shau.

"No problem, you are professionals," the Boss emphasized.

If we survived the climb through the clouds without losing control, the second problem was to find the Boss and join up with him. He said he would keep his lights on for us.

"No sweat," he commented.

Once we joined up, the third problem was spiraling down through the clouds in the middle of the night trusting the radar guys were correct and hoping we would break out of the clouds before hitting the ground or surrounding mountains.

"Piece of cake," he described it.

And then, once we were below the clouds and in the A Shau, how to find the friendly Team in the dark and be able to provide close air support to save them without getting shot down or crashing into the mountain.

"That's what we get paid the big bucks for," he concluded. Around $400 a month, as I recall!

The Boss launched into the dark and a few minutes later called that he was clear on top at around 3,000 feet, our signal to come up and join him.

Mike and I had practiced instrument flying nearly every day on our return to Home Base from our missions, including radar approaches. We felt pretty confident we could fly on instruments if we had to. This would be the BIG test.

Each of us made it through the clouds, turned on our lights, joined up, climbed to 6,000 feet or so to clear any mountains and headed west out to the A Shau.

The radar guys called us when were over the valley. The Boss went spiraling down first. He broke out about 1,500 feet above the valley floor and called us down. We descended one at a time and joined up with him again. We had turned off our red and green position lights on the sides of the helicopters and only had our rotating beacons on, which were mounted on top and hopefully only visible to us and not targets for enemy sharp shooters.

It was really eerie. A near full moon was illuminating the cloud deck above us to a point that we could actually see the valley and terrain around us with the naked eye. We didn't have night vision goggles, GPS or any of the wonderful aids to night flying and navigation that would be invented years later.

We all changed to the Recon team's FM frequency and gave them a call. They came on in a whisper, gave us a short count to home in on them, and told us they had a strobe light in a C-ration can they would use to identify their position. They couldn't set off smoke grenades as we couldn't see the smoke in the dark anyways and the initial explosion would give away their exact position to the bad guys.

I pointed the nose of the Cobra towards where I thought their position was and called them on the radio with a reverse azimuth compass direction so they could point their light towards me.

The strobe in a C-ration can was a great idea. The light would show in only one direction yet be hidden in the can so as not to give away their position to the enemy.

They had told us the enemy had crept up to their night defensive position, climbed into the trees above them and were actually shooting down on them.

I spotted the light almost immediately and told them to get as far down into the ground as possible as I would be firing my wing-mounted Gatling guns in close to saw the tops of the trees down and the bad guys with them.

When they were set, I let loose with the XM-18 mini-guns firing 4,000 rounds per minute from each side. They were like bright red fire hoses in the sky with every 5th round a tracer round.

I aimed just to the right and above their position and, as they held the strobe light steady, walked the fire hoses of bullets to the left across the top of their position. Enemy dead and wounded started falling from the trees while others were trying to escape the onslaught. Mike was behind me in his Cobra and did the same thing with his turret mini-gun as I broke off and came back around to do it again.

Around and around we went until we had emptied our guns on the targets, then started in with rockets, aiming away from the friendlies so they wouldn't get hit by exploding shrapnel as we fired at the retreating enemy.

It was all over in a just a few minutes. The enemy had retreated and the Recon Team thanked us for saving their bacon. Hueys would later go in to extract the Team and their dead and wounded when it got light.

It was still around 0200 hours and overcast clouds. We landed at Firebase Currahee on the valley floor. We had tested our luck at this instrument flying business and wanted to wait until daylight to try and leave the valley.

The firebase Commander went ballistic though and would have none of that idea. We had made a huge racket with the noise of our helicopters and he wanted us out of there pronto, fearing another attack on the base. If we could fly down through the clouds we could damn well fly back up and be on our way. Logical guy.

We did a quick brief, same procedure as we had used at home base, and climbed back into our helicopters to defy death again.

The Boss took off first without any lights on so he wouldn't get shot at and climbed up through the overcast clouds. Once on top in the clear, he turned on his lights and called us to join him. Mike first and then I did the same thing. We headed back to Camp Eagle and each one of us did a radar approach to a successful landing at home base.

Shaky but exuberant, we headed back to the hooch to see if we could get some shut-eye before the dawn came with more missions. With all the adrenalin still pumping, sleep was not to be. It was a night to remember.

Al Goodspeed's Little Bird, December 29, 1969 "10 Days and a Wake Up"

CHAPTER TWENTY-ONE

SPEED CRASHES AGAIN

Al Goodspeed and I joked about how short we were getting. He only had 10 days left in country and I was down to four weeks. He had just turned over command of the Scout Platoon the day before to Roger Courtney in preparation for going home. We talked about being extra careful if we wanted to leave in one piece. Then the both of us laughed. "If you ain't Cav, you ain't shit!", we both said to each other at the same time as we headed out to the flight line.

It was December 1969 and the winter monsoon season still lingered with lots of low clouds, rain and fog. We had the first light mission to check out the A Shau to see if the weather would allow us to operate out there today. It was just getting light as we cranked up the turbines and got ready to head out.

The weather was a high overcast with lots of moisture in the air. Not a bad day to fly, however, we expected to find fog in the valleys, obscuring the hills after all the recent rains.

Sure enough, as we arrived over the A Shau Valley, there was dense fog from one end to the other. We radioed the weather report back to Home Base. No operations possible for a few hours yet. There was nothing for us to do but head back home.

With the arrival of monsoon season, the 101st Division pulled nearly all its forces from the mountainous areas back to the coastal plain. That included the A Shau Valley and all the firebases around there that had been constructed and occupied earlier that year; Airborne, Berchtesgaden, Currahee, Rendezvous, Zon, Cannon, Blaze and others now lay abandoned until next Spring, when the weather would allow operations in the area again.

Except for us in the Air Cavalry. Our mission had always been to be the eyes and ears for the Division, so we still operated out there to keep a look out for enemy activities. If possible, we would engage them with our Cobras and Scouts or bring in the fast mover fighter jets. In limited situations we would do a mini combat assault with our Hueys to put our Blues on the ground to check things out.

We had to be extra careful though as we were the only ones out there and lacked support from other ground forces or Artillery. Hence, the first light weather checks to make go or no-go decisions for us and other aviation units.

As we turned to head back home, I saw a Huey from another unit doing the same as us, apparently checking the weather conditions. He had turned around and was heading back towards the coast as well.

About then Speed called, as we were flying over the eastern ridge of the valley. "Let's do a recon of the road on the way back," he said, as he started descending. "Hokey dokey," I responded and descended to stay on him.

This road was now designated Highway 547, the dirt road that been constructed by the Division engineers last spring, where the convoy had been attacked. As soon as he was down low on the road, he started his usual tactics of weaving back and forth to keep from getting shot down as he scoured the area looking for enemy activity.

As we approached the abandoned firebase at Cannon, Speed called me. "Holy cow, 23! There's all kinds of fresh tracks heading up to those old bunkers on the hill. Foot prints. Water still dripping in them," he reported, as he broke right and headed towards the bunkers.

"Be careful, Speed." I called back, as I slowed to get ready for action.

Captain Seth Hudgins was our new Platoon Leader and I had him in the front seat on his very first flight with us. He was a West Point graduate and very sharp guy. We hit it off immediately.

"Seth, get ready with the mini-gun in case we run into bad guys," I warned, as we kept a hawk eye on Speed.

Then it happened. Speed's Loach pitched straight up for about a hundred feet, then pitched straight down, heading for a huge tree. The nose started coming up as they crashed into the tree, pitching them end-over-end through the air and crashing on the ground right side up.

The tail boom and rotor blades had broken off and the landing gear was flattened. As I circled overhead, I couldn't tell right away if anyone had survived.

"Seth, start firing the mini-gun at those bunkers as we pass them and just keep firing the grenade launcher the rest of the time," I hollered.

Then I instantly got on the UHF radio to the emergency channel that all aircraft monitor. "MAYDAY! MAYDAY! MAYDAY! THIS IS ASSAULT 23 VICINITY FIREBASE

CANNON. MY LOACH HAS BEEN SHOT DOWN AND CRASHED. MAYDAY! MAYDAY! MAYDAY!"

"Assault 23, this is Coachmen. I'm just a few minutes east. Let me know how I can assist, over."

Yay! I couldn't believe it! The Huey I saw a few minutes earlier heard my call and was headed our way.

"Coachmen, Assault 23. I'll keep an eye out for you and escort you in," I called back as we continued to circle the downed aircraft, while Seth fired the mini-gun and grenade launcher.

I could see one of the crew crawling out from the wreckage now and trying to get the other one out too, as I called back to Home Base to tell them Speed had crashed.

Al "Speed" Goodspeed describes what happed.

"I was about 300 to 400 meters ahead of Lew. As I approached Firebase Cannon, I noticed that a large number of suspected NVA had crossed the road headed south and muddy foot prints led up a steep slope and dispersed into an old complex of bunkers overlooking the firebase."

"There were about 15 to 20 bunkers and as I flew down to ground level I could see that footprints lead to every bunker. There was no doubt that the bunkers were occupied."

"By now, I knew Lew was into killer mode. But I didn't draw any fire. I told Lew I was going to fly over the bunkered area again and give it a closer look. Still no fire, so I decided to put some mini-gun on the bunkers. I lined up and was going to run low to high over the complex and fire my mini-gun into those bunkers. That worked just fine until I was at the top of my run, intending to make another run back down."

"Before I even pedal-turned to begin the run all hell broke loose. An AK47 round came through the top of my aircraft and hit me high on my left upper back and penetrated through my chest, exiting from my right upper back. The impact was so violent that both my arms flew straight out and were spasming."

"The next thing I knew the aircraft was diving straight toward the ground. Both my arms were still shaking above my head. It looked like we were going to crash nose first into the ground at a high rate of speed, and maybe hit a tree. We hit the ground really hard and bounced up, flipping end over end. When the aircraft quit flipping, the main rotors and tail boom had been severed from the aircraft and it was lying down favoring the right side of the aircraft. The engine was still screaming at max RPM, allowing what was left of the rotor head to continue to spin."

"My Observer, Sergeant Williams, had exited the aircraft and crawled around to my side to render assistance to me. As I knew he would, Lew had already started attacking the bunker complex with accurate rocket, grenade launcher, and mini-gun fire. This all but stopped the fire that we had been taking when we crashed. Even though I was busted up pretty good, I knew that Lew would fight until his last breath to see that Williams and I were out of the jam we were in."

"After we crashed I was able to get my seat harness off and I was trying to shut down the engine before the fuel around us ignited. I tried to turn the throttle off, but what was left of the control linkage wouldn't allow it to move. Sergeant Williams was lying next to me and saw me struggling with the throttle. He reached in to try and help me close it. I was bleeding so badly from my nose and mouth that I could hardly breathe, let alone talk. Aside from that, I couldn't move anything but my arms. I couldn't feel anything else in my body."

"When Williams reached in to help me with the throttle, I just hit his arm and motioned for him to try to get me out. Unfortunately, I couldn't give him much help. He persevered and dragged me out to where only my feet were still almost in the wreckage. By now Lew had suppressed all of the fire we were taking."

As Williams was struggling to get Speed out of the wreckage, I spotted the Huey coming from the east and flew out to meet and escort him in, explaining the crash site and promising we would cover him the whole time if he would land and assist the crew. He agreed and a minute later we were on low approach to the crash site.

We stayed between Coachmen's Huey and where I thought the enemy location was, while firing rockets at the bunker complex as he landed next at the crash site. We continued circling and firing and covering them as his crew was getting the survivors aboard.

They were airborne just a minute or two later, heading towards hospital facilities 20 to 30 minutes away. All the Huey Pilots knew well the Surgical Hospitals at Quang Tri, Camp Evans and Phu Bai. The call was already in to the 85th Evac Hospital at Phu Bai to get medical personnel ready for the inbound flight of wounded.

Speed continues telling what happened.

"As I lay in the mud next to the crash, it occurred to me that at the very least I had a sucking chest wound. My ability to breathe was diminishing and I was bleeding out. The only fight I had left was to keep my face out of the mud. Frankly, it was a peaceful feeling."

"It was then that I heard rotor blades that could only belong to a Huey. They were landing very nearby and Sergeant Williams was already trying to get me up. I couldn't move. It felt like I was a big bowl of Jello being held together by my Chicken Plate. One of the door gunners on the Huey jumped out and helped drag me aboard. The Pilot immediately took off toward the 85th Evac Hospital in Phu Bai, about 25 minutes away."

"I had been put on the floor of the Huey, lying face up, and this made my breathing even more difficult. But, thanks to Lew's quick action in getting help from the 101st Aviation Battalion the rescue was much quicker than it might have been. Already I was beginning to think that I just might make it. However, lying on my back, blood was pouring into my lungs, risking drowning in my own blood. With everything I had in me, I was able to roll onto my stomach which allowed me to gasp for more air."

"I remember lying on the floor, looking at the Air Speed Indicator between the Pilot and Copilot to see if we were going fast enough to get to the 85th Evac in time. The ASI indicated that we were running at about 135 knots which was about as fast as we could go."

"I was still barely conscious when we landed on the Helipad just outside of the Emergency Room. There was already a crew of medics and nurses waiting for me. They immediately loaded me onto a stretcher to carry me into the ER. I knew that I was in shock and they repeatedly asked me for my Service Number which I repeatedly mumbled back to them. After about four times it dawned on me that they were just trying to keep me talking, so I wouldn't lose consciousness. I even remembered one of the nurses who had treated me for minor shrapnel wounds on another occasion. I finally told them to quit asking my Service Number and that I was not going to lose consciousness."

"After that I kept saying 'Holy Shit, Ten Days,' over and over again. They quit asking for my Service Number and seemed to accept what I was saying as long as I was saying something."

Back at Firebase Cannon, I was helpless to do any more for Speed and Williams and felt sick to my stomach and close to tears as I continued to circle the wrecked aircraft waiting for the Blues and a recovery team from our unit.

I relived the story with Seth of my first flight into the A Shau with Speed so long ago. How he had been blasted by a 12.7mm anti-aircraft machine gun. Watching his rotor blades stop in flight. Seeing them roll end over end as the aircraft came apart. Landing on the trail. Mike Talton disappearing into the elephant grass to help them out. John Hayden's leg nearly amputated by a hit to the femoral artery. Tom Michel coming in with a Scout bird to take Hayden out. Goodspeed banged up but in great shape considering what had happened.

Now I had no idea whether he would make it or not. And less than a week or two to go and he would have been out of here.

One of our Pink Teams arrived a few minutes later to relieve me on station. I briefed them on what happened and where I thought the enemy fire had have come from. They would provide cover for the inbound Blues and maintenance crews that would secure the site and get the wreckage prepared to sling load out and back to Camp Eagle.

The CO was already on his way to the hospital to check on Speed.

The last report we had on Al Goodspeed was that they had nearly cut him in half to repair all the damage to his organs and lungs and his condition was critical. If he lived, he would be evacuated out of country as soon as possible.

As I lay on my bunk that night staring at the ceiling of our hooch and grieving for Speed, I resolved not to joke about being a short timer anymore and concentrate on surviving the countdown to going home; 29 days and a wake-up.

"Speedbird", December 29, 1969

Postscript: It would be 20 years before I would find out that Speed survived, when I attended a very emotional surprise reunion in New Orleans, arranged by the buds in 1990. Here Speed continues the story of his crash as he relates his dramatic experience on arrival at the 85th Surgical Hospital at Phu Bai.

"Though I was still babbling, gasping, and sputtering blood from my nose and mouth, I was relieved when the team of medics moved me from the seemingly unstable stretcher to a wheeled gurney and directly into the ER, while attaching various vitals equipment."

"They moved me off the gurney onto a stainless-steel table where they immediately started cutting off my clothes and boots. At the same time, they inserted IV's into my jugular and carotid arteries, each containing an economy sized bag of whole blood."

"I was still babbling about being SHORT when they flipped me over to check for other wounds. The table was completely encircled by Doctors, Nurses and Medics, calmly attaching more tubes and equipment. Though babbling, I was focused on the two bags of blood hanging over me as they deflated. I could feel the blood going out of the gunshot wounds in my upper back, flowing down the table to a drain somewhere."

"When the surgeon told me that he was now going to insert chest tubes into my right chest and it might hurt, I remember thinking he must be nuts because nothing could hurt any worse. Of course, I was wrong. The chest tubes are about half of a centimeter in diameter and the steel tips are about four inches long. He jammed two of them directly into my chest like spikes! I hadn't been given anything for pain so it was excruciating! More painful than the gunshot!"

"Once that was completed they were ready to move me to the OR where repairs would begin. The last thing I felt was the gurney bumping over the threshold of the OR."

"I awakened about mid-morning on the 30th of Dec 1969, ready to start my new life. Upon wake-up the Nurse at my bedside said that she needed to change my bandages. I asked if I could see the wounds to which she replied that they hadn't been sutured yet. I insisted, and she reluctantly brought me a mirror. I expected to see a couple of small holes. Instead, I saw a huge 4" by 2" gash about 1.5" deep on the entry point side and a gaping round hole about 5" in diameter on the exit wound side. I could literally see inside my chest cavity. I could have put my fist inside it!"

"I asked her, why so big? She said the impact of a supersonic projectile going through the body kills a lot of flesh which must be removed in order to keep from putrefying and becoming highly infected. The hot humid environment in Vietnam was the perfect place for infection for any wound, small or large."

"When she finished bandaging me again she asked me that if I felt up to it, she could have me wheeled outside for some sun. A medic wheeled me out to a patio. With all the attachments and IV's, it was quite a production. For once the unbearable heat and humidity of Vietnam felt wonderful and there was even a slight breeze. It was one of the most peaceful times of my life."

"I reflected on what a hellish year it had been. I thought about the many members of our Troop who had been lost and seriously wounded, and how I'd been blessed to serve with a group of the most courageous, dedicated, and professional men in the world."

"All of us had jobs that could test your skills, your strength, and your sanity. As a Scout Pilot, we were dependent upon the Gunship Pilots who protected us at all costs. This kind of relationship goes way beyond simple friendship. Knowing that there were heroes such as these watching you as if they were mother bears protecting their cubs, made it a lot easier to strap on our small aircraft and fly into an area, daring the enemy to try their luck with us."

"If we were hit, the Cobra Pilots stayed with us until we were rescued. They were all prepared to land and assist us until additional help arrived. If need be they would even strap us to their own aircraft to get us to safety. They were the Top Guns of Army Aviation, and deserved the utmost admiration. These are the men who could be depended upon to get steel on target during tough times. In the end, I decided that the Band of Brothers with whom I'd been surrounded far outweighed the perils I experienced that year of 1969."

"I don't know how long I'd enjoyed the sun that morning, when a medic came out to retrieve me. I was wheeled back to the ward where dedicated Doctors, Nurses and other medical staff were busy caring for the never-ending stream of casualties they tended to every day. I was astounded at their professionalism as they continuously, and passionately, did everything humanly possible to comfort and treat their patients."

"I was at the 85th Evac Hospital for about a week. Once I was out of Intensive Care, I was transferred south to the Hospital in Da Nang."

"On or about the 11th of Jan 1970, I was loaded onto a USAF C-130 Cargo Plane that was packed with racks of stretchers stacked about 12" apart and about 8 high, probably about 120 stretchers in all, plus about 20 regular seats for those who were ambulatory and could walk and sit up. I was one of those in the stacked stretchers. This plane carried us to Camp Zama, Japan."

"At Camp Zama, I was assigned to a 40-man ward and a few days after my arrival they sutured my wounds. Before I went into the OR for the closing I asked the Surgeon how they were going to fill the large tears in my back. He said they would stretch the surrounding flesh and wire them shut. I asked him if he could stretch the flesh that much. He replied that he could stretch it all the way to my asshole if he wanted to. That ended my questions!"

"When I was returned to the ward I met a new patient in the bed next to me. I noticed that he was sporting a colostomy bag on his side. I asked him what had happened to him. He said that he had been in Vihn Long as a Scout Pilot with C/7/1st Cav. He said that he'd been shot in the dick. Come to find out, he had been infused from A/2/17th Air Cav. He had been the guy that replaced me when I went north nearly a year earlier to Alpha Troop! His name was Roger Catlin. I told him I was damned glad we traded places."

"On the 4th of February, I was loaded onto a huge Air Force C-141 Starlifter Cargo Jet, loaded with stretchers, for the trip from Japan to Scott AFB near St, Louis, Missouri. I was ambulatory by this time which made the flight better. There were probably 250 patients on this flight."

"A day after arriving at Scott, I was transferred via a DC-9 Nightingale Jet to the Eisenhower Medical Center at Ft.

Gordon, Georgia. I remained there until late April for treatment and physical therapy."

"My doctor came in on a Friday morning and gave me orders to report to Fort Wolters, Texas. I left the next morning to fly to Love Field in Dallas. I was greeted there at the airport by none other than the Mad Bomber, Eddy Joiner, where we enjoyed one or maybe 20 cocktails until Sunday, when he delivered me to Fort Wolters."

"I must say that the Air Force personnel throughout the journey could not have been more caring." Al concluded.

Twenty years later in July of 1990, several of the buds that I (Lew Jennings) had remained in contact with agreed to meet at a reunion of the recently formed Vietnam Helicopter Pilots Association (VHPA) in New Orleans, Louisiana.

Don Ericksen and Eddy Joiner met me at the airport in a huge limousine for the trip to the hotel downtown. Don was now the president of Summit Aviation in New York, providing jet helicopter tours and service to downtown Manhattan and business jet services to the rich and famous. He also operated a limousine service and was quite the entrepreneur.

When we arrived at the hotel, Don had me wait in the lobby with Eddy near the elevators and disappeared. A few minutes later, the elevator doors opened and out walked Al Goodspeed and his wife Johnny. He still had that big, stupid grin on his face as he gave me a huge bear hug. We all cried elephant tears. It was one of the most memorable moments of my life!

By rare coincidence, Eddy, Al and Don had been assigned together to Fort Wolters, Texas after Vietnam and somehow became roommates at a house they rented off base. They had stayed in touch over the years and had planned this huge surprise for me for months.

We shuttled the limousine back and forth to the airport the rest of the day picking up more of the buds and their wives; Mike and Lydia Talton from Iowa, Dick and Judy Dato from Oregon, Mark and Cathy Stevens from Maine, Mike and Darlene Ryan from Texas and Tom Michel from California. It was the reunion of a lifetime as we partied hard for a week. And we continue getting together from time to time to this day.

Captain Al "Speed" Goodspeed, Assault 16

Assault 27 Mike Talton, left, with Ross Edlin and crew.

Bob Larsen, Mike Talton, Roger Courtney

CHAPTER TWENTY-TWO

GREAT BALLS OF FIRE

The year 1970 arrived with sirens wailing in the middle of the night at Camp Eagle for A Troop, 2/17th Air Cavalry. I was now officially a short timer with less than 30 days to go in country. This was the first time I had ever heard all the sirens going off in the middle of the night. Geezzz. What's happening now?

My crazy roommate, wild man Mike "Warhead" Talton, Assault 27, relates the story of our move north to Quang Tri and his encounter with Great Balls of Fire, or what he refers to as "GBOFs" for short.

"Runners from Flight Ops sprinted from hooch to hooch, throwing open the screened doors, flipping on the lights and calling for all Pilots to report immediately to the Operations Bunker," Mike begins.

"At the Ops Bunker, our Operations Officer, Dick Melick, directed all Pilots to their helicopters with a command to launch immediately."

"No real explanation was offered and we all sensed that we needed to be in the air ASAP. We assumed that our base there at Camp Eagle was in danger of being attacked and maybe over run."

"Pilots and Crewmembers ran up the hill to the flight line. Some were only partially dressed but most of us were wearing combat boots and carrying our flight helmets, flight gloves and the personal gear we always had hanging by our bunks for times like this."

"I swung the blades on the Cobra I had been assigned, climbed in, hit the power and fuel, set the throttle, yelled clear and did a visual check in the dark before hitting the starter. The Cobra spooled up as if it had been hoping some idiot would come take it for a ride in the cooler night air."

"After completing my run up checks and confirming my Copilot was strapped in up front, I made a call to advise that I was departing my revetment for an easterly departure. Then I scrambled out of the revetment and into the air, climbing for altitude and watching for other helicopters, hoping that everyone was running some kind of external lights; rotating beacons or nav lights. I was also trying to find out from Flight Ops who was in charge and what we were supposed to do now that we were in the night skies over Hue and Camp Eagle."

"Somebody told us to fly north to Quang Tri," someone transmitted.

"Follow QL1 north and look for the city on the river," someone else directed.

"Almost none of us had ever flown that far north before, but a few had. One of those few assumed flight lead, a Scout Pilot, but I don't remember who he was. The rest of us sorted our way into a trail 'formation' of sorts. Scouts, Lift birds, Guns, all mushed together, heading north."

"Finally got there. Sort of. Lots of ground lights. A city. Quang Tri?"

"The Scout, our flight lead, decided he had the runway in sight and reported to Quang Tri tower that he was turning final with a flight of ... a lot. Everyone moved into a loose trail and began to follow the guy in front."

"On short final, the Scout discovered that he was actually making an approach to the middle of the main street in whatever city we were over and not the runway at the Military Base. It was Quang Tri but it was not the Quang Tri Airbase. That was north of us on the other side of the Song Thach Han River (didn't know that then, but learned later)."

"Finally got it straightened out, with the help of the Quang Tri Tower folks. All landed safely and thus began several months of life at the former Marine Airbase of Quang Tri."

"Just to the northwest of the town of Quang Tri in I Corps South Vietnam, on a strip of land between highway QL1 to the west and the Song Thach Han River to the east, the Seabees had constructed an Airbase for the US Marines in September 1967. The Marines staged their operations out of the Airbase, known as the Quang Tri Combat Base, for two years until withdrawing completely in October 1969, moving south to the Phu Bai Combat Base."

"Following the Marines' departure, elements of the US Army replaced them at Quang Tri Air base in late 1969, positioning the 1st Brigade 5th Mechanized Infantry Division, the 18th Surgical Hospital, and the ARVN 1st Division in the Marines' abandoned Quonset huts and Base facilities surrounding the airfield."

"Then, in the middle of a January 1970 night, the 101st Airborne Division (Air Mobile) scrambled A Troop 2/17th Air

Cavalry out of Camp Eagle with subsequent orders delivered by radio to the scrambled Pilots flying in a gaggle of circling helicopters, to deploy to Quang Tri Airbase. Get there. Land. Await further instructions."

"Later information revealed that Intelligence reports had indicated that enemy forces were going to come down from the north in tanks and armored personnel carriers (APCs). Although we had evidence of increased activity north of the DMZ and here and there inside of the Demilitarized Zone and at various spots along our side of the "Red Line", the anticipated hoard of tanks and APCs failed to materialize. Regardless, the 101st Division kept A Troop at Quang Tri through the early months of 1970, just in case."

"At one point, due to the expectation of tanks and such, we even received all of I Corps' 2.75 inch rockets mounted with six-pound High Explosive Anti-Tank (HEAT) warheads with point detonating fuzes, a total of only 126 or so. Less than what two Cobras configured as 'Heavy Hogs' could carry in their combined 152-rocket tubes."

"Although we kept a single Cobra on 'ready alert' sitting in a revetment loaded with some of the HEAT rockets, so that we could react quickly if the armored threat showed up unexpectedly some night (and that would have been a serious issue since we had no night vision equipment for either flying or fighting helicopters back in those days), none of us had ever fired the HEAT warhead rockets, and it would literally be a crap shoot to see if we could hit a tank in a spot soft enough to yield to the small shaped charge of a six pound warhead, assuming of course that we could even see them if they came in the night, as we knew they would."

"Regardless of the lightweight warhead or our lack of experience and night vision/sighting equipment, every 'Swinging Richard' in the Snake Platoon was eager to give it a try. Bring 'em on! We'd stick those rockets in the back end of whatever armor they wanted to send into the fight (FYI: the back end of a tank was where the engine was and the least armor and the front end was where the heaviest armor was)."

"Yes, that was us. Young and immortal!"

"We set up housekeeping at Quang Tri and from that night on, we started running all of our missions out of there."

"One thing was certain, the Seabees certainly knew how to build an airfield, and revetments, and Quonset huts, and refuel/rearm points and other such necessary stuff."

"No tanks crossed the border, at least none that made themselves known to us. The armored threat faded from memory. Life settled back into the familiar 'same-o, same-o'."

"So, it came to pass that early on a sunny Southeast Asia morning in January 1970, a heavy Pink Team, made up of one UH-1H as the C&C, one OH-6A as the Scout and two AH-1Gs as the muscle, departed A Troop's northernmost 'encampment' at Quang Tri Airfield and then turned west toward a distant karst known to the Americans as the Rock Pile, and to the Vietnamese as Thon Khe Tri."

"The Rock Pile was a prominent terrain feature that was used by US military forces as a reference point for navigation and directional orientation. It stood essentially by itself, out in the open, on a small plain but surrounded by ridges and mountains in all directions. At about 885 feet above sea level at its peak, it was not the tallest 'little mountain' in the region, but it was readily recognizable by aviators passing through the airspace nearby. It was located just to the northwest of a southerly bend in the highway known as QL 9, approximately 33 kilometers northwest of Quang Tri and approximately 16.2 kilometers northeast of the abandoned Special Forces and Marine Combat Base/Airfield at Khe Sanh."

"So, on the morning we left Quang Tri for points west, the Rock Pile was our intended initial reference point. From there, we would swing to the north toward North Vietnam and start our recon mission. We weren't going after tanks specifically, but if they were there, we wanted to find them. Then we'd find out about those six-pound HEAT warheads, if anyone remembered where we had stored them."

"I was the Aircraft Commander of one of the two Cobras in our flight. My call sign was Assault 27. The other members of our Hunter-Killer team included our new commanding officer, Major Perry Smith, Assault 6, in the C&C Huey, Captain Bob Karney, Assault 16, in the Scout bird and Captain Seth Hudgens, Assault 26, in the other Cobra, my wingman. Each of the four helicopters carried additional crewmembers: some aviators; others enlisted crewmen serving as crew chiefs, door gunners, and Observers. All together, we numbered eight Army soldiers, Americans all, doing our best to keep the Communists out of South Vietnam. Riiiiiight! Actually, that *was* right."

"We reached the Rock Pile after an uneventful journey from Quang Tri playing follow the leader with the Scout in front, the two Snakes weaving back and forth behind him and the C & C Huey riding in trail at a higher altitude. While the Scout and the two Snakes concentrated on preparing to conduct the recon and on providing gun cover for the Team, the C&C bird focused on communicating our position reports and spot reports, and monitoring other radios for the Artillery, TAC air and other A Troop aircraft flying missions elsewhere in the AO or sitting back at Quang Tri on stand-by in case someone got into more trouble than they could handle by themselves."

"The Scout started a right hand turn to lead us northward toward the DMZ, dropping down a bit in altitude but still staying well above the terrain and the jungle below. The rest of us followed, with me maintaining a position and altitude from which I could deliver covering fires for the Scout's protection, and Assault 26 taking up a position to cover me in a similar way for the same reason. The C&C meandered along with us at an altitude selected to keep him out of the range of 'normal' ground fire, 1500 feet or so above ground level (AGL) or higher, if he needed better communications line of sight."

"Interestingly, the Rock Pile stood about 13.5 kilometers south of the 'Provisional Military Demarcation Line' or DMZ (Demilitarized Zone aka 'no military allowed') and about 10 klicks south of the southern boundary of the DMZ. For those who don't know, but might be interested, the DMZ was established in 1954 as an internationally recognized boundary that theoretically separated Vietnam into the North and South components that existed that morning in 1970."

"The 'Red Line', as we called it, stretched from the mouth of the Song Ben Hai river at the Gulf of Tonkin on Vietnam's eastern shoreline for approximately 38 straight-line kilometers to the West, following the windings of the Song Ben Hai river, to a point where it stopped following the river and ran in a straight line further westward for 22.5 klicks, at last intercepting the Laotian border and ceasing to exist."

"Our mission that morning was to conduct a reconnaissance of the area along, but south of the southern boundary of the DMZ, including terrain that ran east-west along the north side of a major ridgeline known to us as the Razorback. Someone in our higher headquarters wanted to know what was going on in the area, so we intended to find out if the bad guys were moving through the area from the Laotian portion of the Ho Chi Minh trail and/or out of north Vietnam through the DMZ into I Corps."

"Aviators flying in a war zone learn things called 'Combat Lessons Learned', either directly from other aviators or indirectly from training materials written by other aviators. Combat Lessons Learned tells us 'to do' or 'to NOT do' certain things. One of those 'to NOT do' things is to fly on constant headings for prolonged periods of time, kind of like flashing a neon sign over our heads saying to any bad guy in the area 'HEY, I'm going to fly over that terrain dead ahead so get ready for me. Here I come!' Another one of those 'to NOT do' things is to fly at the same altitude consistently."

"Well, that January morning, our Scout was not thinking about those particular two Combat Lessons Learned. He was flying the same heading, about due North, and the same altitude for kilometer after kilometer, or nautical mile after nautical mile, if you prefer. He might have been thinking that the shortest distance between two points was a straight line and that our mission didn't really start until we got to the actual area of interest, where he would dive down to treetop level and kick the speed up a notch, until he slowed it down again, just to make his flight path unpredictable and hard to track from a ground based gunner's point of view."

"Assault 26 in his Cobra and I in mine were snaking back and forth behind the Scout for a while, varying route of flight and altitude here and there, but somewhere between that turn over the Rock Pile and eight or nine klicks north of it, I fell into trail on the Scout and was flying his heading and altitude as if I had become hypnotized for the moment. Actually, I was offset just a little in terms of horizontal position, a little to his right, but not much, not enough to matter really. My altitude was a smidgen higher than his, but again, not enough to matter, really."

"Regardless of the reasons, for the moment we were straight and level and making our intentions pretty obvious to anyone observing us and, as it turns out, we *were* being observed."

"I remember looking through the front canopy, past the head of my front seat Copilot, at a long, high ridgeline that stretched east-west across our projected route of flight. Lots of trees and shrubs, and terrain 'fingers' running down from the sharply defined backbone of the ridgeline toward us and into the valley floor to our left and right. The top of the ridge was only a few hundred feet below our current altitude, although it was still sitting almost two klicks away, directly in front of us. Actually, it occurred to me that the southern boundary of the DMZ ran along the back of that ridgeline. It was the terrain feature that someone back in 1954 had chosen to delineate the boundary line, so guys like us would know where it was, so that we could avoid overflying it. Except we looked like we had every intention to do exactly that, and maybe even keep on northbound all the way to Hanoi. In other words, the ridge marked the beginning of the 'No Fly Zone'. We were not allowed to penetrate that airspace, and the bad guys were not allowed to step into that "ground space" on foot, or by wheeled or tracked vehicle either."

"Of course, those were rules made by men back in 1954, and none of them were present at the moment, and, of course, *this was war*!"

"Suddenly, my hypnotic wool gathering was interrupted by a large, probably the size of a basketball, green ball of fire sailing past the left side of my cockpit. Talk about surprise! Then another green ball of fire zoomed past the right side of the cockpit. This must have been what Jerry Lee Lewis was singing about back in 1964! Certainly, these flying pyrotechnics qualified as 'Great Balls of Fire' or what I call 'GBOFs for short."

"Faster than I can tell it, I visually searched for the source of the GBOFs, brought all weapon systems to the ARMED state, confirmed that I was set to fire single pairs of rockets carrying 17-pound warheads from my two inboard M159 19-tube rocket pods, spotted a rapid series of flashes on the ridgeline to our 12 o'clock (dead ahead), advised my Copilot to acquire the flashes with his turreted weapons sight (even though at the moment, we were out of effective range for the mini-gun and the grenade launcher). I visually checked to ensure that my Signal Distribution Panel (SDP) radio select switch was set to the numeral 3 (our VHF air-to-air radio), and pushed forward the 'Chinese Hat' switch on the top of my cyclic control, so that I could direct the Scout to get out of my line of fire (and for those who might wonder, it was going to be easier for Assault 16 to move out of my way than it was going to be for me to fly out from behind him, so that I had a clear shot at whoever was throwing those GBOFs at us. Besides, I was already lined up to shoot just as soon as he was no longer sitting on my gun-target line. I heard the XM-28 chin turret slew and knew that my front seat was ready to rock. We both realized that we could do nothing as long as our Scout was the target that weapons would hit first!)"

"One other thought, since all the while that I was getting ready to wage war, those GBOFs were streaming by both sides of our cockpit at a fairly constant rate. The Scout, bless his little heart, was conducting an excellent screening action for my Cobra, and maybe even for Assault 26 somewhere behind me. I doubt that I actually thought that thought that day, but just wanted to mention it, just in case, in the interest of total transparency."

"16, BREAK RIGHT!" I yelled into my helmet mic with the VHF keyed for transmit. Normally, I'd be the gold standard for the calm, cool, collected, suave and 'dee-boner' (Pilot speak for debonair) attack helicopter Pilot, but the proximity of the GBOFs and the lack of a reaction from the Scout and my frustration about being ready, but not being able to return fire, were combining together in my cockpit that day to cause me to get a bit anxious. The clock was ticking and we were closing the range to the target, a fact that must be making the gunner of that anti-aircraft weapon grin."

"It got worse. Assault 16 did not move. Nothing! Not even a wiggle. And as if he was the 'Man of Steel', he was still flying straight and level pointed at the flashes on the ridgeline, the flashes that were at the point of convergence for all trajectories being burned across the sky by the unceasing stream of GBOFs."

"16, BREAK RIGHT! BREAK RIGHT!" "Again, I 'coached' the Scout to dive off to the right so that I could press my thumb down on the LRB, the little red button on the left side of my cyclic control head, and send pair after pair of 2.75 inch rockets screaming out of my rocket pods to follow the stream of green fire balls down to the anti-aircraft machine gun. Let the man with the bigger balls win!"

"Assault 16 just wasn't getting it! He didn't break right. He just kept on driving straight ahead, getting closer and closer to the ridgeline."

"My right thumb rested on my LRB. My front seat kept flexing his turret. I could hear it slew, probably adjusting his sight's alignment on where he wanted his rounds to impact once the Scout got out of the way. Every time he shifted his sighting reticle in azimuth or elevation, his electro-hydraulic turret followed the shifts, carrying the mini-gun and the grenade launcher to new fire control solutions for the sight-defined gun-target line. We were both anxious to 'let loose the dogs of war'."

"Suddenly, the Scout's left skid tube rose as the fuselage of the OH-6A rotated to the right, slightly, enough to convince my hair trigger mind that he was at last breaking right and that if I fired now, by the time my rockets got to the airspace that he was occupying at present, he would be gone, and the rockets would have an unimpeded route of flight direct to their target."

"That was the plan, formed in an instant, executed even more quickly. So, I pressed the firing button. All systems were GO !! And they WENT!! Two OD painted, M229 17-pound HE warheads riding on their long white Mk40 rocket motor steeds at 2,200 feet per second. Blazing hot, orange-yellow flames streamed out of the rocket motor's exhaust nozzles, four scarfed tubes designed to impart a slow, stability-augmenting spin to the rockets, the projectiles zooming forward at twice the speed of sound. As the rockets left their tubes, four metal fins swung out from their previously folded positions at the ends of the motors and deployed into the air stream, exerting their critical influence on flight stability and ultimate accuracy."

"At last we had steel in the air and they were flying straight, true and hot!"

"Then Assault 16's left skid came back down."

"The fuselage rolled back to the left and leveled again."

"The OH-6A was not going anywhere. Assault 16 was still flying straight and level. He must have been leaning to the right. Maybe he looked out of his empty doorway and unintentionally moved his cyclic to the right as he scanned the terrain below him."

"Whatever, he was dead ahead and so were my rockets, both of them!"

"Time stopped and the angels prayed."

"Time started again, but at quarter speed, and I watched, with my heart trying to decide whether or not to beat again. Without blinking, I stared ahead while first the left-hand rocket and then the right-hand rocket flew past the OH-6A, at the same altitude, even-steven, a mere couple of feet to the left and to the right of the helicopter's thin skin, and then they were gone, flying on to their target, lost to my view because of the God-blessed crew and their flying machine still sitting smack-dab in front of me, now obscuring my view of the ridgeline flashes that continued to spew GBOFs at us."

"I switched my SDP radio selector to the numeral two so that I could attempt to contact Assault 16 over the UHF radio, pushed my Chinese hat forward again, keying the UHF radio for my transmission, and repeated my previous direction to break right. The urgency was past as far as my rockets were concerned. He had 'cheated death' in that regard, but the GBOFs were still in the air and I still had a burning need to launch more of my rocket load. Plus my front seat was chomping at the bit to put his mini-gun to use, at its full 4000 shots per minute potential. I wasn't even thinking about Assault 26 somewhere behind me. I am sure he was trying to position himself for a gun run as well, his weapons HOT and his thumb stroking the firing button."

"Just as I was transmitting my message, unmistakably now a command, or maybe it was a plea, the OH-6A rolled hard right, *extremely* hard right, almost over-onto-his-back hard right, and dove down and to the right, finally and completely out of the way!"

"Rockets on the way!! I may have transmitted the announcement to the world, or at least that part of it to whoever were monitoring our UHF frequency right then."

"Seeing that the first pair had struck the ridgeline, but down and to the left from where the flashes were continuing to blossom into more GBOFs, I applied some Vietnam windage and launched a second pair of miniature 105mm shells, that was supposedly the burst radius for an M229 17-pound warhead, similar to that of a 105mm Howitzer HE round. Seeing the flight of the rockets heading toward the ridgeline as desired but looking like they were still going to strike a bit below where the edge of the ridge fell away to the west, I brought the nose of my Cobra up until the red Pipper of the M73 reflex sight sitting on top of my instrument panel sun screen was high and to the right of my intended target. Again, I fired a pair of rockets, and then a second pair, judging that the first rockets were going to be range and azimuth correct this time."

"My peripheral vision was telling me that the other rockets had functioned as advertised as their grey-black smoke rose out of the trees and brush along the ridgeline. Then something else caught my eye, something further to the left, just down the ridgeline to the west of the source of our GBOFs, which, by the way, had mysteriously stopped flying by our cockpit."

"A second muzzle flash! Actually, a rapidly repeating, uninterrupted series of muzzle flashes. A new stream of GBOFs! A new anti-aircraft machine gun!"

"One AA gun was not all that common in this terrain because of the difficulty of packing it and its tripod and all of its ammunition up and down the steep hills and valleys and across the rivers from wherever it was dropped off by some vehicle to wherever they wanted to deploy it. The machine gun and its tripod, assuming from the size of the GBOF that it was a 12.7 mm or .51 caliber anti-aircraft weapon, weighed over 200 pounds and that is without ammo!"

"Where we were, there were no roads or rails to deliver the heavy stuff directly to the battlefield, and the NVA weren't flying any helicopters out of Laos or down from north Vietnam, at least not in the daylight and not in the mountains. Men were the beasts of burden, most commonly. To have two AA guns in the same area, on the same ridgeline AND inside the DMZ, actually on *our* side of the red line and on its southern boundary at that, well, let's just say it was a surprise, with a capital 'S'. Hats off to the dedicated NVA grunts that had made it happen, not once but twice, and if there were two, there's probably more."

"The way the two guns were placed provided the gunners with overlapping fires and the ability to support each other to a degree, while creating something of a crossfire convergence of their impact zones. They had waited until we were within range of their weapons and their accuracy was close to perfect, but not quite. The guy who pulled the trigger first must have thought we were going to continue to drive forward until we over flew his position and discovered him and his weapon standing on the sharp edge of the ridge with not a lot of options, except to smoke us before we smoked him. It almost worked, but for some reason, I call it the hand of God, it didn't. The dispersion of their rounds as they flew out to meet us was wide enough that they were missing, and misses are good things if you are the target."

"I realized that I had closed the range to the ridgeline to the point that sooner or later one, or both of the 12.7mms was going to get lucky. Probability laws were at work as well and they didn't play favorites, without divine intervention, and I had received more than my fair share of that already."

"Breaking right!" I called to Assault 26 somewhere behind me. I had no idea where Assault 6 and 16 were, but it was now up to them to stay out of the way and out of the fight unless I called for them to do something different."

"I pulled the cyclic control to the right and rolled my Cobra up onto its right side, pushing on the right tail rotor pedal to bring the nose around to the right and pulling up on the collective control for more power and more lift and thrust from the main rotor. I needed to fly us out of the kill zone and into position for another gun run, both to reengage the targets and to cover Assault 26 who I knew was already inbound on a gun run of his own."

"26, there's a second gun down the ridgeline about 300 meters. Take him and then break left. I'll be Inbound behind you! I made the call to Assault 26 as I pulled my Cobra through the steeply banked turn to the right, using every pound of torque I could command from my faithful Lycoming L-13 engine, all 1100 shaft horse power, every pony running at full gallop."

"This was what we had come for, to find and fix and destroy the enemy. The challenge, of course, was that the enemy had come to this place for the same reason, except he was content to wait for us to come to him. And we had. The fight was on."

"I stretched my body around to the left in my armored seat as far as I could during the initial part of my turn away from the ridgeline, trying to maintain my line of sight to what was going on up and down the ridgeline now slipping behind me. I heard our turreted mini-gun working away during our break away from the target and knew that the front seat was filling the air around the target with 7.62mm full metal jacket bullets, every fifth one a tracer burning bright red all the way to the target."

"When I couldn't see back to the target anymore, a matter of brief seconds actually, I looked back to the right and stretched to see up and around my cockpit frame through my rotor blades to make sure I was not turning into Assault 26 or interfering with his run to the targets. There he was, off to my right, higher than I was at the moment but angled downward in a dive to the targets. We were good."

"We passed each other as he flew into the target and I flew away; he on a downward dive and I on an upward climb. I heard my front seat bringing his turret around in case I asked him to engage the target on the next inbound run."

"Rockets blew out of Assault 26's tubes, flying like jet-assisted spears down straight lines back to my right rear. Rocket motor smoke appeared briefly at the wings of his Cobra, but was quickly left behind by his increasing velocity and further dissipated by the strong downwash of his massive 540 rotor system and those wide blades with their 27-inch cord, sucking in huge volumes of air and beating it downward and rearward as they propelled the sleek Cobra into battle."

"I knew that the enemy on the ridgeline were hearing 26's Cobra literally roar as it charged toward them, the noise from its main rotor increasing in volume and severity as the airspeed increased and combined with the rotational speed of the advancing rotor blades. I had always loved that sound, 'the sound of freedom' one fellow Cobra Pilot had once called it, but for the enemy right now, the roar must be making the hairs on the back of their necks stand up as they watched streaks of fire and smoke scream down to them as if Thor himself was flinging lightning bolts from the heavens."

"Trying to finesse my Cobra into gaining more altitude while maintaining airspeed was a struggle. I was still heavy with fuel and unexpended ordnance. My front seat had used some of his 7.62mm mini-gun ammo to cover our break at the end of our first gun run but not much, not enough to make a difference in our Cobra's performance. The hot, humid air was making it difficult to climb and 'streak' at the same time, and I had traded off all of the airspeed I could spare in an effort to scramble upward for my next run in."

"Looking back again at 26, I saw him starting his left break off of the target and simultaneously I heard him call.

'26 Out'. A simple transmission to make sure I knew he was outbound from the target and that I was clear inbound."

"He needed my rockets on that ridge to cover him during his outbound leg, so I immediately rolled right and established a run into the second target."

"27 Inbound," I called, making visually sure that 26 was clear of where my rockets would fly and impact."

"Both our C&C and our Scout remained silent on the radios, at least on the three frequencies I was monitoring, the ones we were using for in-flight communications. I wasn't thinking about it at the time but C&C was probably engaged on his other radios in continuous communications with our higher Headquarters (Squadron) and with our Troop Operations Center, reporting to the former that we were engaging a 'discovered' enemy and commanding the latter to spin up additional Scouts and Cobras and even another C&C bird for an anticipated relief on station. For all I knew, 6 was calling for Artillery support or TAC air, maybe both. One way or another, if this fight continued, we would run out of bullets or fuel or both before long."

"As I began our dive toward the ridge, neither target was firing. Given our current range to the ridgeline, somewhere over 1000 meters, I had to estimate where the second target was located as I could not actually see the machine gun or its crew. Fortunately, 26's rockets had 'marked the spot' well enough for me to align my rocket sight in azimuth and elevation, using the smoke and debris from his warheads. I adjusted the collective to stabilize power (torque), made a slight cyclic adjustment to compensate for the 'heavy' 17-pound warheads and their need for some super elevation, and pressed my wing store fire button, the LRB."

"This time I fired pair after pair after pair, walking them up the ridgeline from left to right, from the second machine gun position to the first. Again, I broke right at the end of the run, switching from my inboard rocket pods to the outboards as I simultaneously coordinated the covering fire of my front seat, ensured that we were clear outbound, pulled our Cobra through the turn and made my radio call."

"27 outbound. This time we'll be inbound from the east."

"Roger that. 26 inbound."

"Partway through my right-hand turn, I jinked back to the left so that I could end up in position to attack from the east instead of from the south as I had previously."

"Another of those Combat Lessons Learned: 'do NOT use the same attack route repeatedly' or maybe it was 'more than once'. Anyway, we were going to fire them up from the east this time along the back bone of the ridge, instead of from the south."

"I saw 26 streaming rockets into the target area, adding his high explosives to mine and covering the ridgeline with High Explosive Composition B4 fire and smoke, black and grey, lots of it."

"As 26 broke away from the target and called his break, I estimated that he would be clear by the time my rockets arrived at the target and I unleashed the hounds from hell from my outboard M157 rocket pods. Whereas I had been carrying 26 pairs of rockets when we started this dance, I now had 7 pairs left in the two pods hanging on my outboard hard points. I used them all."

"26 followed my lead and expended his rockets into the firestorm that we had unleashed on the ridgeline jungle, chosen by our enemy as their 'mountain fortress'."

"We both added copious amounts of 7.62mm ball ammunition and 40mm HE grenades to the mix, finally giving our front seats the opportunity to flex their considerable firepower up and down the ridge. Both the M134 mini-gun and the M129 grenade launcher were considered area fire weapons and lacking any visible targets at the moment, that is how we employed them, firing up the area, with an emphasis on the top of the ridge and into the brush and trees along the upper slopes."

"My own personal Combat Lesson Learned regarding airborne ordnance; 'never take home what you carry to the fight, give it to the enemy, leave it on the field of battle'."

"Finally, it was time to take a breath and to determine what we had accomplished. Notably, the air was clear of all GBOFs. Notably again, no GBOF had found a home in any of our four helicopters. We were 'unscathed' as they say in the funny papers, despite how close we had come to being otherwise."

"We needed to conduct a BDA, 'Battle Damage Assessment'. We *wanted* to conduct a BDA. Higher HQ wanted to know what happened and so did we, *but*, we had a problem. Normally our Scout, in this case Assault 16, would fly over the target area at a suitable altitude and speed while visually assessing the results of our attack and radioing his observations to the rest of the Team. Our SOP required that the Snake or Snakes in the Team provide the necessary gun cover for the Scout during the BDA. Keep him safe. That was our rule. Exactly what we Snake drivers do for a living, except in our excited enthusiasm while caught up in the heat of the moment, we had expended all of our rockets and bullets and grenades. We had nothing with which to provide the requisite 'gun cover'."

"The one trump card we still held was that the bad guys didn't *know* that we were dry on ordnance. Plus, after all of the high explosives and steel that we had thrown at them and the fact that they weren't banging away at us with their 12.7s, we let ourselves conclude that we had either killed them or had driven them underground, assuming that they had constructed underground tunnels, spider holes and other such earth-based fortifications as part of their decision to set up shop on our side of the DMZ."

"So, as the lead Cobra Aircraft Commander and the guy who should have made sure we had kept something in reserve, I 'volunteered' my front seat and me to make the BDA, while 26 in his Snake, 16 in his Scout and Assault 6 in the Huey maintained overwatch and acted in 'threatening manners'. 26 could make gun runs as if he was going to dump more stuff on the ridge, and the Scout and the Huey had three guys with M60 machine guns in case they saw any movement on the ground as we flew the BDA. Small potatoes and flakey, but still..."

"We decided to test the waters before diving in, so we made a fast run over the ridgeline. Then we made another one from a different direction over a different crossing point. The idea, of course, was to entice some trigger happy bad guy to pull the trigger, and hopefully miss, so that we would know if someone was still watching and still ready to fight."

"We ignored the fact that we were crossing the southern boundary line and flying into the DMZ itself. This was one of those moments when you did what you had to do, not stopping to ask permission, but not wanting to ask for forgiveness later either. No one said anything on the radios, and neither my front seat nor I scolded each other."

"Neither fly-over drew ground fire. On neither run did we see any bad guys, alive or dead. If we had killed them on the ridge, either we had blown them to smithereens (wherever that was) or someone had carried off the bodies, a thing that happened a lot if they had the manpower and the time. Of course, we didn't know if they had enough of that either, just that they weren't there."

"Then I saw it, a Chicom 12.7mm anti-aircraft machine gun still standing on its tripod with ammunition belt attached, all black and threatening and apparently unharmed. It was the first gun that had fired at us when the fight began. It was sitting smack dab in the center of a very narrow strip of the ridgeline spine at the point of highest elevation, surrounded mostly by brush, its three legs straddling a footpath that appeared to be well used."

"I wanted that gun! Somehow, I had to 'capture' that machine gun and take it back to Quang Tri with us. If we (note the 'we', even though my front seat did not realize that I had mentally included him in a scheme that would require him to exit the aircraft in bad guy land, unless he could talk me into doing it) could get that beauty to fit onto one of our open ammo bays."

"As I focused on the 'trophy' and noodled on how to make it mine, I mean 'ours', I reported my discovery to the Team over VHF, and flew closer to the prize, and lower, and slower, until there I was, hovering next to the object of my insane fascination, actually just above it, keeping my rotor blades out of the trees while trying to decide if I had enough room on the ridgeline for my skids."

"I needed seven feet of real estate to hold the width of my skids. Of course, seven feet was a spec number and didn't allow for any margin at all. It didn't matter because the footpath was not that wide anyway."

"I could always straddle the ridge, letting the skids find their footing on the slopes of the ridge while centering the spine between them, aligning the longitudinal axis of our Cobra with the long axis of the ridge. But there were complications with that idea, involving things that extend downward from the fuselage that don't do well when jammed into the dirt, things like radio antennas and such."

"Landing perpendicular to the long axis of the ridge *might* work except we would need 53 feet of clearance from trees and other things just to fit us onto the ridgeline with main rotor and tail rotors spinning, absolutely no margin for error, but once again, it didn't matter because we just did not have the space."

"Those SOBs had planted that gun in a pretty inaccessible spot, for a Cobra anyway. But the Scout! So much *smaller*, but no, that was out. If something happened to him while he was trying to grab that machine gun, nothing I could ever say or do could compensate."

"A grappling hook and rope?"

"I checked with Assault 6, just in case someone on his bird had had the forethought to bring such a useful tool."

"He wanted to know why I wanted such a thing. I hesitated to tell him, but only for a second."

"I tried to explain how we had an opportunity to reduce the enemy's ability to wage war, but my explanation sounded weak even as I tried to fabricate it. If I couldn't convince myself that it was a good idea, how could I ever convince him? Even if he did have the grappling hook and a rope thick enough and long enough, I doubted that he would have been reckless enough to sit at a hover in his UH-1H, presenting the bad guys with a fairly large and stationary target, while one of his crew tried to grapple the 12.7 and then either drag it aboard or secure it on the rope for a ride down to the valley floor. Plus what if it had a round chambered and something we did triggered it?"

"Belatedly, I arrived at the door marked 'It Ain't Gonna Happen' and resigned myself to the fact that someone else would have to capture the machine gun, or maybe we could use Artillery or TAC air 'snake and nape' to blow it and burn it."

"Then I glanced at the fuel gauge and saw that we were approaching 'bingo' state, that point in the mission where we had to depart the mission area while we had enough fuel to get back to Base, Quang Tri."

"Reluctantly, I maneuvered our Cobra so that I could dive off of the ridgeline and follow its slope toward the valley floor back into South Vietnam, accelerating into forward flight in the process. With a final visual check of the area surrounding us and seeing no one pointing a weapon at us, I increased collective pitch and pushed gently forward on the cyclic."

"27 coming out," I called to the Team on VHF."

"As if she was ready to call it a day herself, our Cobra smoothly transitioned from a low hover into flight and away we went, skimming at tree top level down the long slope until our airspeed passed 100 KIAS. I may have clenched my teeth just a bit as I waited to see if that 12.7 was going to stitch my backside with GBOFs. Easing back on the cyclic while maintaining our takeoff power setting, we rapidly climbed through the altitudes vulnerable to ground fire and rejoined our flight, talking with Assault 6 as we took our position behind our Scout."

"While I had been focused on my NVA disarmament action, 6 had coordinated a replacement team to relieve us, and there they were, coming up from the southeast. After a mission handoff over VHF that stressed the fact that two 12.7mm machine guns had been on the ridgeline and that at least one of them was still standing, and yes, somehow the second gun had escaped total destruction as well but at least it appeared damaged, we departed the AO for the return flight to Quang Tri, leaving a second heavy Hunter-Killer team to develop the situation."

"Actually, the situation got a lot more complex after we left. Turns out the NVA had moved into that area with intent to stay a while. They did indeed have underground 'facilities' established, and the men and equipment to go with them. Things got very interesting in the days that followed, but that is a story for another day."

"Oh, later on I talked with the NCO who was riding as Assault 16's Observer. When I asked if he had heard my radio calls to break right, he acknowledged that he had but that 16 had not. Seems that 16 was talking to the NCO over the intercom about all of the things that he was seeing down below them as they flew along and that he either had the toggle switch for the VHF radio flipped down or the volume of the radio turned down to the point where he did not hear the radio traffic, when he had his intercom ICS switch keyed and was talking."

"I asked him if he knew how close he had been to finding out about the afterlife, and he looked at me and nodded. His face reflected that not only did he know how close he had come, but that he might have gotten a glimpse through the pearly gates. Then he volunteered that he knew they were in 'trouble' when he saw a rocket fly by his empty doorway. Since his seat was on the left side of the cockpit, I knew exactly which rocket he had seen, as I had watched the same rocket go sliding by him."

"I didn't ask him if the rocket was flying in slow motion as it passed him, but I did ask how closely it had passed."

"Almost close enough to touch," was his answer and then he spread out the three fingers and thumb of his right hand in a four-pronged gesture, 'and those fins in the back were all open like this'."

"Then he added, 'When I saw that, I yelled at the Captain and pushed the stick to the right. He looked at me and then out his door at another rocket that was passing his side. I think we both heard you tell us to break to the right. The next thing I knew, we were up on our right side and then diving for the trees. I was holding on'."

"Thankfully, both rockets had passed their helicopter before they decided to make their break, otherwise ..."

GBOFS!

CHAPTER TWENTY-THREE

I'M HIT!

It was January 2, 1970. Only days to go on my short timer's calendar to catch my freedom bird back to the good old US of A. We had been flying out of Quang Tri way up north, conducting reconnaissance missions all along the DMZ to the Khe Sanh plain and west to the Laotian border in an area called the Salient, a parrot's beak shaped area of the border that was a main ingress point for NVA forces coming down from North Vietnam.

Nearly every day for a week now, we had been finding small elements of enemy forces along a major trail that came in from Laos near the old QL-9 highway and meandered south towards the A Shau valley. Most of the enemy forces we were engaging appeared to be engineers improving the trail in groups of 3 to 5 soldiers with mostly small arms weapons, AK-47 assault rifles.

Eddy Joiner and I were coming back in the late afternoon from a mission way out there, when Eddy in his Scout bird spotted some smoke rising from a grassy knoll off to our right.

"Hey 23, 11. Check out that smoke up on the hill at our 2 o'clock." Eddy called. "Let's check it out," as he dove towards the ground and started bobbing and weaving towards the smoke. I already had all my systems armed and finger resting on the firing button for the rockets as I warned my front seat gunner to get ready for action.

As Eddy approached the smoke, he called out the dreaded words: "TAKING FIRE! TAKING FIRE! THEY'RE IN THE OPEN ALL OVER THE PLACE! TAKING FIRE!" as he broke left.

My front seat gunner instantly laid down fire from the turret-mounted Gatling gun at 2,000 rounds per minute as he covered Eddy's escape, while I waited half a second for Eddy to clear and started firing my 17-pound high explosive warhead rockets, then breaking off to the left as well so I wouldn't overfly the target and maybe get blasted at close range.

"There must be at least a Company (40-50) of bad guys down there," Eddy called when he was clear. "They were cooking food and scattered throughout the area in the elephant grass," he further explained. "You have any nails on board today?" he asked.

"Sure do," I replied.

"Nails" is a slang term we used to describe our flechette rockets. These rockets were especially effective against enemy troops in the open and not under protective cover, just like in this situation.

The flechette rocket warhead contained 2,200 20-grain steel flechettes that looked like tiny steel darts about an inch long. The flechettes were packed into the warhead side by side, one facing forward, one facing aft. The result was that when fired, the rocket would head to the target and as it got close, the warhead would explode, sending the forward half of flechettes immediately towards the target area. Those facing aft would be delayed a nano-second while they turned around to streamline into the wind, providing a one-two punch of thousands of nails.

The flechette rocket was also a "wide area" weapon. The flechettes dispersed over an elongated area that could cover the size of a football field depending on the distance to the target.

I had 14 flechette rockets on board in the two outboard 7-shot pods. I called to Eddy to stay well clear as I set up for the rocket run at quite a distance and low slant angle to the target. The bad guys continued firing at us trying desperately to knock us out of the air, as I slowly fired one pair at a time, expending all 14 rockets and covering the entire hill with 30,800 nails. I'm sure I killed a lot of enemy soldiers that day. A hell of a way to die, but we had gotten away unharmed for the moment.

It was just the two of us, a long way from friendlies and getting dark, so we didn't stick around to try and do a battle damage assessment or the proverbial body count. We headed back to Quang Tri as darkness fell and called in our report so others in the night, like the Air Force "Spookys", could take over.

The next morning it was up early to head back out to The Salient and see if more enemy activity was in store for us. Anticipating trouble after our encounter with the large enemy force the previous evening, the Boss had assembled a heavy team of two Cobras, two Scouts and him in his C&C Huey.

We were still nearly ten miles away when we started seeing a sight we simply could not comprehend. The "trail" coming in from Laos we had been reconning for the last week was now clearly visible as a doggone highway!

Major Trombley came over the radio. "This is Assault 6. Obviously, something has happened overnight and looks to be very dangerous. Are you all ready to continue the mission?" he asked. Each of us called back in the affirmative, as we continued to approach the road.

The two Scouts dove for the dirt, bobbing and weaving down the new road as me and the other Cobra stayed close behind covering them. The Scouts started chattering over the radio in awe of what they were seeing. Huge tire tracks like Russian assault vehicles and thousands of footprints were visible as what had been a well-camouflaged trail up until now, had been laid bare. The enemy had apparently crossed over the border from Laos during the night in force. Maybe by the thousands! We cautiously continued following the road, waiting to be attacked at any second. Until we reached the end of the road, finding nothing.

"6, 11, we don't see any people or vehicles. Should we head back up the road?" Eddy asked the Boss.

"Okay everyone, let's be alert. We know they're around here somewhere. 11, let's start heading back up the road and widen our recon on both sides," Trombley directed.

Sure enough, they were all around us as Eddy called out a minute later; "TAKING FIRE! TAKING FIRE! THEY'RE ALONG THE RIGHT SIDE OF THE ROAD AT THE BASE OF THE HILL WITH TRUCKS CAMOUFLAGED UNDER THE TREES!" We immediately started laying in rockets and mini-gun fire, as the Scouts lobbed Willy Pete white phosphorous grenades to mark the target and broke away. It seemed like we were taking fire from all directions.

The Boss had already called for backup in the form of a Forward Air Controller (FAC) that was high overhead ready to direct in Navy, Marine and Air Force fighter jets. He called to say he would have fighters inbound in a few minutes loaded with "Snake and Nape" (high explosive 250 or 500 pound bombs and Napalm liquid gas canisters). We continued to shoot more rockets and mini-gun as the Scouts cleared the target and then we all stood off a half mile or so away to watch the fighters come in on their bombing runs.

The smoke from the white phosphorous grenades was dissipating by then, so we told the FAC to tell the jets to simply aim their bombs at a lone tree on top of a small knoll, because the trucks and bad guys were hidden in camouflaged fighting positions at the base of the knoll, about 50 yards east of the tree.

The fighter jet guys, God bless 'em, screamed down from the heavens, still on oxygen, and dropped their loads, hoping to come within a football field off the target, so we were totally amazed when the first fighter on the first run dropping Napalm actually hit the tree instead of the bad guys. The rest of the bomb runs hit the intended target area though, as we prepared to go back in.

As soon as the fighters broke off and we headed back in, all of us started taking heavy fire. The C&C bird called in that he had been hit and had taken a round through the floor.

I was already setting up for another gun run when a bullet blasted though the Plexiglas canopy of my cockpit, just inches from my face, slamming into my instrument panel. Pieces of Plexiglas hit me, slicing across my lower cheek. Luckily, I had my helmet visor down or some really serious damage would have been done to my stunning good looks!

My engine instruments were jumping around. My rotor rpm was way too high. I instantly thought maybe we were experiencing engine governor failure or worse. Without thinking, I instinctively reduced rotor rpm with a toggle switch on the collective. The RPM gauge still indicated it was too high, but the aircraft was starting to wobble as if the rotor blades were going too slow. Things were turning to shit in a hand basket quick.

"I'M HIT! I'M HIT! THIS IS 23, I'M HIT!" I shouted over the radio.

We were some 30 miles or more from the nearest friendlies and into some really serious doo doo. The CO's bird had been hit, the Scouts were still taking fire and now, for the first time in my tour and only days to go on my short timer calendar, I had taken a round through the cockpit and appeared to be in serious trouble.

We all broke off from the fight and the team gathered around me for the flight back to Quang Tri. I was uncertain how much longer I could keep the Cobra flying. My Copilot, Stan Shearin, and I started assessing the damage and going through emergency procedures while continuing to provide updates to the rest of the team over the radio.

Stan was not injured. He hadn't been hit or taken any rounds up front.

I was OK, just a little bleeding from my left cheek and there was a big hole in the left window in front of my face.

The bullet had gone into the instrument panel and damaged or destroyed many of the engine instruments. I wasn't sure what was or wasn't working, nor did I know if we had taken more rounds elsewhere in the airframe. My teammates flew in close to look for additional damage, as we all headed back.

With a huge sigh of relief, Quang Tri finally came in sight. My rotor rpm, while the gauge indicated it was still too high, was actually too low, so I declared an emergency to the control tower and set up for a "running" landing to the runway. The running landing allowed me to keep some airspeed up and to better control the helicopter as we landed at 30 to 40 knots and skidded down the runway until coming safely to a stop. The fire trucks and emergency crews were there in a jiffy, but thankfully we didn't have to use them. The Cobra didn't catch on fire and was towed to the maintenance area for further evaluation and repairs.

The CO's Huey did not sustain major damage. The Scouts were in good shape too. Another Cobra was brought out for me. My Copilot and I transferred our gear into the new bird and got it ready to go out again.

That night, we were in the mess hall for a debriefing when the CO, Major Tom Trombley, pulled me aside. "Lew, you only have a few days left in country. I don't want you going out with us to The Salient any more. I want you to pack your gear, return to Camp Eagle and help Maintenance with test flights until your DEROS (Date of Estimated Return from Overseas Service)."

"Yes Sir," I replied. It was over. Just like that.

We shook hands and I headed to the Quonset Hut to pack my stuff and fly south to Eagle in the morning.

Len Constantine and Lew Jennings (very skinny at the end of my tour). "Mr. Hollywood" Bob Larsen back from the hospital in Japan – crazy guy.

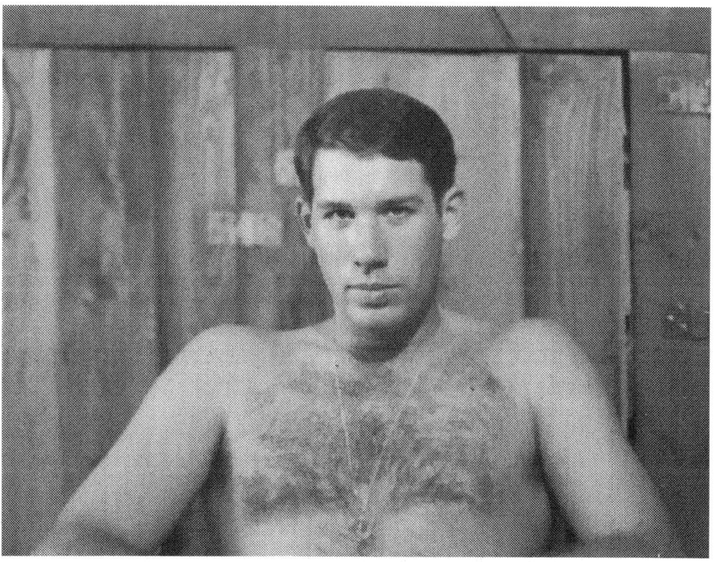

CHAPTER TWENTY-FOUR

AUSSIE FAREWELL

The night before, our Commanding Officer, Major Tom Trombley, had ordered me back to Camp Eagle to conduct maintenance test flights. After nearly being shot down with a bullet into my cockpit and an emergency landing, I think he just couldn't stand the thought of losing another Pilot who was within days of going home, like what had happened to Al Goodspeed.

I said my goodbyes to the buds at breakfast and headed to the flight line at Quang Tri to take a Cobra back to Eagle. Mike Ryan would be flying a Scout bird back there with me, carrying my duffel bag in the back of his Loach. It was a flight of sheer joy that morning as we raced each other down the QL-1 highway, super low level at 100 knots for some 50 miles, all the way back past the ancient capital city of Hue and into the Scabbard Pad at our Home Base at Camp Eagle.

After shutting down and securing the Cobra and unloading my gear back at the hooch, I headed to Operations to check in with Captain Dick Melick and Staff Sergeant Saunders.

"Hi Lew. Welcome back. Why don't you check with Keith Finley and see if he needs some help with Cobra maintenance," Dick told me.

Keith had taken over maintenance duties from John Bacic after John had been wounded in the crash with Mike Talton. Keith and I got along great. He lived in a hooch across from mine, with a nice bar built in. Over the next two weeks we enjoyed many an after-hour drink he made with some orange flavored powder that was popular at the time. I started sprouting warts from my face and neck within the next few days. Seems Keith had mixed the orange powder with some bad water. I soon stopped drinking the stuff as it was ruining my good looks!

The next two weeks were focused on maintenance test flights to keep our Cobras up and running and mission ready. Most of the flights were less than an hour. Many times, I would fly the Crew Chief in the front seat, so he could get some flight time in the bird he spent so many hours maintaining. It was especially a treat for him to test fire the weapons from the front seat when we were out over the ocean and in the clear.

It wasn't long though before I got called to Operations.

"We received a Mission Request to conduct reconnaissance of an area near Firebase Barbara," Dick Melick explained. "Everyone is committed up at Quang Tri so I need you and Ryan to go out there to do the mission. Your contact is an Australian advisor to the ARVN (Army of Vietnam) Artillery Battalion on the firebase."

So much for maintenance test flights. Three days and a wakeup!

Keith Finley volunteered to be my front seat as we joined up with Mike Ryan for the short flight north to the vicinity of Firebase Barbara. The firebase was located about 20 miles north of us in the low foothills about ten miles inland from the coast. We checked in on the radio and started a reconnaissance in ever-widening circles out from the firebase, mainly focusing on the hills to the north and west.

We didn't expect to find any enemy activity so close to our friendly locations and the coastal plain, however within an hour or so Mike Ryan spotted a campfire with cooking utensils that appeared recently abandoned. The search was on.

In minutes, he tracked footprints to a nearby well-camouflaged and fortified bunker. We called in a report to our Aussie advisor. There were no reported friendlies in the area and we received permission to conduct reconnaissance by fire. Ryan flew low over the bunker and dropped a CS gas grenade to see if we could detect anyone in the bunker. Sure enough, two NVA soldiers emerged firing automatic weapons and the fight was on.

We quickly dispatched the two enemy soldiers and continued to recon the area, finding more traces of enemy activity and a fairly large complex of bunkers. I called in an Artillery mission to the firebase to lay in some delayed-fuze high explosive rounds to try and penetrate the bunkers.

It turned out the location of the bunker complex, just a few kilometers from the firebase and deep down in a ravine behind a ridge, proved too difficult for the Artillery guns. At low angle fire, the rounds would hit the front of the ridge and at high angle they would land beyond the bunker location. The only way to get at them was to fire rockets into the small bunker openings with the Cobra or bring in some fighter jets with 500-pound bombs. Most of the bunkers proved to be too difficult to locate and fire rockets into the entrances, so fighter jets were the order of the day. We continued our reconnaissance and using TAC air fighter jet support to attack the bunker complexes.

The next morning, we were out there early checking in with our Aussie friend. By now everyone on the firebase was on high alert, knowing there was extensive enemy activity right in their back yard so to speak. As we continued our reconnaissance, we discovered many small groups of enemy soldiers in prepared fighting positions that had been previously occupied and abandoned the month before by the ARVNs (Army of the Republic of Vietnam). We called in the reports and this time, were handed off to the Navy to employ naval gunfire from a ship offshore.

This was a first for me. The procedures for employing and adjusting Naval gunfire weren't much different from Army Artillery. I called in the location of the enemy activity in six-digit coordinates within 100 meters of the center of the target area and the ship fired a spotter round. I adjusted from there, long or short (which is 'Add' or 'Drop' in Artillery speak) and left or right, in 50 meter increments and it was only a few minutes before all the guns on the ship were firing huge delayed-fuze projectiles that literally ripped the enemy fortifications apart. It was quite a sight to behold and the sailors aboard ship were ecstatic when we reported the substantial number of enemy dead and fortifications they had destroyed.

Our Aussie advisor was grateful too, however, he was very concerned with all the enemy activity so close to their position. I had radioed in our sightings continually to our

Home Base and they in turn had passed them to higher Headquarters. That night we were congratulated on discovering all the enemy activity and were told planning was underway to conduct a major air assault of Infantry in the area in the next day or two.

The following morning Mike Ryan, Keith Finley and I were out there again. It seemed so ironic that everyone was up on the DMZ and out in the Khe Sanh plain where we thought most of the bad guys were, only to find them right in our own back yard.

We found blood trails from the previous day's battle and more enemy activity. We had some skirmishes with small groups of NVA throughout the day and employed Artillery fire from the firebase.

As I was checking out on the radio with our Aussie friend, he said he looked forward to working with me the next day and hoped I would be there coordinating things. I told him sorry, no, someone else would be out to support him. It was my DEROS date and I was catching my "Freedom Bird" home. "Good on 'ya, Mate," he replied and with that I wished him good luck and a fond farewell. My last mission was over!

The next day a few of the buds drove me in a jeep to the airfield at Phu Bai. I caught a flight to Cam Ranh Bay and two days later found myself standing in the terminal at the Seattle-Tacoma International Airport, awaiting a flight home to San Francisco. I started my tour in Vietnam at 167 pounds and now only weighed 138 pounds. My khaki uniform that had been in my duffel for a year was baggy and wrinkled and I needed a shave badly, so I headed to the airport barbershop.

There were two barbers who looked up as I entered. "Hi, I'm Lew Jennings, just back from Vietnam. I look and feel like crap. I hope you guys can clean me up before I meet my family in San Francisco."

"Sit right down here son," one said, as he motioned me to the empty chair as the other started getting some hot towels. "We'll have you looking great and feeling good as new in no time."

As I leaned back and closed my eyes, I whispered; "Thank you God, this must be Heaven," as the first hot towel caressed my haggard face.

It was 2 February 1970. I had officially survived 58,560 minutes flying Army helicopters in combat in Vietnam.

Chief Warrant Officer Lew Jennings, Assault 23, 1969

CHAPTER TWENTY-FIVE

THE HELICOPTER WAR

A lot of us survived being Army Helicopter Pilots in Vietnam. So maybe it was a bit of a stretch to believe we only had "19 Minutes to Live" as had been reported in the media.

On further reflection however, the statistics reveal some incredibly brutal facts about helicopter combat in Vietnam and the dangers faced by those that carried rucksacks and rifles.

There were nearly 12,000 helicopters deployed in Vietnam by all the Services that flew over 10 million flight hours. Almost half, 5,086 to be exact, would be lost.

Of the approximately 1,100 OH-6A Light Observation Scout helicopters employed in Vietnam, we would lose 842 or 80 percent.

Of the estimated 950 AH-1G Cobras, we lost 270, nearly 30 percent.

The Hueys would accumulate 7,531,955 flight hours in Vietnam, making it the most combat seasoned aircraft in history. Of the 7,013 UH-1 Hueys deployed to Vietnam, we lost 47 percent or 3,305.

And while all of us thought we were young and immortal, we lost just under 5,000 helicopter crewmembers killed in action or 10 percent of all the casualties of the Vietnam War, plus an untold number of wounded.

Those that carried a rucksack and a rifle faced unbelievable danger as helicopters carried them into combat. Once the enemy was located, helicopters would fly them directly into combat in minutes, time and again, day in and day out. The average GI, Army or Marine, experienced 240 days of combat in a one-year tour of duty.

The average "tooth to tail ratio" of 30 to 70 describes the relationship of fighters (30 percent) to support personnel (70 percent) in a battlefield situation. Using that ratio, of the 2.6 million service members who served in Vietnam, approximately 780,000 would be involved in combat, many carrying a rucksack and a rifle. There were over 58,000 killed in action and 304,000 wounded in the Vietnam War suggesting that nearly 40 percent, or one in four of those carrying a rucksack and a rifle would become a casualty.

The helicopters that carried soldiers into battle however, were the saviors of the wounded as well.

During World War II, there were less than 25 medical evacuations by helicopter as there simply weren't very many helicopters produced at that time. The death rate for casualties, once they reached medical facilities, was four percent.

During the Korean War, the OH-13/Bell 47 bubble helicopter of MASH fame performed over 25,000 medical evacuations and was credited with reducing battle casualty death rates at medical facilities by half compared to World War II; from four percent to two percent.

Over 500,000 helicopter medical evacuations were conducted during the Vietnam War, transporting nearly 900,000 sick and wounded patients, reducing casualty death rates at medical facilities to less than one percent. Most wounded were airlifted to medical facilities within an hour (known as the "Golden Hour"). This resulted in the lowest casualty death rate in the history of warfare and ushered in the use of helicopters world-wide to provide emergency medical transport for civilian populations.

"Dustoff" was the call sign of those courageous helicopter crews dedicated to medical evacuation of the sick and wounded from the battlefield. The Dustoff call sign was acquired in 1964 by the 57th Medical Detachment (Helicopter Ambulance) by the outgoing Commanding Officer, Major Lloyd Spencer and maintained by the new incoming CO, Major Charles L. Kelly, who himself would become a legend in the Dustoff community as "Combat Kelly" and lose his own life saving wounded.

Over time, Dustoff became defined as Dedicated Unhesitating Service to Our Fighting Forces. And Combat Kelly's response, when prompted to leave a landing zone while under fire; "When I have Your Wounded" became the battle cry for all Dustoff Pilots and crewmembers.

While most, if not all Huey crews conducted medical evacuations, Dustoff helicopters were dedicated, unarmed Air Ambulances displaying the Red Cross, whose sole mission was to evacuate the wounded from the battlefield to medical facilities. Needless to say, they were all miraculous, courageous helicopter crews who saved thousands of lives and suffered severe casualties themselves in the process.

Three Dustoff crewmembers would be awarded the nation's highest decoration for conspicuous gallantry, the Congressional Medal of Honor; Major General (then Major) Patrick Brady, Chief Warrant Officer Michael J. Novosel and Chief Warrant Officer (then Sergeant First Class) Louis R. Rocco. They epitomized what all of us flying helicopters in combat were dedicated to - supporting our fighting forces.

That's also why I love Helicopter Pilots in general. I don't know a single one who wouldn't try to save a life if they were able.

In this day and age of evolving technology and especially the development of drones to perform missions such as reconnaissance and evacuation of wounded from the battlefield that will surely save lives, I'm reminded of the sage advice of Chinese General and military strategist Sun Tzu who prophesized over 2,000 years ago in his treatise *The Art of War:*

"The supreme art of war is to subdue the enemy without fighting."

May it someday be so.

Lew Jennings, Major, US Army (Retired), July 2017

2,202 Helicopter Pilots and 2,704 Helicopter Crewmembers were Killed in Action. An untold number were wounded.

The buds in Alpha Troop, 2/17th Air Cavalry 1969 (Top) Steely-Eyed Lew Jennings (below)

EPILOGUE

AFTER VIETNAM

Major Lew Jennings, US Army, 1985

The Army awarded me a Direct Commission from Chief Warrant Officer to First Lieutenant on my return from Vietnam in 1970. I retired as a Major in 1987, after assignments in the US at Fort Ord, California, in Europe with the 2nd Armored Cavalry Regiment, back in the US at Fort Knox, and four years of duty with the Navy and Marine Corps, including two years of sea duty coordinating helicopter and search and rescue operations throughout the Pacific for the U.S. Navy's Third and Seventh Fleets.

I met many talented, wonderful people of all ranks in all the Services during my military career and cherish their friendships to this day.

After retiring from the Army, I flew commuters for American Eagle out of San Francisco and jumbo jets for World Airways out of Kuala Lumpur, Malaysia and then pursued the corporate world starting my own Company, Performance Education Systems (PES), helping companies organize and train for national expansion.

In 1995, my wife Anneke and I sold our home in Seattle and moved aboard our 41-foot sailing ketch *Unicorn*. We sailed off over the horizon to seek adventure and follow our dreams as long as we were healthy. We fell in love with the tiny fishing village of La Cruz de Huanacaxtle on mainland Mexico just north of Puerto Vallarta, where we built and operated an oceanfront bed and breakfast resort for several years.

We returned to the USA in 2005, retiring to Lago Vista in the Texas hill country near Austin. I had just spent several months based near there, flying volunteer missions to aid survivors of Hurricanes Katrina and Rita. I thought the area was beautiful and the people great.

I came out of retirement in 2008 to fly secret Intelligence, Surveillance, and Reconnaissance (ISR) and Logistics missions in Iraq for two years. My old friend and Vietnam bud from Alpha Troop, Mark Stevens, joined me over there to terrorize the terrorists. The efforts of our group of "Gray Hairs" helped save thousands of lives of US soldiers, coalition forces and innocent Iraqi civilians.

Aviation has always been a passion for me. I continue to stay involved in general aviation, restoring and building airplanes and participating in aviation groups like the Experimental Aircraft Association, Old Bold Pilots, Palm Springs Air Museum and Quiet Birdmen. And I always enjoy telling stories and doing presentations on Vietnam – The Helicopter War.

We currently live aboard our restored motor yacht "Le Rêve" ('The Dream' in French) near family and friends in the beautiful Santa Cruz Harbor in California. I grew up here as a child just a few blocks away and it's nice to be back home.

Thank you for reading my memoir. I hope it provided some insights into the life of an Army Helicopter Pilot in Combat in Vietnam and a renewed respect and admiration for those that carried a rucksack and a rifle.

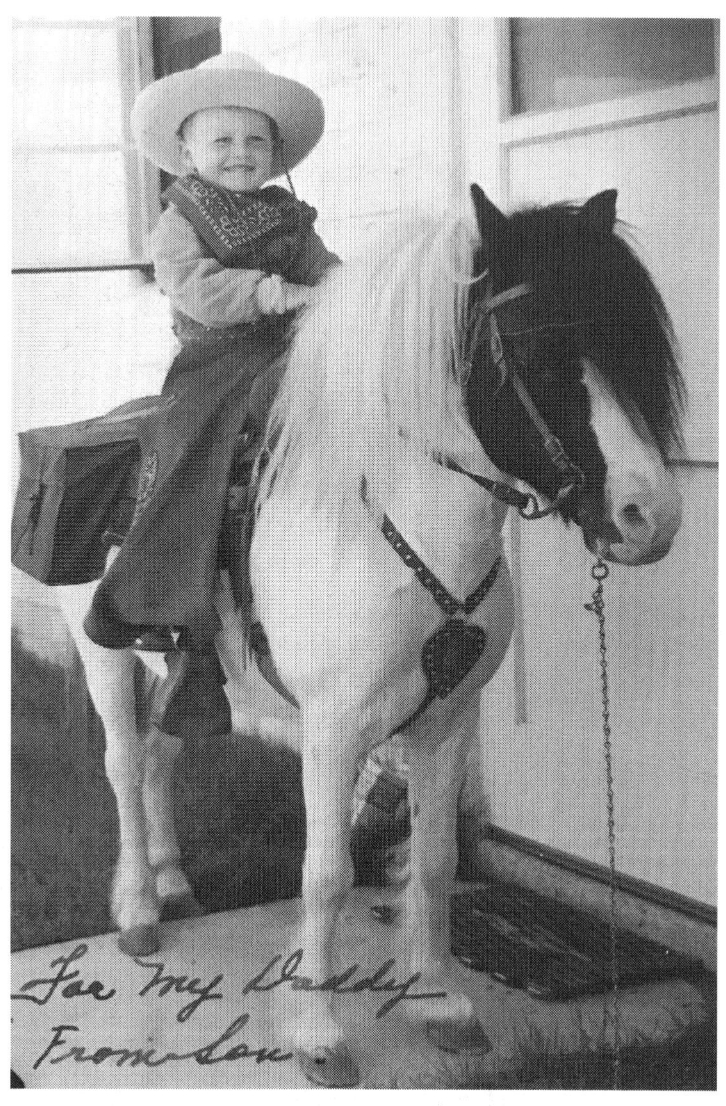

Lew Jennings at 4 Years Old. "Meant to be Cav!"

ABOUT THE AUTHOR

Lew Jennings is a retired Army Officer, former airline pilot and business executive. He flew 726 Air Cavalry Cobra helicopter gunship combat missions in Vietnam, receiving over 50 combat decorations including three Distinguished Flying Crosses for Valor and 36 Air Medals. He is a Life Member of the Vietnam Helicopter Pilots Association, the Distinguished Flying Cross Society, the Disabled American Veterans, and an active member in the Experimental Aircraft Association, Old Bold Pilots and Quiet Birdmen. He and his wife Anneke live aboard their restored motor yacht in the harbor at Santa Cruz, California.

www.19minutestolive.com

Made in the USA
Columbia, SC
07 January 2019